Andrei
Sakharov
and Peace

D0324667

Andrei Sakharov
and Peace

Edited by

Edward D. Lozansky

AVON
PUBLISHERS OF BARD, CAMELOT, DISCUS AND FLARE BOOKS

Acknowledgments

"The Persecution of Andrei Sakharov" by Lawrence Elliott, reprinted from the November 1984 *Reader's Digest*; copyright © 1984 by The Reader's Digest Assn., Inc.

"Andrei Dmitrievich Sakharov" and "Sakharov and the Bomb" from *Russia and the Russians* by Kevin Klose; reprinted by permission of Kevin Klose.

"Elena Bonner's Complaint" copyright by Khronika Press.

"The Sakharovs in Gorky," interview between Vladimir Tolz of Radio Liberty and Natalya Hesse, March 1984; reprinted by permission of Natalya Hesse.

"Who's Braver—the Cosmonaut or the Dissident?" by Vassily Aksyonov, from the September 15, 1984 issue of *TV Guide®* magazine; copyright © 1984 by Triangle Publications, Inc., Radnor, Pennsylvania. Reprinted by courtesy of Vassily Aksyonov.

"A Generation that Failed" by Robert Kaiser, reprinted from the September 23, 1984 edition of *The Washington Post*; copyright © 1984 by The Washington Post.

"Sakharov's Contributions to Science" by Andrew M. Sessler and Yvonne Howell, excerpted from "Andrei Sakharov: A Man of Our Times," reprinted from the May 1984 issue of the *American Journal of Physics*; copyright © 1984 by the American Association of Physics Teachers.

Articles by Andrei Sakharov: "Police Dictatorships" from *Sakharov Speaks*; "The Liberal Intelligentsia of the West: Its Illusions and Responsibilities" from *My Country and the World*; "The Carter Correspondence" from *Alarm and Hope* reprinted by permission of Alfred A. Knopf, Inc.

"Andrei Dmitrievich Sakharov" by Vladimir Voinovich and "Andrei Sakharov and the Russian Intelligentsia" by Valery Chalidze from *On Sakharov*, reprinted by permission of Alfred A. Knopf, Inc.

Articles by Andrei Sakharov: "An Autobiographical Note," "A Letter from Exile," "A Letter to My Colleagues," "Andrei Sakharov's Appeal on Beginning His Hunger Strike," copyright Andrei Sakharov; reprinted by permission of Efrem Yankelevich.

"A Message from Gorky" by Andrei Sakharov, copyright © 1983 by Andrei Sakharov; "The Danger of Thermonuclear War" by Andrei Sakharov, copyright © 1984 by Andrei Sakharov; both reprinted by permission of Efrem Yankelevich.

"Chronicle of Disappearance" compiled by The International League for Human Rights; reprinted by permission.

"When Honor and Conscience Are Lost" by Sidney Drell; reprinted by permission.

Contents

ANDREI SAKHAROV AND PEACE

Foreword by
Edward D. Lozansky

AT THE PRESENT TIME THE THREAT OF NUCLEAR
war is the major concern for people around the world. And
it seems that we do not have clear ideas as to what should
be done to prevent nuclear confrontation between the superpowers. A continuous and accelerating arms race is certainly not the answer. On the other hand, the possibility of
total nuclear disarmament is an absolute utopia, at least for
any foreseeable future.

Ironically, the important message to the West on how to
deal with these issues comes from Andrei Sakharov, a man
who put one of the most destructive nuclear weapons, the
H-bomb, into the hands of a totalitarian government which
by its nature and definition is the main threat to the world's
peace. Sakharov, at great risk for himself, is telling us what
we should do to avoid nuclear war and, at the same time,
to survive as free people. This is why his popularity is so
strong here in the United States, and in the rest of the free
world.

Some people might argue that this is an overstatement.
Americans and Europeans admire Sakharov and speak out
in his defense because they feel sympathy for the man who
shares their values, who speaks out with an impressive degree of courage, and who has become a martyr for the cause

of human rights and peace. I think this is only partially true. In this tough and egotistical world one should also look for some other reasons why the story of Andrei Sakharov has received so much publicity around the world. Why are so many influential people on both sides of the Iron Curtain now involved in his case? Why are people of sharply differing views on politics and the economy, of different religious backgrounds and beliefs, now joining hands in the fight for his liberation? Since there were and still are many other well-known dissidents in the Soviet Union who have suffered much harsher treatment than Sakharov. So why all this outcry for this particular man? I think that the answer lies in the fact that in addition to our respect and admiration for Sakharov, we also intuitively understand that we need him perhaps even more than he needs us.

In his books, articles, and statements Sakharov repeatedly reminds us about the true nature of the Soviet regime. He teaches us how to deal with the Soviets, how to read their Byzantine politics, and what should be demanded from them as a guarantee for a mutual trust. "A most important concept, which in time became the cornerstone of my position," writes Sakharov in his letter to Anatoly Aleksandrov, president of the USSR Academy of Sciences, "is the indissoluble bond between international security and trust on the one hand, and respect for human rights and an open society on the other . . . I have discovered the massive and cynical nature of the violations in the Soviet Union of fundamental civil and political rights . . . A society which fails to respect these rights is a 'closed' society, potentially dangerous to mankind and doomed to degradation."

I think this is a very important message which should be read and understood by all those who are concerned with the preservation of peace, and especially by those who believe that peace can be achieved mainly through public pressure on democratic governments.

Responding to this pressure, the governments of demo-

cratic states are very often forced to make unilateral concessions and sign agreements which could be hardly helpful to
the cause of peace but which will be definitely beneficial
for the Soviet tactical and strategic interests. At the same
time, those rebellious few in the Soviet empire who are
trying to organize independent peace groups in their countries are quickly silenced in jails or mental institutions.
Unfortunately, only a few leaders of the Western peace and
nuclear freeze movement are raising voices in their defense.

The Soviets understand perfectly well what advantages
the so-called fight for peace can bring to both their domestic
and foreign policy, and when it comes to the exploitation
of people's aspiration for peace, or of their fear of nuclear
holocaust, the Department of Agitation and Propaganda under the Central Committee of the Communist Party and the
KGB's Department of Disinformation suffer no shortage of
funds or ideas. "... The people's deep wish for peace is
exploited," says Sakharov in his May 1980 "Letter from
Exile," "and this is perhaps the cruelest deception of all.
The deep yearning for peace is used to justify all the most
negative features in our country—economic disorder, excessive militarization, purportedly 'defensive' foreign policy measures (whether in Czechoslovakia or Afghanistan),
and lack of freedom in our closed society." And later, in
the 1981 article "How to Preserve World Peace," Sakharov
continues: "... the Party authorities continue traditional
Russian geopolitics but now on a worldwide basis—taking
advantage of the enormous resources of a totalitarian system, a unified and slanted but clever and consistent propaganda both inside the country and out. It quietly penetrates
all the cracks in the West and employs subversive activities
there; it exploits the increased though one-sided resources
of its economy for unrestrained militarization."

One of the most clever and at the same time reprehensible
examples of Soviet propaganda deals with the huge number
of Soviet people who died during World War II. How often

do you hear the Soviet leaders and spokesmen trying to mislead public opinion using the following line: "We lost twenty million people in the war! In every family there were men killed and missing in action. The war causes so much grief and destruction. How could anyone believe that we would want a repetition of all the horrors of war?"

No one questions that a nation that has suffered such horrible losses yearns above all for peace. The only problem is that in the Soviet Union the interests of the nation and its leaders (*nomenklatura*) do not necessarily coincide. For a party which has never allowed free elections it is difficult to claim that it serves in the best interest of the people. History teaches us that it does not. The value of human life is not very high in the USSR. Stalin liked to repeat, "*Les rubyat—shchepki letyat.*" When you chop wood, splinters are going to fly. So what is twenty million splinters? It took no war for them to send twice that number of people to their deaths in prison and labor camps, and no one was ever punished for it. On the contrary, Solzhenitsyn, Sakharov, and all those who demand that the monstrous crimes of the Stalin regime be completely disclosed are prosecuted for alleged slander. Stalin is dead, but the political and economic system of Stalinism is very much alive.

The Soviet Union sends its troops to crush any attempt to achieve independence and freedom in the countries they have seized without any regard for the number of casualties inflicted. They are committing genocide in Afghanistan; they arrest people and place them in mental institutions for doing nothing more than calling for the observance of their own constitution. Moreover, it seems that at the present time Stalin's resurrection as a great national hero goes ahead with full speed.

The point is that the Great Terror is a logical outgrowth of the system and not just the aberration of a bloodthirsty maniac. There is little doubt that the communist authorities will not hesitate to return to the days of the Great Terror and, if necessary, to destroy another twenty million Soviet citizens in order to retain power. This is something that all of us should realize if we want to learn how to deal with the Kremlin.

Sakharov is telling us to be firm, to display unity and readiness to reject and eliminate the dictates and demagoguery of the USSR. He stresses that "genuine security is possible only when based on a stabilization of international relations, a repudiation of expansionist policies, the strengthening of international trust, openness and pluralization of socialist countries, and the observance of human rights throughout the world..."

Four members of the USSR Academy of Sciences, Anatoly Dorodnitsyn, Aleksandr Prokhorov, Georgi Skryabin, and Andrei Tikhonov, know English very well but on orders from the Kremlin they "translated" Sakharov's message as a request to the United States to launch a nuclear attack on the Soviet Union. This accusation was later picked up and widely spread by the Soviet media in order to convince the Russian people that Sakharov is a traitor. The participation of the Academy of Sciences—the most prestigious intellectual body in the USSR—in this slander puts another shameful stain on Russian history. But every normal human being understands that Andrei Sakharov has proved to be a great Russian patriot. He sends us a message of hope that despite her horrible violent history Russia still can produce people of the highest morality dedicated to the cause of peace and democracy, which means that there is a chance that not everything is lost yet.

"The patriotism of Andrei Sakharov, to his native land and to the entire world," said the late president of the National Academy of Sciences, Philip Handler, "is a noble beacon for us all. May that light continue to shine, penetrating the dark corners of repression and the gloom of despair."

We need Andrei Sakharov and he needs us. The world's

public opinion has not been able to shield Sakharov completely but at least has saved him so far from much harsher treatment. "Our only protection is the spotlight of public attention on our fate by friends around the world," says Sakharov. We hope that this book will help to increase and maintain this attention.

"THE WELCOMES"*

Alexander Solzhenitsyn

THE APPEARANCE OF A NEW JOURNAL, *KONTI-nent*, also stirs new hopes. For the first time since attempts in the U.S.S.R. to publish *samizdat* journals in no way subservient or conforming to the official ideology were nipped in the bud, and since the only honest and serious journal, *Novy mir*, was ravaged, the Russian intelligentsia is attempting to unite its thoughts and works without regard for either the will of officials or its own division by political boundaries. This is neither the ideal form nor ideal territory for the publication of a free Russian journal; how much more joyous our hearts would be if all the authors as well as the publisher itself were located on native Russian soil. But under present-day conditions this is clearly not possible.

However, the plan of the journal reveals to us a new side of its task: *for a start*, it will be published in Russian and German and we may clearly expect editions in other European languages. And so our straitened and scattered condition is turning into a new hope: the journal would like to become international, to combine the efforts of not just Russian writers and concentrate the attention of not just Russians. Today, when all the dangers and tasks of society cannot be contained within national boundaries, such a turn is natural and fruitful.

If we read the proposal even more carefully, we see that

---

*Written for the first issue of Russian *Kontinent* in 1973.

it contains names that are highly esteemed and widely known in Eastern Europe; so that, considering the honorable array of board members and the make-up of the editorial committee, we can expect a preponderance of voices and opinions from that part of the world. From this we can see an even more interesting prospect for the journal: it may become a genuine voice of Eastern Europe aimed at those Western ears which have not been blocked off from the truth and want to hear it. Only forty years ago, it would have been inconceivable that Russian, Polish, Hungarian, Czech, Rumanian, German, and Lithuanian writers might have a similar life experience, draw similar bitter conclusions from it, and have almost identical desires for the future. Today, this miracle, for which we have had to pay so dearly, has come to pass. The intelligentsia of Eastern Europe speaks in a single voice of suffering and knowledge. May great honor come to *Kontinent* if it can express this voice effectively. Woe to Western Europe (and very soon) if its ear remains indifferent.

Wishes often exceed what later actually happens. May it turn out differently this time.

Andrei Sakharov*

THE CREATION OF A NEW JOURNAL OF LITERA-
ture and public opinion seems to me very necessary and
timely. Its task now is to provide a maximum of factual
information about the socialist countries and about the entire
world.

I expect the literary section of *Kontinent* to shed light on
the more profound aspects of life which are accessible to
an intuitive perception of art. I am certain that the journal
will make its contribution to the extremely important process, common to all mankind, of forming and reconstructing
the philosophical, moral, and ethical values so lacking in
contemporary humanity, which is preoccupied with the present day and is disillusioned.

I hope that all sections of this new publication will be
interesting, talented, diverse in genre and subject matter,
and will bring the reader not only knowledge, but spontaneous joy as well.

Kontinent has one particular feature that I should like to
say a few words about. Its contributors are people who have
spent a significant part of their lives in socialist countries.
The reality of these countries is a historical phenomenon
very poorly understood in the West. Its social, economic,
and spiritual characteristics cannot be comprehended from
the window of a tourist bus or from the official socialist
press. Therefore, these people have something to tell the
world and it would be hard to overestimate this opportunity.

I hope this new journal, born in difficult conditions, will

---

*Written for the first issue of Russian *Kontinent* in 1973.

find its reader and be of help to people and liked by them.

Unfortunately, I can merely dream that this journal will be available not only in the West, but to many people in the East, too. All the same, let us hope!

KONTINENT

Kontinent—literary, sociopolitical, and religious magazine
Editor-in-Chief   Vladimir Maximov
Deputy Editor-in-Chief   Natalia Gorbanevskaya
Editor of the English Edition   Edward D. Lozansky

Editorial Board:
Vassily Aksyonov, Zenko Barev, Alain Besanson,
Nicholas Bethell, Enzo Bettiza, Joseph Brodsky, Vladimir
Bukovsky, Robert Conquest, Jozef Czapski, Milovan
Djilas, Cornelia Gerstenmaier, Jerzy Giedroyc, Aleksandr
Ginsburg, Paul Goma, Pyotr Grigorenko, Gustav Herling-
Grudzinski, Sydney Hook, Irina Ilovaiskaya-Alberti,
Eugene Ionesco, Naum Korzhavin, Edward Kuznetsov,
Nikolaus Lobkovicz, Ernst Neizvestny, Amos Oz, Nor-
man Podhorez, Aleksis Rannit, Andrei Sakharov, Andrei
Sedych, Victor Sparre, Strannik, Carl-Gustav Strohm,
Armando Valladares.

Kontinent was founded in 1974 by exiled Russian writer
Vladimir Maximov. The task of the magazine, as the Editor
and Editorial Board see it , is not only to engage in political
polemics with militant totalitarianism, but above all to confront it with the combined creative force of East European
literature and spiritual thought, which have been enriched
by the most bitter personal experience and by the resulting
perception of a new historical prospect. The major principles
of the magazine which editors formulate for themselves are:

ABSOLUTE RELIGIOUS IDEALISM,
that is, with a given dominant Christian tendency, a constant spiritual union with representatives of other faiths.

ABSOLUTE ANTITOTALITARIANISM,
that is, a struggle against any variety of totalitarianism—Marxist, nationalist, or religious.

ABSOLUTE DEMOCRATISM,
that is, consistent support of all democratic institutions and tendencies in contemporary society.

ABSOLUTE NONPARTISANSHIP,
that is, a categorical refusal to express the interests of any existing political group.

Members of the Andrei Sakharov Institute receive English Edition of *Kontinent* free of charge. The Institute was founded by a group of leading American scientists to defend Sakharov and to promote his scientific and humanistic ideals. To join the Institute or to subscribe to *Kontinent* please write to:

> Andrei Sakharov Institute
> 508 23rd Street, NW
> Washington, D.C. 20037
> Tel. (202) 364-0200

ACKNOWLEDGMENTS

The Editor is grateful to George Bailey, Barbara Futerman, Arina Ginsburg, Irina Ilovaiskaya-Alberti, Edward Kline, Vladimir Maximov, Ludmilla Thorne, Efrem Yankelevich, and the French office of Solidarity for their help in preparing this book.

ACKNOWLEDGMENTS

National Andrei Sakharov Day

By the President of the United States of America

A Proclamation

Dr. Andrei Sakharov has earned the admiration and gratitude of the people of the United States and other countries throughout the world for his tireless and courageous efforts on behalf of international peace and on behalf of basic human freedoms for the peoples of the Soviet Union. In recognition of this work, Dr. Sakharov was awarded the Nobel Prize for Peace. Soviet authorities prevented Dr. Sakharov from receiving this award in person by prohibiting him from leaving the Soviet Union.

In the face of continuous harassment and mistreatment by the Soviet authorities, Dr. Sakharov has continued his work for peace and individual human rights. Despite his exile to the remote city of Gorkiy on January 22, 1980, and despite continued efforts by the Soviet authorities to deny Dr. Sakharov the means of continuing his work and of maintaining contact with the outside world, the example of Andrei Sakharov's courage continues to shine brightly.

The Congress, by Senate Joint Resolution 51, has designated May 21, 1983 as "National Andrei Sakharov Day" and has authorized and requested the President to issue a proclamation in observance of that day. On this occasion, Americans everywhere are given the opportunity to reaffirm that, despite attempts at repression, the ideals of peace and freedom will endure and ultimately triumph.

NOW, THEREFORE, I, RONALD REAGAN, President of the United States of America, do hereby proclaim May 21, 1983 as National Andrei Sakharov Day. I call upon the American people to observe that day with appropriate ceremonies and activities.

IN WITNESS WHEREOF, I have hereunto set my hand this eighteenth day of May, in the year of our Lord nineteen hundred and eighty-three, and of the Independence of the United States of America the two hundred and seventh.

Ronald Reagan

FOR ANDREI SAKHAROV

Natalya Gorbanevskaya

And he looked about him, and his soul was filled . . .
the orchestra thundered to choke his wounded breast.
Then a Leninist sleeve, like a searchlight, fumbled
to silence, stifle and crush them all.

The queue from the concrete armoured car
has travelled across us all,
and if we're not exceptionally alive
all the same we've survived the times.

But until the speech that divides us
from beasts has decayed and ossified,
we won't have occasion to hold our tongues:
the orchestra plays a firing-party march.

And he looked about him, and his soul . . .
another looked about now wounded.
A third fumbled instinctively
to heal the broken joints of time.

trans. Mark Jacob

FAREWELL TO RUSSIA

by Vladimir Maximov

1

FOREST FIRES WERE BLAZING AROUND MOSCOW. Blue smoke shrouded the town roofs, crept into all crevices and openings, blocked the lungs, stung the eyes, letting up neither during the day nor the night. Though it was only the middle of summer, the scorched leaves were already rustling on the asphalt roads and sidewalks, crackling and crumbling underfoot, ready to be reduced to colorless dust at the first hint of a breeze. But there was no wind and from day to day the suffocating heat became increasingly intolerable. The Moscow fires roared on.

All living things seeking escape were fleeing in all directions, running from the hellfire of the capital out into the peaceful backwater of outlying areas spared by the raging elements. The city was being drained of its population, the few remaining signs of life preferring cooler and more secluded hideouts. At times like this even flies would like to go off duty, just to avoid having to buzz around, move and breathe. But the System whose spiderweb trapped the country and its people operated at all times of the year and under all weather conditions. With the System there were no days off, no holidays, no lunch breaks. The System was always on the alert.

Once Vlad had been incorporated into its field of vision, the System kept him under constant surveillance; following

1

attentive analysis came an official summons slip, a peremptory signal from the Moscow section of the Writers' Union:

"You are requested to attend the prose section meeting," etc., accompanied with all the usual trimmings.

And Vlad understood that the bell had tolled for him with full force, but instead of giving over to distraction or despair, it rather filled him with joyful frenzy: if die we must, let's go to the sound of music!

Without wasting a minute, he sat down and in a half hour's time covered a page and a half, sending the System a resolute signal back: "We are letting slip the dogs of war!"

"As I have been informed, the secretariat of the Moscow Section of the Writers' Union of the Russian Soviet Socialist Federative Republic and the bureau of the prose section are jointly preparing a discussion on my novel, with all the practical conclusions that are to be drawn. I have nothing to apologize to you for, nothing to regret. I am the son and grandson of hereditary proletarians, a man of the working classes, and I have written a book relating the dramatic dénouement of an affair for which my father, grandfather, and the greater part of my ancestors on either side of the family gave their lives. For me this book is the result of many years of reflection on the dispiriting and already irreversible train of present-day events and also the bitter fruit of personal experience. If, left to yourselves, you were to look open-mindedly and courageously into the face of reality, I am convinced that many of the same "Why's" which beset me during the course of my work on this novel would also occur to you.

"Why is it that in a country of victorious socialism alcoholism is becoming a national tragedy? Why is it that after half a century of existence this country is being torn by the forces of pathological nationalism? Why is it that indifference, corruption, and theft are well on the way to

becoming the norm? What are the real reasons for all of
this, what is the root cause behind this state of things? These
are roughly the questions which were in the fore of my mind
when I set to work on this book. I don't know whether I
have been able to answer even one of these questions in an
adequately convincing fashion, but you have no grounds to
doubt the sincerity of my intentions. It was with the same
urge to help their country and their people sort out the
contradictory phenomena of modern life, so that once the
weight of past errors had been cast off they could make
fearless progress, it was with the same urge that my predecessors, from Doudintsev to Solzhenitsyn inclusive, wrote,
each of course working within the extent of his talent and
strength. Unfortunately, those who should have armed themselves with these books not only remained deaf to the voices
clamoring for truth but actually gave them a hostile reception. It is hard for me to judge why and who stands to
benefit from this ill being propagated in the tissue of our
society, but the inevitable end of this sort of treatment is
incontrovertibly evident to me: repercussions cannot be in-
ventoried, nor disasters plainly listed. If our society does
not face this today, tomorrow will already be too late.

"I harbor no feelings of bravado; I will be leaving the
organization of which I was a member for almost ten years
with a feeling of sorrow and loss. That organization has
numbered and continues to count as members people who
taught me how to live and work. But sooner or later each
and every one of them will nevertheless have to make the
same hard choice. The Writers' Union, and more particularly its Moscow section, is gradually becoming the exclusive domain of minor political marauders, of errant literary
shopkeepers, of all the Mednikovs, Pilars, and third-class
Yevtushenkos, the acolytes of spiritual parasitism.

"I am perfectly aware what awaits me after my exclusion
from the union. But when all's said and done, I cherish the
conviction that in the farthest reaches of the country, behind

the wick and kerosene lamps as well as behind modern electric lamps, sit the children who will follow in our footsteps. They sit, wrinkling their Socratic brows, and they write. They are actually writing! Maybe it will not be up to them to change the woeful image of reality (after all, this is not the task literature puts before itself), but there is one thing I'm sure of: they won't let their state be dug under on the quiet, though that is the design of the spiritual gravediggers of all colors and persuasions."

So on the appointed day, when Vlad appeared before the clear eyes of his prosaic colleagues, the lines of battle were clearly drawn and the positions entrenched. True, among the "colleagues" present he didn't notice any well-known faces or names, with the possible exception of the chairman—an inveterate liberal from the old "rootless cosmopolitans" who had taken on the disreputable task of drowning a fellow writer who had transgressed into taboo, in exchange, as it came out later, for a tourist trip to America.

"Lord, what a commission, especially that chairman," thought Vlad as he sat down to face them and remembered an old joke.

This was the legendary Soviet liberal with a never-changing motto on his fawning lips: "Better I than another." Many an ode and oratorio had he composed in the honor of his soul's anguish and moral tribulations, in his attempt to approach the coveted feeding trough where those most fortunate receive quite appetizing crumbs from the master's table! There was no baseness or perjury to which he would not stoop in his quest to always belong to the permanent opposition, all the while basking at every opportunity in the sun of kindly consideration from above. But his inspired face always continued to bear a martyr's expression; he was in danger, in distress, he was on the way to Golgotha!

May the exacting reader pardon Vlad, but he always preferred to deal with the orthodox school; at least they never had to wax hypocritical with him.

Once, Ernst Neizvestny[1], responding to Vlad's usual bewilderment, defined his perplex state even better:

"You ask, what is a Soviet liberal? All right. Imagine
our wise leadership as an enormous rear, mind the metaphor,
surrounded by a group of orthodox ideologians single-mind-
edly engaged in licking this ass, for which activity they
receive tidy dividends. They lick and lick, but their position
is scarcely comfortable since the present-day liberals are
pushing from behind, trying to elbow into position and get
their share of the goodies. The orthodox chaps obviously
don't want to share with them, they kick up a fuss and try
to convince the ass that what the newcomers want is to bite
rather than lick. The ass should of course realize that licking
and not biting is the name of the game, and that the newcomers are quite willing to do it better for less pay! Come
to think of it, the ass seems to be coming to that conclusion
itself, how clever of it!"

In Paris once, soon after his arrival, a great singer was
telling Vlad about the fate of a really great, possibly even
the greatest composer of our time:

"If only you knew what they drove him to, he even
starved—I used to bring him canned goods from abroad!"

"?!"

"Well, just look at the crowd he had to feed: his family,
the maid, the secretary, the chauffeur, the dacha guard! It
was no easy task to keep the larder stocked!"

The Lord will forgive Vlad for such blasphemy, but he,
as the son of humble Tulin shoemakers and the offspring
of the urban poor, who had gone through years of his life
half-hungry, thought to himself: "I should have that composer's worries!"

The play was meanwhile unfolding according to the rules
and the prepared scenario:

---

[1]Ernst Neizvestny is a prominent Russian sculptor. Now lives
in New York.

CHAIRMAN (his round little face triumphantly strained, eyes cast downwards, chubby fists placed on the table before him—he is distressed, it's hard, but he is only fulfilling his party duties):

"Well, comrades, let's start, who would like the floor?"

FIRST "COMRADE" (his last name either Strichnine or Struchnine,[2] or a combination of the two for that matter!):

"Comrades, when I read this, if I might say so, novel, I remembered my youth on the front—I was working in the Special Section of the army at the time. To speak frankly, we used to get lots of Vlassov leaflets that sounded the same as this, but in those grim years I knew how to deal with those who produced and those who read such trashy anti-Soviet ramblings" (and here the blood began to rise to his puffy face as he recalled the past, and Vlad vividly imagined what would have befallen him had he come within the other's power at the time). "Is it for this breed of, if I may say so, confabulator that you and I, comrades, shed our blood in the years of the Great Patriotic War?"

CHORUS OF "COMRADES":

"No, not for such as he, Vasilii Sidoritch!"

"Shame!"

"Whoever let him into the union in the first place?"

"All kinds push their way in!"

"He certainly needs to have his knuckles rapped!"

"Let's get right to it!"

SECOND "COMRADE" (with hooped brow, bulging eyes, and a hemorrhoidal face looking as though once he had accidentally stepped on a pile of his own shit and couldn't get it off):

"Comrades, you know me, I'm a working man, from a working family" (if one were to count as work the time his father had done in labor camp, then he really could lay claim to the bluest possible proletarian blood), "my writing

---

[2]Translator's Note: Play on words: poison/coward.

is on workman's themes and that is why I am outraged on behalf of the whole working class, of all the workers of our country! Where, for example, could Samsonov have met the sort of workers that he depicts? What bars did he have to comb, in what doorways did he pick up his characters, let him answer, if he dares?"

AGAIN THE CHORUS OF "COMRADES":

"Attaboy, Anatole, give it to 'im straight!"

"Drunken city bums, that's what they are!"

"A fat lot of work he must of done in his life!"

"In any case, he's supposed to have a dark past!"

"And a double-barreled name to boot!"

"It's in three parts!"

"Why lose time, just turn him out, it's just incredible the kind of literary blather they dare put about!"

"What's the point of any further discussion—the matter's so clear-cut!"

CHAIRMAN (now this bacchanalia sickens him, his liberal soul is disgusted with all these unrestrained thugs: he shakes his little head in disapproval, presses his puffy little hands to his chest in appeal, but checks himself in time—there is that trip to the U.S. after all):

"Believe me, Vlad, I don't agree with our comrades, I don't fundamentally agree" (and here there's a heroic pause, as though it's his last step before the guillotine), "it's not a matter of ideological error—if that's all it were, it would be easy to make good, I would sit down with you myself and we would come to an agreement, because you know how I care for and value your talent. But, as I was saying, that's not what's at stake, it's just that your novel is bad, hopelessly lousy, it's a flop, a creative failure, believe me, Vlad, believe I'm talking to you as a friend. You seem to have written yourself out, you've dried up; why don't you go hole up somewhere, work in a factory, get close to the people, and then we'll take you back into the union, you'll get back into our creative community!"

Well, maybe my novel, Alexander Mikhailovich, sir, really

is bad, but frankly speaking, it's a funny time and an odd place for you to come out and say so!

Vlad felt that he was about to throw up with all this pompous obscenity, and blew up in fury:

"That's enough of that, you distinguished pinheads! If you're not tired of talking, I'm tired of listening to you. Your lack of literary talent is only equaled by your lack of rhetorical talent, so why don't you look for someone else to practice your mudslinging on! Do you really think that I'm going to take your distortion seriously? Whom do you take me for? For instance, you—Struchnine or Strichnine or whatever you call yourself—what do you keep going on about your youth on the front for? Do you really think I don't know what you were really doing in the Special Section of the army? If there was any blood shed by you there, it certainly was somebody else's, because the only thing you've ever leaked is piss and it's your hands that are dripping blood. And as for you, Moudannikov, Medannikov, or more exactly Mednikov, what have you ever handled except for an office pen for signing denunciations, or maybe it's that your daddy, a first-class wheeler-dealer with dubious connections, counterfeited a nice certificate of proletarian heritage for you? As for you, Alexander Mikhailovich, since you're one of those who have forgotten much but learned even more, you've stuck it out, but, may the Good Lord forgive me, wouldn't it have been better for you to have died of a heart attack in '49, then at least your own children would respect you, instead of which the only thing your old hangmen ever taught you was their trade. How ever are you going to face your Maker? As for the rest of you, despicable buggers, I won't even stoop to talk to you, you'll rot even without my help. Damn you all!"

Vlad left the room to the sound of their enraged squawking, and, blinded to the faces and objects around him, flew down the stairs, through the oak room, tea room, lobby, the double doors at the entrance, and rushed headlong into the street where even the unhealthy stifling air of the town seemed refreshing for once.

In the state he was in, he didn't even notice that he had wandered near a familiar theater, of which for some time now, or more exactly, ever since Eugene Sh. had introduced him to the stage manager, he had become a habitué; to make up for time lost, he turned into the service entrance.

The theater had always been Vlad's hidden weakness. Having caught the bug while still in the provinces, he saw many stages, met numbers of stage managers and even more actors, but never before had he seen a drama performance which so unceremoniously toppled all his ideas about the theater and the dramatic trade as a whole. Unlike the theaters he'd come up against, here the stage manager and the show merged and became one, for the man played and worked for everybody—from the hero-lover to the makeup assistant and the set worker. It was a theater where the heart and will of one man permeated everything and created a theatrical miracle. When later Vlad was to remember in Paris what condescending little smiles the arrogant public there bestowed on the director's self-immolation and denunciation of Moscow snobs, he would feel fed up with the pretentious shamanism of the French maîtres, and always want to curse outright: You're lying, you S.O.B.'s, this has never ever been seen before!

As soon as he saw him enter, the stage director broke the rehearsal up with some excuse and sprang down from the stage with a nimbleness that belied his age, asking him with concern, "Well, what happened?"

"Just as was to be expected, Yuri Petrovich."

"So they finally dared?"

"They didn't even hesitate."

"The fools!" sprang from his lips, but he stopped short and tensed in concentration. "Stay on for the last show, Vladislav Alekseyevich, I'd like to introduce you around— you won't be sorry you stayed."

So Vlad stayed. For someone familiar with the life of this theater backstage and behind the scenes, its very existence was a socialist enigma. Rehearsals here consisted in the preparation of some complex military operation against an unnamed but universally assumed opponent (the producer, the actors, the technical staff were all in this together), and the show itself was a battle each one of them projected against this imaginary opponent. Before the play commenced, during intermission, and at the end, both around the theater and in it reigned the heavy atmosphere of a shared secret, an entente, a conspiracy, an expectation of something that would right away make a change in the world, a metamorphosis and a flowering forth. Believe it, comrade, and it will come to pass!

But the most dumbfounding part of the general mystery was that it involved not only those who inspired it but also those it was directed against. Since there were no official boxes, the audience was undifferentiated in rank and position and had to file into the ground-floor rows in random order; thus, no one was surprised when a member of the Politburo sat next to a dissident just back from labor camp, when a general of the Defense Department in his civvies sat next to an implacable Zionist, when a Central Committee Secretary for Propaganda rubbed elbows with a fledgling literary "Vlassovist." Furthermore, there was no guarantee that under certain circumstances many of them wouldn't be switching seats.

That evening the play was *Pushkin*, in which a man poisoned by his own chimerics paces about the stage in various personae, sharing with the audience one single endless torment: "No, I will not wholly die..." But this was not declaimed in dogmatic affirmation, rather couched in a beseeching, invocatory, questioning manner.

The first person Vlad bumped into in the lobby over intermission was E. K., an old friend who had done time in the camps, the darling of the capital's social life, who had perhaps set off the literary metamorphosis of Vlad's generation.

"Let them all go to hell, Vlad old boy," said the other, nearsightedly peering at him and clumsily trotting alongside him. "There's nothing more we can do here, as they say, the situation is exhausted, all lived out, so to speak; we have to leave or else we'll suffocate. Look at Brodsky, he got the point, packed his bags and—good-bye. I don't know what will become of him there, but here it wouldn't have clicked in any case."

This said, he melted into the crowd without taking leave, not that he had to say good-bye since they had yet a long way to go, living and seeing each other not often but under other skies and circumstances.

In the buffet, his friend from Igarka came up to Vlad, bent a raven brow over him, and sighed in sympathy:

"I heard about it, kid, bad news always travels fast," as he laid an arm on his shoulder. "God bless you, Vlad, I doff my hat to you; had I known back then in Igarka how this would end! Well, don't forget the old man, drop in one of these days!"

No, Yuri Yosifovich, he wouldn't be dropping in anymore, caught in the vortex of the impending departure, but the thankful parting words would be remembered lifelong.

Just before the second act, Idashkin appeared suddenly next to Vlad.

"Forgive me, Vlad," he mumbled, avoiding his glance in embarrassment, "of course my expressions of sympathy are neither here nor there, but I'm truly sorry that we didn't make it together. Maybe it could have worked out otherwise, but in any case, please don't bear me a grudge!"

But it wasn't up to him to sit in judgment over you anyway, Yuri Vladimirovich, you judge yourself and things will then turn out differently.

After the show, the stage director took him along upstairs into his office:

"He's waiting for you already, Vladislav Alexeyevich, try not to scare him off—he's quite susceptible, you know."

And indeed upstairs he saw a light-haired loafer, about fifty years old, with premature bald patches coming in on his large head and the face of a methodical drinker.

"Always in the opposition, just can't seem to change, eh, Yuri Petrovich?" The blond man was speaking to the manager, as though deliberately ignoring Vlad's presence. "When will you quit teasing fate, our old diehards are going to have your head one of these days—they won't listen to what we have to say . . ."

He went on in a similar vein for about five minutes, after which he got up, nodded to the boss, indicating they should continue outside, and then left without addressing Vlad.

The stage manager hurried after him but returned soon, making a point of properly closing the autograph-laden door; he then came up close to Vlad and whispered loudly and meaningfully:

"You can hand in your documents, Vladislav Alexey-evitch."

"You're sure of that?"

"You can take it from me—at this level, there are no idle words."

And he was right: the level was indeed high, and the value of the words even higher, as it proved, for once Vlad crossed over to the West, he found in John Barron's book entitled *KGB* a photograph of a certain familiar-looking light-haired man, with a telling caption underneath: "Sitnikov, Vasili Romanovich—Head of the Department of Disinformation of the KGB of the USSR."

From here, from afar, Russia still seems to be like that theater hall where no special seating is provided for those in positions of power and where, consequently, everyone is constantly risking having to switch roles with his neighbor. And when he thought about this, he usually remembered Sasha's wife's (Angelina Galich's) story:

"I remember how we rented a dacha for the summer in Jukovo. You know the scene—a closed area, a reserve for vacationing leaders, but hierarchy in no way becomes unimportant for all that. There's a store for them called Greece—remember as Chekhov put it in *The Wedding*: 'In Greece, they lack nothing!'—well, there they 'lacked nothing.' For us common mortals, there was an ordinary corner grocery where the usual commodities are available: cheap sausage, butter, sugar, milk, day-old bread, and, on a lucky day, some leftovers from Greece. One morning I went into this little store and couldn't believe my eyes: there was the usual line, but mixed in with the usual everyday customers were various historically eminent figures, just standing there with banal shopping bags in hand—Molotov, Kaganovich, Bulganin, and just two people away from me 'their sidekick Shepilov' as they say, who, to be fair, did lean more to the people after the burnout. So we were just standing there as though there was nothing unusual about it, when, all of a sudden, a thirtyish red-haired man in bedraggled jeans runs in, plunks a bag full of empties on the counter, and throws off to the cash-register girl:

"'Hey, Nattie, ya have twenny-one liter empties here, for one rub' 44; I'm givin' you three kopecks on top o' that, so ya just ring up 08 after 1 rub' 47!' The girl put the glassware away without a rejoinder, and brought out a bottle. Nobody even put up a fuss, or maybe they didn't want to get involved. Just some old lady, a maid in one of the dachas, standing in front of me grumbled, 'Sure, why not, if you're Stalin's grandson!'"

As one poet with talent who'd written himself out once put it: "Other times, other people." It happened to be his case too.

2

"February. Fill the inkwell and cry." But that winter didn't incline Vlad to righteous labor, or to tears, for that matter.

A snowstorm was blowing away the new-fallen layer, thaws turned to frosts, a blinding sun broke through dark cloud masses, and yet the awaited answer failed to come. The days dragged on slowly and boringly, only occasionally brightened by various social gatherings at home or out; the circle of old friends which only yesterday had seemed indissoluble painlessly excluded him from its midst and closed its doors behind him, continuing its own life according to the same perennial rules. Nobody repudiated him, God forbid, no one broke off relations, rather the contrary: most of those whom he considered as being close friends, given the opportunity, would try to stress their closeness with him. It was just that each and every one of them, quite unconsciously, had crossed him out, and divorced him from his own sphere of concern and his own existence. Leave us, proud man.

By that time Tatiana had moved in with him completely, and they lived under one roof, recognizing outright that there was no backtracking possible, that the future held no promises for them, but rather a doubtful unknown, and that from now on they were forever bound together with the lifelong chains of a single and unique destiny.

At first, Vlad anxiously watched his wife, searching for signs that this life of theirs, somewhere between heaven and earth, would eventually make her feel afraid or unsure of herself—but the days passed and she remained the same girl he had first met: even-tempered, attentive to others, and kind. Behind an apparent pliability lay the deep-seated stubbornness of an integral and independent nature, which yielded under pressure yet sprang right back, ready for ceaseless opposition.

Having become used to weakness in women and not strength, at first he was on his guard, under the impression that the two traits combined could pose a threat to his usual grasp on himself. But little by little as time went on, he was able to get over his initial watchfulness without noticing it. He calmed down and relied on her tact and sensitivity.

So, when finally, in the middle of the second week of February, the phone rang to summon him to the Visa and Registration Office of the Ministry of the Interior, he was not surprised by her immediate decisiveness.

"I'll go alone," she stated quietly but firmly. "One never knows what to expect if they were to refuse—you'd fly off the handle; it's better not to tempt fate. I'll phone you right away from a booth."

Awaiting her call, Vlad paced back and forth nervously, alternately imagining the best and the worst possible scenarios. "Who knows why they do what they do, today it's one way, tomorrow another, and they have the upper hand in any case!"

Her voice sounded so ordinary over the phone, just as though they were talking about the weather:

"They said no. Didn't even want to discuss it, they said that with private invitations they only give the green light in the case of relatives."

Rather than disheartening him, the news left a hollow feeling. The tension of the past weeks was replaced in a flash of fatigue and apathy—whatever happens, may they all go to hell, he'd had enough of blowing his life out to the gusts of their whims and fancies!

Vlad did actually get up enough strength to phone his theater friend and tell him briefly about everything that had happened. The reply he got was an earful of long and unconvincing explanations, with references to the clumsiness, routine, and indifference of the bureaucratic machine, but all that didn't change anything for him; he just let the words go past, finally coming to terms with the fact that all things have an end and that the mousetrap had snapped shut.

That night they didn't exchange a single word. It was as though each of them was offering to the other an opportunity to draw conclusions about the past, reflect upon the present, and weigh the future, while standing at the threshold of the unknown, to which there was now to be no end. Time to ponder and to decide for themselves once and for all whether they should go their separate ways or stay together.

Getting up in the morning and going out to the kitchen, she casually asked:

"Tea or coffee?"

It must have been then, with those few words, that their life as a couple must really have begun.

However, towards the end of the week, answering a routine call, he suddenly heard a woman's voice on the other end, speaking in feline tones: "Hello, Comrade Samsonov? You are requested to come at 10 A.M. tomorrow to the office of the deputy head of the Moscow Visa and Registration Office, Comrade Fadeev. The address is..."

The rest sank into his head, but through cotton wool. "What could this mean?" A hot wave of variegated possibilities lashed through his mind. "Had the red tape finally wound up, or had something happened?"

The answer came that very evening. He had gone out for the papers and upon his return, his wife called out in alarm:

"Natalia Dimitrievna called saying Solzhenitsyn has been arrested and to spread the word around!"

It was too much to take for one single day. His recent slight sense of relief disappeared, like the air escaping from a balloon, leaving in its stead the sticky emptiness of inexplicable fear. If they had decided to cut off the top of the pyramid, then certainly they wouldn't hesitate to blow up the rest, and in that case, the fates of people like him, Vlad Samsonov, would be deemed totally expendable. May the vanquished shed tears!

Nightmarish fears invaded his heart and held him in their grip. It was the first time in his life that he distinctly felt one could really sense a scorching earth beneath one's feet. The ground was truly burning under his soles, beating him back into the snowy corner of the twilight city, circling through the streets and in the lanes, giving him no rest, no respite.

The debilitating fear that wore him down became increasingly mixed with fury: Why was there always this all-invasive fear tracking him down, winding over and through him and destroying his soul? Did he owe anybody anything? Was he obligated to someone? No, he'd had it with paying this price for leading a vegetative existence on earth! If there were no breakout possible, wouldn't it be vastly better to put an end to it by cutting the knot and to hell with the rest!

But as his memories welled up, outstripping his flight from himself, he heard the admonishing voice of Sergei in the corridor of the Tagansk underground:

"Listen, please, remember everything, we'll get our own back, our time will come! Don't forget, Vlad old boy, I have no one else but you!"

And following hard upon, the condescending tones of Boris Yesman:

"The temple remains standing, Vlad, and quite a temple from what I hear!"

His wife probably guessed his state of mind and shadowed him around silently, and that late night their blind erring through the town helped them closer together, the better to face the abyss opening up at their feet.

Midnight found them in her old apartment. After having spent a sleepless night tossing back and forth until the first glimmer of dawn, they left on foot as before, heading towards Kolpachny Street, where their lot was to be decided today, to meet their fate, their destiny, the unknown.

Moscow in the thick freezing white fog lay before them, a big ink blob with the sparks of remaining lights all along the way. The city was rubbing its sleepy eyes open and starting to cook up its usual daily turmoil. Visibility gradually improved. But the nearer they got to their destination, the heavier his heart felt.

"Will they take me right on the spot, or will they play cat and mouse with me some more?" Vlad wondered.

More than all else, Vlad was worried sick about his wife. If they were to take him, she would be forgiven nothing, neither her links to him, nor her break with her family, not even her presence here with him in the Visa and Registration Office. Whatever its weak points might be, as Vlad knew from personal experience, the System in whose web they had somehow managed to be born was quite mercilessly consistent when it came to vengeance. In your righteousness, Lord, spare her this misfortune!

At this, Vlad found himself at the destination. Though the hour to go before opening was rather early, there was quite a motley crowd lined up stamping its feet and shivering.

In the midst of the usual conversation, confessions, and verbal skirmishes, Vlad came to his senses somewhat, and his spirits lifted a bit. So when he heard his name over the loudspeaker in the reception hall, he was braced for anything that could happen as he entered the office sanctum.

A man in civilian garb, with glowing coals in his cruel eyes, glossy hair looking as though it had just been to the barbershop, with a black part running down the small head, received him standing up and looking somehow through and over him and rapped out indifferently:

"The authorities have decided to grant you a one-year visit to France. Your return will be predicated on your behavior abroad."

"I have to think this over." Vlad surprised himself by hardening. "You are aware of what happened yesterday evening?"

"What are you referring to?" There was no curiosity in the voice, just complete indifference. "I'm listening."

"A writer was arrested yesterday—"

The man didn't allow him to finish, but broke in with sharp scorn:

"That is no concern of mine. That's all. You may leave . . ."

Vlad returned to his awaiting wife.

"I can leave."

He was having a hard time coming to his senses.

"Why don't you go on home and I'll take a walk, get back by dinner..."

He absolutely had to be alone, to think about what had happened and how to behave in the days remaining before his departure, so as not to give Galina Borisovna an excuse or possibility to use his present situation to her advantage.

Though yesterday's surprise didn't put Vlad in a position to choose between "leaving or not leaving"—he was doomed to go now that it had been decided—the circumstances now were such that even the slightest false step might prove very costly. First of all, he had to explain, to himself and those around him, to what extent the two administrative decisions were interconnected or were coincidences—the arrest of the one and the legal exclusion of the other. Just the thought that this coincidence could and certainly would make for misinterpretation pushed him into a total sense of prostration. He had become "the Grand Duchess Maria Alekseyevna"! Perish the dreadful thought.

Vlad found himself on Chkalovo Street, near Sakharov's house. The academician opened to his knock and showed neither worry nor surprise.

"Why, hello, Vlad, come on in for a cup of tea and we'll talk things over afterwards."

He continued while ushering in his guest:

"We've worked up a text with our requirements in several paragraphs, the main one of course calling for the immediate liberation of the arrested writer, which I think you should be the first to sign, if you see what I mean?"

The master of the house set about clumsily arranging the tea set in front of him.

"And you do have to leave the country, Vlad; someone who will be listened to has to be abroad right now."

He let himself into a chair and gazed at him aloofly.

"You must give careful consideration, however, to exactly what you will be saying there..."

The academician's ability to keep his spirit clear and his

mind on a fine-honed edge even in troubled circumstances had always amazed Vlad. His approach to things and his tone of conversation didn't vary according to the importance of the person he was talking to, or depend on his or her affiliation. In speaking, he never pressed a point but rather just spoke his thoughts out loud, giving his opinion as though it wasn't meant to commit anybody to anything, but it always came out so simply and with such trust that willy-nilly it made even the most inveterate opponent answer him in the same spirit. Though he had other prepossessing traits, it was this more than all else, to Vlad's mind, that drew such a large number of completely different individuals to him, even people who were diametrically opposite. As the saying goes: To each tribe its leader. Without a leader of his caliber, not only the tribe but the nation and its people as a whole would not resist.

Vlad left his house in a calmer frame of mind, and when he placed a call from a pay booth on the way and learned that the writer who had just been arrested the day before had already landed at Frankfurt Airport, he felt much better still and even waxed merry:

"Let's get going!" as a certain Smolensk workman with a princely name once put it, as he set off for outer space.

From that day on Vlad found himself spinning in the routine farewell merry-go-round. The phone rang almost nonstop, interest in his case grew by leaps and bounds not daily, but hourly, the importance of the event linked to him gradually overshadowed his modest person. Journalists and diplomats from half the world over, close friends and un-named well-wishers, mere acquaintances and half-forgotten girlfriends sprang up all of a sudden and started inquiring as to his state of mind and his plans for the future. If one were simple-minded one could conclude that prodigal mankind had finally reached maturity and was rushing now to make amends.

Even an unexpected guest turned up, one of the active

members of the Igarka amateur troupe, remembered chiefly for his poisonous mockery and tiny buttonlike nose.

"Well, well," he surmised, flaring his little nostrils in curiosity and screwing up his drooping face, "they're getting harder to come by every day, these writers; they must have put the squeeze on your fellow pen pusher. The best of luck to you anyway!"

Upon which he disappeared, as though he'd never happened. Vlad kept wondering for quite a while why he had come by and why he'd even bothered remembering him, but he couldn't find any satisfactory explanation.

The day prior to his departure, a black Volga with official plates parked on the square in front of Vlad's house, proclaiming to all and sundry "The fatherland sees all, knows all!"

It was interesting to note that the car didn't give any signs of life, and its passengers, including a woman, also looked totally immobile to Vlad as he passed by; they resembled some stylized car fair display. Very very occasionally, the Volga seemed to come to life, unwillingly discharging its hateful duties, taking some of its daily guests to the closest trolley stop, after which it returned to its immobile station.

At first the Volga parked outside annoyed Vlad to a certain guarded degree, made him feel vulnerable faced with this impudent indifference, but by the end of the day, he got used to seeing it as he took his visitors to the door and paid no further attention to its silent presence—if that's all it took to make them happy!

Towards the evening guests were flocking to his door, which scarcely even had time to shut as it let the visitors file in. And though his circle of friends and acquaintances was rather large, yesterday he would never have thought that there could be so many and such a mixed bag.

The guests kept coming in, mixing, then disappearing, to be replaced immediately by others. But before they went on home, all the members of this motley crowd managed to circle around in the mill, in his tiny crowded living room, renewing old acquaintances, rehashing the most crucial world problems, arguing and picking fights, and once again swearing friendship till the grave and slipping in a couple of drinks on the way, finally forgetting what the point of their visit here was in the first place.

Vlad met and accompanied each one to the door, listening to and voicing the words which are customary in such cases, shook hands, drank his farewell toasts, registering neither the faces nor the hearty words of parting.

They wended their way past him, past friends and future enemies, ignorant of their role in his life, as though they were cards coming out of a pack at random: King of Spades or Queen of Hearts?...

The flowing Santa Claus beard of a certain translator from the periphery of the dissident movement spread before Vlad; this belonged to an inveterate liberal who comfortably married his liberalism with the young Marx who was so dear to his loving heart.

"Here, Vlad, something to remember me by."

He was literally radiating simplistic good-heartedness. "It's a boxful of Russian earth, so that you should never forget our Russian earth, Vlad!"

The words "Russian earth" were delivered by the translator with such emotion and feeling that one could surmise that he was the only collector thereof, and that he had a monopoly on bestowing such boxes to those whom he considered to be deserving of such a high honor.

What a combination—human vanity multiplied by certified idiocy!

After him Vlad's focus went to another face in the crowd, its contours sharp but already somewhat softened by a drunken high; the man was a famous writer and literary bully whom he had known only casually up until then, with a reputation for hospitableness, and a love of drinking sprees.

"Alekseich, let's toast this one," as he rolled over towards

Vlad with a jigger in hand, "though it's scarcely an adieu, we'll probably be meeting soon."

At this, he gave a stubborn shake to his rapidly graying locks.

"I can't take it anymore, it's enough, when I have to go, I don't want to croak in this outhouse. Want to go see the big wide world, God knows."

He downed his ration and winked as he parted.

"So wait a bit, Alekseich, all's not yet said and done."

If you remember, Vlad had read his book in his youth, in the communal living quarters at the Ashkhabad construction site. He'd gulped the book down at one sitting, thrilling at the smells of the dug-out trenches, of the soldiers' sweat, tempered with those of alcohol disinfectant and burning powder, of smoke, tobacco fumes, Volga water. He was to carry this book around a long time on the tortuous roads of his odyssey, until he gave it away on a whim to a drinking companion who was also a shameless lover of the printed word.

He was far from thinking at the time that roughly fifty years later they would meet again in a literary get-together, and yet still later would be joined by fate in the chains of emigration. Who knows how their common toils will end, but whatever the outcome he would never outlive his gratitude towards this unwilling cotraveler, who unbeknownst to himself was the first to give him a crystal ball through which he saw reality in its true light. Here's to your health, Victor!...

Sasha Galich's patrician head was already approaching, tears brimming in his sorrowful gaze:

"It'll be boring for me without you, Vlad, oh so tedious, it's really too much, but as for deciding to leave myself, don't seem to have the gumption for that either..."

He sighed beseechingly.

And yet you'll have to, Sasha, sure enough. You'll pluck out all your roots and ties and you'll throw yourself into the rarefied atmosphere of exile and you'll stifle in its impenetrable deafness and torpid indifference, maybe to be saved by (may the Lord forgive me!) a chance death from even more excruciating suffocation. But then, who is to know? Now, after everything that had happened he was ready to cry the words "Be seeing you, Sasha!" after his friend's parting back.

Pretty soon Vlad stopped registering his surroundings. The faces blurred, the voices mixed and garbled together, and in his pounding head one exclusive rhythmically returning thought: This is the end, this is the end, this is the end!

He came to in an empty room, surrounded by the mess of the night before. It was a wintry morning, and the window let in the promise of a very cold day and sunshine for the road.

"Time to get up, Vladik," called his wife, seeing he had woken up and looking at him from the other side of the table with exhausted eyes.

"The car's due to come in ten minutes."

"Nobody's left?"

"Young Slepak and the kids went to sleep in the kitchen, they're to go demonstrate on Old Square today."

"They couldn't find a safer place?"

"Guess not."

"Well, it's up to them. Tired?"

"A little."

"Scared?"

"A little."

"Just hang on a tiny bit longer, it'll soon be over."

"I'm hanging on."

Then off they went through the murky daybreak, riding along the new-fallen snow on Dmitrovsk Road, going towards Sheremetyevo Airport. There they were drawn into the crowd of people seeing off travelers, they lined up for customs inspection, went through the passport and ticket control, and, upon finding themselves in the waiting area for international passengers, realized abruptly that this was really the end and that there was no return...

Down there in the hall, behind the glass partition, were the people whom he more or less counted as being a part of himself and of the existence that was now coming to an end. One could still reach them with a glance, wave another good-bye, and maybe even try to silently pronounce some words for them to lip-read, but though they seemed accessible, they all, both taken together and separately, were from now on beyond the pale of his present life.

"Attention to all passengers, the flight to Paris is now boarding..." This came out first in Russian, then English and French.

Going past the bar, Vlad couldn't resist and went up to the counter and said to the aging curly blond waitress:

"Let's have one for the road, and pour it just to the brim..."

Downing the burning liquid, he threw the change on the counter and joined the line, without a backward glance: "Headlong I go, all precaution thrown to the winds!"

"The seat-belt sign is on. Please refrain from smoking."

The soot-covered wings of the airliner suddenly tore away from the earth, the earth of his fatherland.

"Miss, could I have a drink?"

3

All right, that's the end and it's time to stop. He probably had only been able to express a fraction of what he would have liked to say, but memory picks and chooses what it wishes to retain as being important and that was the logic the author followed unquestioningly. Maybe it's in the apparently random words and utterances that the truth of his life lies, a truth free from deliberate flirtatiousness, playful reticence, and fake philosophizing. He had told the story first and foremost for his own benefit, as though drawing conclusions from the byways he had traveled, but nevertheless also with the timid hope (man is weak, after all) that this long tale would serve as a lesson and a moral for those who are possessed with the same ambitious intentions and who are setting out on a similar road.

And besides, this book is also a farewell—when people take leave of each other they are not always able to say everything that should be said to one another. However, what is given here ought to be enough for the past to be left alone, for old vengeance and ancient quarrels to be forgotten, for yesterday's grief and mutual pretensions to be dropped. He had called it quits with his life, and all inventory of mutual ills, insults, and sorrows had become irrelevant.

Another destiny was in the offing, the roads of which meander through the cold perspective of the unknown. Who knows how long the wandering would prove and where a final resting place would be found? He harbored no illusions: there was no return possible, though the hope was stronger than the reality, and this was the source of his thirst to be, to want, to act—without it, life would indeed have long lost its meaning.

He knows that his cup would have to be drunk to the last drop, but a certain realization went along with this: rage unaccompanied by compassion fostered strength but emptied the soul. For this reason, when he looks back, from wherever fate has led him, he sends you not curses but bottomless gratitude. For even the part of you that he had been able to carry out (on the soles of his shoes) would suffice for him to adore you, O Russia, with the rage and compassion of a son!

HOW SAKHAROV KEPT ME WARM

by Eduard Kuznetsov

> Wilt Thou destroy and not spare the place for
> the fifty righteous that are therein? . . . And He
> said, I will not destroy it for ten's sake.
> —Genesis 18:24, 32.

LOOK AT AKHMATOVA IN LIDIA CHUKOVSKY'S
double-volume work on her. For some these are new ideas,
different renderings of already well-known lines. For others—more than that. "Anna Akhmatova lived her life trapped
in a torture chamber. She demanded of herself and others
unstinting homage to that torture chamber and despised those
who acted as if it did not exist."[1] For me that exalts Akhmatova to a higher plane, and Mandelstam's characterization
of her poetry as the "symbol of Russia's grandeur" takes
on a higher meaning, one of morality.

Thus I'm inclined to think that the saint is seen differently
by the ruddy-cheeked servant of the cult on the one hand
and some dying leper on the other. For one of them the
saint's hagiography glistens with deeds of glory for the
church, for the other the canonical recounting is a tale rife

---

[1.] Lidia Chukovsky, *Zapisi ob Anne Akhmatovoi*, vol. I, p. 9.

with false hopes of healing ulcers. The truth lies with neither but with the one who synthesizes all, the one for whom all has meaning. And I would continue to say: the fact that Sakharov is a scientist is of little consequence. Scientists abound. As the prison-camp saying goes: "There are a plenty of people but few human beings."

And now about the hunger strike.

TO: Major Rukosuev, Camp Warden
FROM: Prisoner Goremykin

I hereby begin a hunger strike to the death because without boots I'm a goner.

Everyone else was given boots. I wasn't. I request that I be given a pair of boots.

Someone else might go on a hunger strike demanding immediate changes in the constitution, or maybe the dismantling of all Soviet missiles.

"Go on, fast away," my keepers nod approvingly. "You'll kick. Won't bother a soul."

As a rule that's true. But what of reason, and what of despair? Is there any room for reason once all one's patience is gone?

The prison camp is a monster with many faces, each with its own set of fangs. What I'm talking about is those things that threaten the soul with death and destruction.

Every hour of every day, year in and year out, the prisoner is trapped in the omnipotent grip of his masters' hand, which can squeeze him ever so slightly or for an instant set him free only to grip him even more tightly. Or, should it so desire, it could flatten him, cutting him up into small bits and pieces, rubbing him into mush. And this, I suppose, is one of the most basic lessons set forth by the masters of this country, a great portion of whose population has come into contact with those soul-grinding, soul-mincing prison camps. Moreover, the powers that be are unrepentantly cynical, and the more unrepentant, the more a soul trembles and bows down before them. And one quickly realizes he is nothing but meaningless ash. And I've observed that that works.

But a hunger strike, whatever its formal motives, is in part a desperate attempt to escape the masters' omnipotence, their power, from which the soul, dying of fear and worry, tries to hide, if only for a short time: it sits and licks its wounds, trying to restore its sense of self. *They* have an instinctive nose for the fugitive nature of the hunger strike. And even though they never tire of egging you on: "Come on, you'll croak all the sooner," that sort of mumbling really comes more from an inertia forced on them by virtue of their own position than anything else. The fact is that they secretly shudder: the slave has fallen from slavery; he's stopped trembling. He has refused the most basic of the camp's rewards: bread. He has by his own will placed himself at the mercy of the camp's harshest lash: hunger. If he is numb to the temptation of the reward and does not fear the lash, even for an instant, then what is to be done with him? The entire Cheka universe begins to rock off keel. But then, just as everything had its number for Pythagoras, *they* believe that everyone must fear something. And after a while they switch from the lash of hunger to something else. Cold, for example.

TO:
FROM:
Everyone else was given a pair of boots. I wasn't. I request I be given a pair of boots.

And after three weeks or maybe after two months they carry the poor wretch out of his solitary cell. No boots. It matters not. He has won a more important battle. Moreover, he might not get his boots, but he still has a chance at some sandals if he waits awhile. The powers that be sometimes will make concessions in the face of such desperate pressure tactics. They'll sputter and jerk, perhaps not instantly and not in the direction they're being pushed in. But again, that matters little for the hunger striker. What does matter is that by taking refuge in the fortress of the hunger strike, the faster has warded off a feeling of helplessness, despair, and the hate produced by them, a soul-consuming hate which penetrates beyond one's enemies to encompass nearly the entire world. It's a world that appears quite cold when you're looking from inside the barbed wire out.

So at the close of 1977, I too began a hunger strike. Why not put my neck in the noose? It's true, I wasn't demanding boots, just a general amnesty. Why not?

I was unbelievably fortunate. Alik Murzhenko's[2] wife was allowed to see him, and he was clever enough to hint that I wasn't fasting just to fast. His wife returned home through Moscow where she went straight to Sakharov. Of course, I didn't have the foggiest notion, since I was in solitary, in a cell one by two meters, not only behind a set of double doors, but also ensconced in the deepest corner of the block, cut off by a set of bars from the rest of the corridor.

I got used to the feeling of hunger fairly quickly. We know that by the end of the second week the body switches over to self-consumption, and the stomach stops crying for food. But then the cold caught up with me. It was December; the twentieth had already come and gone. And the temperature was also under twenty below. The powers that be work in tandem with the cold, just as they do with hunger. They know that the cold rips through a thin man much harder, and so my furnace was kept no warmer than a corpse. The draft is cold enough *with* prison clothes, and now they'd gone and taken away any extra clothing. They would pass me a teakettle with hot water twice a day. I would warm my hands on it. Then I would wrap it up in a blanket and

---

[2.] Murzhenko was arrested and sentenced to fifteen years in jail together with Kuznetsov for the attempt to hijack the plane with Jewish refuseniks from Leningrad to Stockholm in 1970.

press my feet up against its rounded sides. Only when at last it had cooled down would I lean forward towards the tin spout. The warm water gave off a scent of despair.

Closer on towards noon the barred door to my hole would clank, and I would hear a hopeful rummaging about near the furnace.

"Hey, you," I'd cry out through the door, "how come you don't turn the heat up right?"

It wasn't the stoker who would answer, but his supervisor: "You're getting the heat the rules allow: eight kilos a head."

I'm not hearing this for the first time, and God only knows, sixteen pounds of wood isn't much, but it should be able to heat the furnace for at least a couple of hours or so. But nope...

Later I found out what had in fact been going on. The stoker was one of us, but an obsequious groveler, scared into his place long ago once and for all, whose face would turn yellow at the sight of military brass. They actually *were* giving him an eight-kilo bundle, but not from the woodpile under the tarp, but some old rotten aspen wood. The most important thing was that they weren't letting him stick around the furnace until the wood caught. He would light the fire and leave. Then they'd lock up my cell and that was the last anyone would get close to the stove. The wood just sat there to rot away. Sometimes towards nightfall when my hopes for a second visit from the stoker had just about gone up in smoke, I'd dump out the kettle into the latrine urn and start banging on the bars. The iron-clanging din made your ears ring. A good while later the officer on duty would appear. Our exchanges sparkled with variety. I say to him, trying to breathe evenly: "I'm freezing." He, tauntingly: "You're getting everything the rules allow." There was another one, who, when feeling up to it, would walk into my hole, put his palm up against the furnace plate only to jerk it back as if he had been burned.

But then one day early in the morning there was a strange squeak from the corridor cell door. I heard the timid steps of someone stealing down the corridor. The feed door opened, and there I saw the drunken mug of one of the supervisors, not exactly the soul of kindness, but no mean bastard either. The main thing was that he had known me for fifteen years from my very first day in the can. And then in a low whisper he informed me that waiting at the prison gates demanding to see me were Sakharov and his wife. They had been there for five days already. And it was all over Western radio.

It was getting on towards noon when the brave Colonel Romanov squeezed into my cell, not without some difficulty. Romanov was the number one KGB man for all the Mordovian camps: ruddy-cheeked with a potato nose but a sharp eye; devious and clever and evasive.

And for the first time instead of the traditional "Go on, fast away," I heard the first attempt to reason with me.

And why not! With Sakharov's arrival my hunger strike was no longer a local stink, and Moscow had thundered down from on high: "Make him stop!" After all, Moscow on high couldn't care less about either Romanov or me, as long as the unsanctioned noise ceased. They certainly weren't going to play games with some backwoods screw-up colonel who couldn't take care of things. And on top of that this was *Sakharov*, and he wasn't exactly coming to some collective-farm tea to complain about bugs. He was all over town talking up the natives. That meant putting a stooge behind every bush and getting a report off to Moscow every night. And even Bonner's son had shown up suddenly for some reason. And who knows what he had come out for and what he would do once he got back to Moscow. The worst was having to guess what all of this was about. There was no way that *the* Sakharov had come all the way out to filthy old Mordovia just to cheer up some prisoner. No-o-o, sir, no way things could be as simple as that!

Of course, it could all come out looking very flattering on some local KGB man's record if he sent in all sorts of reports to his Moscow bosses, but then if something went wrong . . . After all, no matter how you play it, they'd blame him for this whole stink. The hunger strike was, after all, his department. Sakharov and his wife spent a full ten days plowing around the snowdrifts surrounding the prison camp. Needless to say, they didn't get their requested meeting with me. They knew from the start that they wouldn't.

I told Romanov: "How am I supposed to sit down and reason when my teeth chatter so much I can't talk? And anyway," I bluffed, "the worse you are to me, even if it's only with this cold, the meaner I get. It's the only thing that keeps me going." And I narrowed my brow and sharpened my glance into a look of hate.

The colonel left. Soon afterwards the corridor cell door clanked open, letting in the stoker. He dropped a load of dry wood on the floor and then another and another. . . .

And then the feed door opened up to the same drunken face:

"How much longer is he going to be here?"

"Who?"

"Sakharov."

"How should I know?"

He shot back an incredulous glance.

"What is it to you?" I answered suspiciously.

"It's just that there's grub in the store. It's like they're putting on a show for Sakharov."

I'm not sure if that was entirely the case; I later heard from people on the outside that the Sakharovs came into the local store one day, and as usual there wasn't a thing to be seen on the shelves. They ended up having to call Moscow to have some friend or relative bring them something edible. That got the people upstairs nervous, and two or three days later they had milk and butter brought into the store . . . to the delight of the local inhabitants.

I fasted for quite a long time after that, six weeks in all. But now I not only wasn't freezing, I was trying to pry open the window. But in vain; it was nailed shut summer and winter: fresh air was forbidden.

My furnace breathed forth unbelievable heat. Even the

ice caked up on the outside of my window melted down, baring the original outer oval frame. I stand up on my bunk and stretch my neck up and sharply to the right so that the muzzle-faced bars of my window lined up with the outside frame: beyond the web of barbed wire hanging over the wood fence I could see the dirty seam of the railroad bed. A lethargic steam train, all hidden in a white cloud of smoke, would roll on by, its wheels, barely audible, clicking laggardly and unevenly along the track. If I strained a bit more, leaning farther to the right, I could see a clump of field covered by ice-blue snow under an unhappy-looking sun, as if part of the backdrop for some awful fairy tale. And a gray, bumpy path winding its way in and out of the snowbanks. Every now and then I would see awkward figures in black, bent over furtively, rushing about, slipping and sliding. There was one—quite tall. No, that couldn't have been him. He had already left. Besides, he would never shuffle about all hunched over like that. He walks upright. . . .

No, everything's just fine. I'll make it. It's not that hopeless.

I don't dare touch the furnace. I could cook *bliny* on it.

THE PERSECUTION OF ANDREI SAKHAROV

by Lawrence Elliott

© *Courtesy of* Reader's Digest

IT IS JANUARY 22, 1980, A COLD, GRAY TUESDAY IN Moscow. A policeman stands in the center of Leninsky Prospekt, one of Moscow's main streets, searching the south-bound traffic. At 2 P.M. he sees what he is looking for—a black, chauffeur-driven Volga limousine—and signals it to the curb. A stoop-shouldered man with a wisp of white hair and deep-set eyes is sitting in the back.

Passers-by turn to watch while plainclothes police, whose high-handed self-assurance marks them as KGB, get into the car, which then melts into the traffic. One more comrade is being hauled off to confront the error of his ways.

But there is a difference. This comrade is Andrei Sakharov—one of the towering intellects of our time and the outspoken soul of the beleaguered human-rights movement in the U.S.S.R. Unable to silence him, afraid to rouse the ire of the civilized world by murdering him, the Kremlin has decided to isolate Sakharov.

It all goes quickly. Sakharov is driven to the office of the procurator general of the U.S.S.R. and informed that for anti-Soviet activities he is to be stripped of his decorations and awards, and deprived of the right to live in Moscow,

35

the city where he has spent nearly his whole life. That afternoon, he and his second wife, Elena Bonner, are flown 250 miles east to Gorki, a drab military-industrial city closed to foreigners and far from the academic stimulation essential to Sakharov's work.

On days when the wind wasn't blowing too hard, the exile would walk in the dreary district where he was made to live. Usually Elena Bonner walked with him, slowly, both with ailing hearts, both suddenly turned old. Sakharov would carry a heavy shoulder bag crammed with manuscripts, journals, a radio. He took it everywhere, even when he went to buy bread. Why? "Because the police would break in, smash the radio and steal the papers," said the exile. They had done it before.

Ironically, Andrei Sakharov had once been a pillar of the establishment, among the most privileged of Soviet citizens. Although he never joined the Communist Party, the men in the Kremlin considered him one of their own, *their* scientific prodigy. They showered him with every honor and material comfort.

But Sakharov was not one of them. In 1953, he had made the decisive contribution to the Soviet hydrogen bomb in the belief that once both superpowers held this catastrophic weapon they would be forced to negotiate their differences. Gradually he felt driven to speak out against the nuclear threat to humanity. Then he began raising issues that no one wanted to talk about, taking the side of those who were in trouble with the KGB because of what they said or believed.

Dissent in the U.S.S.R. is a lightning rod; eventually it called down on Sakharov's head the thundering fulminations of the wardens of Soviet orthodoxy. He was unmoved; he did not lust for power or the material rewards that separated the classes in the so-called classless society. But to people who spend endless hours waiting in line just to buy the day's necessities, Sakharov was impossible to understand. "What does he want?" they asked in bewilderment. "He had everything and he threw it away."

The Sakharovs are installed in a KGB-controlled apartment: four small rooms on the ground floor of a building across from the police station. The police can—and do—look directly into their windows. There is no telephone; soon after they move in, a police post is established outside their door—a table, a chair, four six-hour shifts every day.

Still stunned by what has happened to them, they are grateful for the couple across the hall. "If you need anything, just knock," says the husband. A woman who lives upstairs befriends them; her child suffers from an allergic rash, and Elena Bonner, a pediatrician, prescribes a successful treatment.

But the KGB sees everything. One day the couple deliberately turn their backs on the Sakharovs. And when the woman upstairs next sees Bonner, she cries out, "Whore! It would have been better for my child to rot than be touched by your dirty hands!"

Andrei Dmitrievich Sakharov was born in Moscow on May 21, 1921, and grew up in a lively, intellectually invigorating household. Like many Russian families, this one suffered during the Stalin terror—nine close relatives were arrested as "enemies of the people," and seven of them disappeared in camps or internal exile. But Andrei's father, a well-known author and physics teacher, was spared, and the boy went on to Moscow State University. He was the most brilliant physics student anyone there could remember.

Graduated in the spring of 1942, Sakharov was detailed to a munitions factory on the Volga, where he could apply his genius at physics and mathematics to solving engineering problems. Afterward he returned to Moscow, pursued his studies, married, published several significant scientific papers. Then, one day in 1948, he disappeared from public view; not a word was heard of him for nearly ten years. In deepest secrecy, Sakharov had been put to work with the handful of scientists racing to develop a thermonuclear weapon.

On August 22, 1953, the Soviets successfully detonated a hydrogen bomb, and three months later, at age 32, Andrei Sakharov was secretly elected to the Soviet Academy of Sciences, the youngest man ever so honored. But his subsequent efforts to stave off the "criminal" multi-megaton tests in the atmosphere brought a warning from Premier Khrushchev: those decisions would be made in the Kremlin; they did not concern scientists.

It was a turning point. When the tests went on, Sakharov was "seized," as he put it, "with an awful sense of powerlessness . . . it was terrible. After that I was a different man."

He protested other government policies: openly disagreeing with Khrushchev's plan to send students to work in factories or on farms; opposing the influence of Trofim Lysenko, the quack geneticist whose malign power had debased Soviet biology and genetics; decrying the industrial pollution of Siberia's once-magnificent Lake Baikal. In 1966, after writers Andrei Sinyavsky and Yuli Daniel were sent to prison for "slandering the U.S.S.R.," Sakharov and other intellectuals wrote the new Soviet leader, Leonid Brezhnev, that a revival of the Stalinist repression would be "a great disaster."

Still, the men in the Kremlin were willing to gloss over his addled notions—what could a nuclear scientist understand of politics?—if only he would shut up. Not one understood the passion that drove him. The year was 1968 and Sakharov's "manifesto," *Progress, Coexistence, and Intellectual Freedom*, a major statement of his world-view, was already circulating in the Russian underground press. In it, Sakharov detailed his vision of a future free of the tensions and repressions afflicting men and nations, and with an enlightened Soviet Union joining the West to save mankind from the disasters of civilization—war, pollution, starvation.

When the document was published in the West, it made Sakharov world-famous. But the more he was hailed abroad, the testier grew the Soviet leaders. They began to react with venom: Sakharov's security clearance was abruptly canceled; he was dropped to the lowest possible work for his academic ranking, his brilliant career forced into a scientific backwater. In the midst of these travails, his first wife died of cancer.

By the terms of his exile, Sakharov is forbidden to leave Gorki or communicate with foreigners and "criminal elements." Friends are turned away at the door and threatened with jail if they return. Whenever Sakharov steps out of his building, plainclothes policemen follow. Once, he and Elena Bonner are walking in a thick aspen grove, and their guards lose sight of them. Within minutes a helicopter comes booming out of the sky to search for the couple.

More and more Sakharov's first concern was to help victims of the Soviet system. And more and more his own fate became intertwined with theirs—human-rights advocates, Tatars not allowed to live in their Crimean homeland, fundamentalist Christians persecuted for practicing their faith, Jews who had lost their jobs because they asked to live in Israel. He spent days answering the thousands of letters that now came to him, writing appeals, interceding with the authorities or consulting lawyers on behalf of imprisoned dissidents. It was a struggle with few victories. But he did not give up.

He began to appear at the trials of those charged with political offenses. It was at such a trial, in October 1970, that Sakharov met Elena Bonner. She was a force in her own right, a tough-minded activist, 47 years old. Her mother had spent 17 years in labor camps and internal exile, and her father had died in prison, before both were "rehabilitated" by a regretful motherland. Sakharov, the middle-aged widower with three grown children, and Elena Bonner, long divorced with two grown children, fell deeply in love. They were married the following year.

The government-orchestrated pressures against Sakharov built relentlessly. Two alleged Arab terrorists broke into his apartment in 1973 and threatened him with "something worse than death" if he continued to make public statements about Israel. In Moscow—where there are no street maps worthy of the name—the idea that two foreigners could even locate Sakharov's apartment without police connivance is ludicrous.

Around the same time, Elena Bonner's daughter was expelled from Moscow University and her son was denied entry. She herself was called in by the KGB four times and abusively interrogated. Depressed, the weariness in his face reflecting tremendous burdens, Sakharov protested against this official "thuggery."

Elena Bonner is his lifeline. As long as the police allow her to leave Gorki, she travels to Moscow regularly and is able to let the free world know something of Sakharov's life in exile. Returning, she brings news, scientific books and papers, and fresh food rarely available in Gorki.

But the KGB watchdogs are biding their time; they know what to do. When Sakharov is effectively isolated, when the world can no longer learn what he is doing or thinking, or the state of his health—in short, when he has become a non-person—the Kremlin will have resolved the Sakharov problem.

In December 1982, Bonner is subjected to a humiliating body search aboard the Moscow train, put off and forced to walk to the nearest station. The following April in Gorki, she suffers a massive coronary seizure, but appears to recover. Later in 1983 she suffers a second severe heart attack. But she is indomitable. In only a few weeks she is bound again for Moscow, carrying what she fears may well be Andrei Sakharov's last messages from exile.

In October 1975, electrifying news came to Sakharov: he had just been named winner of the Nobel Peace Prize. His friends around the world exulted, certain this new high exposure would ensure his safety. But the fury in the Kremlin was now unbounded. No Soviet citizen had ever before been so honored. That the coveted prize should now go to their most dangerous and implacable foe was intolerable. With malice aforethought, the hierarchy refused to grant Sakharov a visa to accept the award when he applied. In the end Bonner went to Oslo and read his speech to the distinguished gathering.

Democratization of the Soviet system is essential to world peace, he said, and international security inconceivable without an open society. He called for an amnesty of all Soviet political prisoners, named 120 "known to me" and begged forgiveness from others not mentioned. "Every single name, mentioned and unmentioned, represents a hard and heroic destiny, years of struggling for human dignity."

When Soviet forces invaded Afghanistan in late December 1979, Sakharov condemned this brutal violation of international law. Three weeks later, he was exiled to Gorki without even the pretense of a trial. But he continued to plague the Kremlin leaders. When they refused an exit visa for his daughter-in-law, Liza Alexeyeva, who wanted to join her husband in the United States, he and Elena Bonner began a hunger strike that riveted world attention on this latest Soviet exercise in malevolent injustice. After 18 desperate days, during which both Sakharovs came close to death, the Kremlin capitulated. Liza Alexeyeva was given her visa.

But that success was only one more score to be settled. In the fall of 1983, following Bonner's second heart attack, Sakharov petitioned the state to permit her to go abroad for treatment. He feared for her life if she were to be hospitalized in Russia, he said frankly, "and her death would be my own." Last February Sakharov petitioned once more. There was no reply.

On April 24, friends in Moscow received a telegram from Elena Bonner saying she would arrive on May 2. When she did not appear, it was recalled how she had repeatedly emphasized that her failure to keep prearranged travel plans could mean only that she was being held against her will.

On May 6, Irina Kristi, a close friend, took the train to Gorki and, as specified in a contingency plan long before, met the Sakharovs in front of their apartment building. Hastily they gave her the grim news: that Bonner was confined to Gorki and under investigation for "defaming the Soviet state," and that she had also been threatened with a charge of treason, a crime that carries the death penalty; that Sakharov had begun a hunger strike on May 2 and meant to "fast to the end if they do not let her go abroad for medical treatment."

At that point, an impenetrable curtain of silence descended around the Sakharovs. Official disinformation abounded, however. At the end of May, Soviet officials blandly declared that Sakharov "was well, eating regularly and leading an active way of life." But subsequent evidence passed on to the international press by reliable sources inside the U.S.S.R. suggested that Sakharov was being force-fed in a Gorki hospital and treated with mind-altering drugs. Responding to rising concern in the West, the Soviets released a month-old videotape late last August. In it, Sakharov appeared to have aged "significantly and dramatically," according to his son-in-law Efrem Yankelevich. Around the same time, it was reported that Bonner had been sentenced to five years of internal exile after being convicted of "slandering the Soviet state."

In the judgment of Elena Bonner's daughter, Tatiana Yankelevich, who lives in the United States, the Kremlin's goal has been "to bury the Sakharovs in Gorki—alive or dead."

Will the Soviet authorities succeed? So far, they have ignored the formalized representations of Western leaders. But can they turn a deaf ear if ordinary people from all over the world join their voices in a combined crescendo of protest?

ANDREI DMITRIEVICH SAKHAROV

by Kevin Klose

© Courtesy of Kevin Klose

> Today, as always, I believe in the power of reason and the human spirit.
> —Andrei D. Sakharov

I

TUESDAY, JANUARY 22, 1980, DAWNED COLD AND uncomfortable in Moscow: bundled crowds scurried and queued beneath a seamless, iron-gray sky. Smoke, steam, and urban grit shimmered on blasting wind. The harsh moment matched the mood and expectation of the Russians.

Less than a month earlier, Soviet paratroops and airborne had ridden the hulking freighters of Aeroflot's military arm into neighboring Afghanistan and, in a bloody coup, had killed the Marxist strongman then holding Kabul and replaced him with another Marxist more to the Kremlin's liking. Reinforcements were moving down from marshaling points in Soviet Uzbekistan and meeting fierce resistance. Russians were killing turbaned Moslem tribesmen in the

45

name of Lenin, which was permissible. But the Afghanis were fighting back, spilling Russian blood in the name of Allah.

Very little about this remote adventure was familiar: it bore no comforting resemblance to Hungary in 1956 or Czechoslovakia in 1968. National television showed friendly Afghanis welcoming their Soviet comrades, but tales of maiming and butchery accompanied the coffins homeward from far mountain passes where the young men were dying. Soviet troops were at war for the first time in thirty-four years and Moscow stood condemned by most of the world. State propagandists portrayed the intervention as aid to a fraternal regime endangered by imperialist subversion, but most statesmen of the world regarded the surprise invasion as a historic new step by Moscow toward a prize that had beckoned Russians since czarist times: access to a warm-water port on the Indian Ocean. Even though the Western powers had all but abandoned assistance programs to Afghanistan in the 1970s, the overt Soviet move had turned a buffer zone into a battle zone. Few world leaders applauded.

American wrath went beyond words. Just seven months earlier, Jimmy Carter had embraced and kissed Leonid Brezhnev in a moment of saccharine sentimentality at the signing of a new strategic arms treaty in Vienna. The invasion ridiculed Carter, whose domestic popularity was plunging to new lows anyway because of the Iranian hostage crisis. The president reacted with startling fury to the Soviet incursion, suspending all bilateral exchanges and canceling a massive grain shipment to Russia that Moscow had counted on to help feed its vast, undernourished livestock herds through the winter. There even was a move to boycott the Summer Olympic Games, scheduled to open in Moscow in mid-July. The Soviets had sought the Games for years and spent hundreds of millions of rubles to build new sports facilities and face-lift ancient cathedrals and other neglected historic sites in Moscow and other major cities. The Games had long been planned by the Brezhnev Kremlin to showcase

Soviet-style communism while reaping millions in hard currency from Western spectators. Now, it appeared, cynical Washington was acting as though there never had been a Vietnam war, as though Moscow had not negotiated some of the most important post-war agreements with the Americans, including the first strategic arms limitation treaty in 1972, even while U.S. bombers were blasting Moscow's staunch ally, North Vietnam. Carter alone wanted to kill détente.

Incredibly, there was a powerful voice from Moscow itself joining the American hardliners. Dr. Andrei Dmitrievich Sakharov, the much-decorated nuclear physicist who was the country's most influential political dissident, supported stern countermeasures by the West to punish Soviet Russia for invading Afghanistan. Though millions of Soviet citizens had never heard of him, and millions more thought him an anti-Soviet wrecker, there were other millions who silently agreed with Sakharov when they heard his calls for political, social, and economic reforms broadcast back into the country by Western radio stations. And in an interview a few days earlier with ABC correspondent Charles Bierbauer that now was being repeated by the foreign stations, Sakharov had supported most of the Western sanctions, including an Olympic walkout.

Winter had hardened into a bleak passage of time. It was about to get worse. Around 2 P.M., a black, official limousine could be seen moving through traffic on broad Leninsky Prospekt west of the Kremlin. It was a car from the prestigious Soviet Academy of Sciences, making a weekly trip from an apartment in central Moscow to the famed Lebedev Physics Institute. The sedan's lone passenger was a tall, stoop-shouldered man with deep-set eyes, a straight nose, and a high, intellectual's forehead that arched upward to a bald dome ringed by a nimbus of wispy white hair. Although his income was enormous by Soviet standards—about seven hundred rubles a month—his clothing was nondescript, even shabby, in the genuinely offhand manner of most Russian intelligentsia. Fatigue and age lined the corners of his mouth and nose; his skin was so pale that in places, especially around the eyes, it seemed almost transparent, a chalky gray. Such a pallor is common in wintertime Moscow, when lack of sunlight, exercise, and fresh fruits and vegetables visibly drains the inhabitants of vigor. But chronic heart disease and immense, inconsolable human burdens had etched themselves into the man's demeanor as well: he seemed surrounded by stillness and silence, and his face in repose carried a solemn, somewhat guarded, mournful expression. At 58, Andrei Sakharov had spent most of his life in titanic struggle and he looked far older than his years.

In recent years, the state had grown tired of Sakharov's criticisms and had become increasingly concerned about the effect of his views on the citizens. The KGB had tried persuasion, vilification, threats, intimidation, and denunciation to deflect Sakharov from his dissent. All to no avail. He continued speaking out and the regime had to accept the bitter truth that its attacks not only had been ineffectual but, perversely, had strengthened Sakharov by making him a martyr. For example, when the organs in 1973 opened a press campaign against Sakharov which may have been designed to prepare the country and the West for his arrest, prominent Americans and West Europeans bluntly warned that scientific exchanges would be halted if Sakharov were not left alone. The Western threats were taken seriously by the more than three hundred other men and women who, like Sakharov, were full members of the Academy of Sciences, an institution venerated in the country as the flower of Soviet intellectual might. These scientists, who cherished their trips to the West as confirmation of their own status, were deeply worried by the foreign reaction to the attacks on their colleague. Such meddling in internal Soviet affairs was intolerable. But the party capitulated since the exchanges were proving vital to efforts by KGB agents and Soviet scientists to glean information from the technologically advanced Americans.

The situation of Sakharov vs. the State took on new dimensions in 1975, when the rogue scientist was awarded the Nobel Peace Prize. Kremlin outrage was boundless. No Soviet leader had ever won the prize, and 1975 seemed ripe for Leonid Brezhnev, whose statesmanship was viewed in Moscow as the key to the successful signing of the Helsinki Agreement on European Cooperation and Security. The accord had strengthened understanding between the USSR and Western Europe—and extended legal recognition to Soviet hegemony in the East European bloc. But Sakharov had gotten the prize instead—for what the regime could only consider as his seditious activities against the motherland.

Despite the affront to Moscow, the Politburo had allowed Sakharov's wife, Elena Georgievna Bonner, to travel to Western Europe and, while there, deliver an acceptance speech for the Peace Prize. The Kremlin could not punish her as it was inclined to do, since the Helsinki Agreement purportedly guaranteed rights to free expression among the citizens of the signatory nations. An effective program to counter this aspect of the agreement had not yet taken full form in the policies of the Kremlin's police organs.

This was the web of circumstance that had protected Sakharov down through the years. But now, the Afghan invasion and the West's bitter reaction had swiftly altered the equation. Washington itself had called a halt to the scientific exchanges, threatening to break all dialogue until the Soviet Army returned to Soviet territory. But Moscow already had secretly extended the military defense perimeter of the USSR to include all the territory of Afghanistan, making retreat unthinkable. The dimensions of the commitment were so great that, in fact, if foreign forces crossed the new perimeter, Soviet national interests would be at stake. Moscow at that moment had no intention of quitting Afghanistan, regardless of Western pressure. Furthermore, it no longer mattered that Jimmy Carter had once tweaked the Kremlin by sending a personal letter of support to Sakharov via the U.S. embassy, or that Sakharov had impudently used his revered position as an Academician to summon an Academy limousine to retrieve the letter. The way now was clear to deal with Academician Sakharov.

A traffic policeman on the busy boulevard suddenly pointed his white-tipped baton at the Academy car and flagged it to the curb. Nothing unusual here: corrupt police scour for bribes everywhere in Moscow, regardless of weather conditions. But now, the policeman departed from the usual script: instead of putting out his hand, he ordered the passenger from the car. Sakharov gathered his ever-present briefcase, pulled his overcoat more tightly around himself, and clambered out. In moments, he was ordered into another car and whisked away.

Sakharov's next stop was the Moscow procurator's office. There, he was taken before deputy state prosecutor Aleksandr M. Rekunkov, who informed him that, this time, Sakharov had gone too far. The state would no longer tolerate his anti-Soviet activities. He was to be stripped of his awards and banished from Moscow. His wife, Elena, would go with him for now, although the exile would not apply permanently to her. He was to call her and tell her to be ready to leave in two hours.

At that moment, Sakharov's wife was at home in their apartment on the Chkalov segment of the Moscow Ring Road. The eighth-floor flat, No. 68, consisted of two high-ceilinged rooms with a view to the southeast toward the modern antiseptic bulk of the Rossiya Hotel and the ancient spires of the Kremlin beyond. The apartment was crammed with books, papers, mementos, and photographs. There were several typewriters and tape recorders scattered about and multiple onionskin copies of *zayavlenie*, declarations, by dozens of disgruntled and disaffected Soviets. For years, the flat had been a mecca for an endless stream of Russians seeking solace or, at least, a sympathetic hearing of their complaints. Almost every day, new faces appeared at the large, heavily framed wooden door to beseech a brief moment with the physicist. Sakharov seldom turned people aside and, as a result, along with the rows of international scrolls, declarations, and medals struck, illuminated, or embossed in his honor and smuggled into the country by sympathetic Westerners, the apartment also was a repository of the unanswered hopes and demands of scores of plain Russian citizens. To the KGB, all these items, from scrolls to medals to zayavlenie, were fair game to be confiscated and held as "evidence" against Sakharov in any future criminal prosecution. Even the typewriters were supposed to be registered, for, under Soviet law, reproduction equipment of any kind other than pen and paper should be registered with the state.

When the telephone rang, Elena was having coffee with her 79-year-old mother, Ruf Grigorevna Bonner, a slip of a woman whose voice had sunk to a throaty baritone after decades of chain-smoking heavy Russian-style cigarettes with ready-made paper holders attached. With the two was Yelizaveta Konstantinovna Alexeyeva, a young Eurasian woman who had been virtually disowned by her own parents for falling in love with Alexei Semyenov, Elena's son by her first marriage. Liza had lived with the Sakharovs for more than two years while waiting for permission from the state to emigrate from Russia to join Alexei, who had been allowed to leave for America in 1978. She was a lissome country girl with jet-black hair and eyes and a gentle manner that concealed a stubborn resolution.

When Elena put down the receiver, the other two knew a crisis was at hand. Her hand flying, Elena desperately dialed some numbers on the apartment phone. Ever since 1974, the Sakharov telephone had been cut off from any international calls. But local and long-distance calls inside Russia had been possible despite the harassment of interrupted conversations and the whirs and clicks of recording devices tapped onto the line. Now the KGB's attention to detail on this arrest showed: even as Elena spun the dial, the telephone went dead. Quickly, Elena dispatched Liza to run to any pay telephone that worked and try to get word to the foreign newsmen. Ruf Bonner "was to go as my bodyguard," Liza said later. The women feared that the KGB would try to snatch the girl if they found her alone on the street.

They bundled up, took the elevator downstairs, and burst onto the sidewalk expecting the worst—a cordon of cops. To their astonishment, there wasn't a uniform or an agent in sight. They walked down the hill and over the small bridge that spans the Yauza, the little Moscow River tributary that meanders through the city northeast of the Kremlin. Two blocks from their building, they found a working public phone. Dropping a two-kopeck piece into the machine, Liza made a call to a longtime close friend of Sakharov's. Then she called a Western correspondent. And then that phone went dead.

But it was enough. By the time a cordon of police and plainclothesmen assembled around the heavily built gray stone apartment building, the word was out. From their offices all over downtown Moscow, the Western press corps was streaming toward the apartment.

Correspondents rushed to the address and took up a vigil outside the guarded building. Burly uniformed police refused entrance to any foreigners and only allowed residents of the building inside. "There's been a robbery," lied one of the cops. When American television crews arrived, the police retreated inside. As night fell, Elena was escorted from the rear of the building by some agents and bundled into a battered police van whose windows were incongruously covered by small, neatly hemmed tan curtains. The van took Elena to her husband while we raced back to our offices to file fragmentary reports.

Elena's destination turned out to be Moscow's main international airport, Sheremetyevo, north of the city, where she was delivered to the police headquarters station. Andrei Dmitrievich walked out of the building and, for the first time, she knew he was safe. Then, they were driven to Domodedyevo, the sprawling airport to the east that handled hundreds of flights daily to the remote interior. They were put aboard a special jet and flown to Gorky, a city two hundred fifty miles east of the capital and closed to foreigners. This was to be the place of exile.

II

If Andrei Sakharov had not existed, someone likely would have had to invent him as a way of illuminating in vulnerable human terms the transcendental cruelties of our atomic age. For the contradictions of his life up to the moment of his arrest were nightmarish.

As a patriotic young scientist, he made crucial contributions that put thermonuclear weapons in the hands of Soviet leaders. But as he matured and his knowledge of the world grew, he came to see Russia's rulers as expansionist despots, immeasurably strengthened by the weapons he had helped perfect. Where once he viewed the United States and the West as adversaries of his long-suffering nation, he had come to sense that it was his own country's leaders who were more dangerous and perhaps only the United States possessed the power—and hopefully the resolve—to hold them in check. Once, the totalitarian essence of Soviet rule had not concerned him; now, he demanded democratic reform, political pluralism, and personal freedoms never tolerated by the Communist regime.

In a simply stated yet complex and almost mystical vision of man's fate in the nuclear age, Sakharov had come to believe that genuine guarantees of human freedom were not simply desirable, but indispensable if the species was to have any chance of avoiding an inevitable plunge into devastating atomic warfare. Control of these ghastly weapons demanded the full interplay of every level of a society, so that every facet of its concerns—and its humanity—could be brought to bear on the struggle to subdue the instinct to destruction. Totalitarian rule stunted political maturity by demanding passivity from the people. The leadership's easy and unchallenged use of force to solve internal political questions posed immense dangers when such a regime was confronted by external problems. Beyond all this, denial of freedom throttled the dialogue, so vital to any society, over the nature and implications of the vast power it possessed— and how to wield it. From reflecting on the course of his own life, Sakharov well knew how impenetrable and formidable state power could be in brushing aside moral issues. He had come to realize that these moral questions—rather than matters of weapons and hardware—must be the starting point for any nation's leadership debates over the nuclear arsenal. Sakharov had been preoccupied for years with defining and giving voice to his views; the effort had carried him to the most anguished corners of human experience and the long journey had transformed him.

Andrei Sakharov was born on May 22, 1921, the first of two sons of a prominent Moscow physics teacher, Dmitri Ivanovich Sakharov. He grew up in a communal apartment in the historic city which the Bolsheviks recently had made their capital. Most of the flat's occupants were relatives of one degree or another, and this seems to have significantly strengthened the tall, dreamy child's sense of well-being and personal isolation from the tumultuous world the Communists were intently rebuilding in the war-ravaged country. The focal point of this large and intelligent clan was Sakharov's paternal grandmother, Babushka Maria Petrovna Sakharov, who was 59 when Andrei was born. Of mixed Polish–Russian descent, she had borne and raised five children, most of whom lived in Moscow and were part of the daily scene of the little boy's life. "Our home preserved the traditional atmosphere of a numerous and close-knit family—respect for hard work and ability, mutual aid, love for literature and science," Sakharov reminisced fondly from exile. But even then, the family was not immune to the cruelties of the new age. The émigré Soviet demographer who calls himself by the pseudonym Maksudov has carefully studied the Sakharov and Bonner families and found that the strife of the Revolution, and subsequent Civil War, is reflected in their family trees.

"Seven members of the family took part in World War I, while [later] five persons—four men and a woman—participated in the Civil War. Three of these fought with Kolchak, and one was mobilized by Hetaman Semenov but then [was] transferred to the Red Army. Four members of the family died of typhus and famine during the Civil War." Sakharov himself has said nothing of this aspect of his childhood; as with so many Russians, the notion of sacrifice and loss beyond normal endurance is simply part of the fabric of life.

As a well-known author of sixteen books popularizing science or teaching physics, Dmitri Sakharov pursued a rewarding career regardless of the new politics of the country. He was an excellent classical pianist and Andrei Dmitrievich Sakharov recalled hearing his father happily fill their home with the works of Beethoven, Chopin, Grieg, and Scriabin.

"Without evident social dislocation," observed Maksudov in his study of the families, "without emigration, change to physical labor, or insurmountable difficulties in obtaining higher education, this family of the Moscow-Russian intelligentsia became Soviet intelligentsia. Most probably, the process wasn't entirely smooth. Some members of the family must have found it hard to adjust; the lawyers and soldiers had to change jobs. But outwardly, these changes are not very noticeable."

The marriages of collateral relatives of the future Nobel Peace laureate brought other ethnic groups into the essentially Russian family tree: Armenians, Jews, Poles. (Many years later, the KGB would circulate rumors that Sakharov in fact was not a Russian at all, but a Jew who had changed his surname from Tsukerman, or Sugarman, to the Russian version of the same name. This was one way the political police sought to explain the physicist's deviance to the narod. Moscow's Jewish activists regarded this effort as being in the anti-Semitic tradition of most Central European police forces.)

In many respects, Sakharov's childhood was idyllic. "Family influences were especially strong in my case, because I received my early schooling at home and then had difficulty relating to my own age group," he commented later. But the idyll was not to last. Having emerged by the close of the 1920s as first among party equals, Joseph Stalin was about to begin the destruction of all opposition to his rule. In December 1929, the prelude to the Terror began, with Stalin's demand that forced collectivization of agriculture begin immediately, accompanied by the liquidation of landed peasants, the kulaks. The country was warned that foreign spies and turncoat collaborators were conspiring to undermine the state, and a wave of denunciations and espionage arrests began.

In 1930, before Andrei Sakharov had reached his tenth birthday, a talented uncle, Ivan Sakharov, was arrested by the secret police on suspicion of espionage. Ivan, an assistant director of the new Soviet state bank, had had the misfortune to have a close friend who went abroad as part of an official Soviet delegation—and defected. In the witch hunt that followed, the uncle was arrested and sent into internal exile. He worked for years as a draftsman and hydrologist on the Moscow–Volga Canal, and once escaped from his banishment long enough to attend his mother's funeral in 1941. Eventually, he was to die in a Gulag prison hospital in Krasnoyarsk during the war.

Ivan Sakharov's punishment was just the start for the family. By the time the terror-filled decade had run its course, four other immediate relatives were imprisoned: Uncle Vladimir in 1935, Uncle Konstantin in 1938, and Uncle Gennadi in 1941; Aunt Tatiana was arrested as the wife of an enemy of the people in 1938. But she was lucky: like another woman who had married into the family and later was arrested as the wife of an enemy of the people, Tatiana survived and returned to the family in 1943. The others died in prison.

Looking back on this grim chapter, demographer Maksudov commented: "In the 1930s, like all families in the country, the [Sakharov] family was chopped a fearsome blow. Nine members were repressed in the Terror. Ivan Sakharov had the longest camp experience. He died in prison after thirteen years of exile and imprisonment. Those men who were arrested between 1935 and 1938 died more quickly—in one to three years. Not one of the imprisoned male members of the family lived to be released, but both women who were arrested lived through their terms of five and eight years, respectively. . . . They were charged with espionage and sabotage, contact with enemy peoples, Trotskyism, etc. The targets of repression belonged to the Soviet intelligentsia proper. These were young, energetic people who had taken part in the war (four of the five who had fought in the Civil War were arrested), who had been educated in Soviet institutes, and who held leadership jobs. It's quite clear that their arrests threw not only their own lives into disarray, but also those of their relatives who remained free.

"Imagine the sleepless nights . . . how much suffering they must have endured for their near and dear who were in jail. . . . The Terror dealt a shattering blow to the older generation. It carried away a third of the men born before the Revolution and was the cause of death for two-thirds of the men who died between 1920 and 1943."

The young Andrei Dmitrievich and his immediate family came through all this tragedy safely. Andrei's thoughts delved deep in the austere riches of math and physics, subjects at which he proved remarkably gifted. The phenomenon of science's attraction as a refuge from the complexities of politics or repression is well known.

Whatever his later brilliance, Sakharov's high school years moved at a normal pace, and he was graduated with honors in 1938 and followed his father's footsteps into physics. With a group of other gifted Soviet youngsters, he moved into university-level studies.

When the Germans smashed across the Russian border early on the morning of June 22, 1941, panic swept Moscow. In the war's early months, Sakharov's classes were evacuated to the remote desert city of Ashkhabad, the capital of Soviet Turkmenia, then—as now—the most backward of all the USSR's fifteen republics. Its population of nomadic Moslem tribes tended scrawny sheep in the wastes of the Kara-Kum desert, seemingly more a part of the era of spears and shields than of Stuka and panzer. The changed locale did not interrupt his studies and Sakharov was graduated with honors in physics. In 1942, he and other promising new scientists were detailed to a large munitions factory on the banks of the Volga which manufactured artillery shells and other ordnance for the Red Army.

He arrived at a moment of supreme crisis. The motherland was in mortal danger, with the Nazis battering at the gates of Leningrad and pushing deeper into the vital innards of central Russia. The Red Army was being thrown back on almost every battle line. One of the military's greatest problems was obtaining an adequate supply of reliable artillery shells. In Sakharov's factory, teams of young women peered at each casing under a bright light, searching for flaws that could cause the shell to burst in gun barrel or at the muzzle. The work was exhausting, time-consuming, and inaccurate. Sakharov began analyzing the problem. Shortly, he hit upon a solution that allowed the inspection process to be mechanized, greatly speeding production and quality. He received the first of what would become a lifelong flood of citations, all of them marking him as a man with prodigious powers of concentration and analysis.

With the war ended, he got married, returned to Moscow, and enrolled in graduate studies at the Lebedev Physics Institute, perhaps the most prestigious of all the physics institutes in the country and the match for intellectual talent of the best physics research facilities in the world. Soon his wife, Klavdia, gave birth to the young couple's first child, Tatiana, named after the aunt who had been arrested seven years earlier.

But the cozy, sophisticated life of a Moscow professional which Sakharov himself had enjoyed while growing up was to be denied his own children. For the young physicist was about to join a titanic scientific-engineering effort that would cloak his next twenty years in the deepest secrecy. Instead of comfortable quarters and access to the best that Soviet society and culture could offer to residents of the capital, Sakharov and his family would spend most of the next decade living in remote regions of the country on the job. He was to be barred from ever talking about his work, and sometimes he would seem almost phantomlike, coming and going without warning and living apart from his family despite his love for them.

As Sakharov was to find out to his own dismay many years later, those lost moments could never be regained. He learned too late that family ties never forged could not be created two decades later. That was to be one burden of the post-war years. The other was that, with the power of his intellect, Sakharov helped vault his backward motherland into the forefront of the nuclear age.

SAKHAROV AND THE BOMB

by Kevin Klose

He was, as they say, a crystal of morality among
our scientists.

—Nikita S. Khrushchev

I

THE EVENT THAT PERMANENTLY ALTERED SAK-
harov's life and joined his fate with our own occurred thousands of miles east of Moscow, when a single B-29 bomber
wheeled in the clear air over Hiroshima, Japan, on the
morning of August 6, 1945, and released an atomic bomb.
The fireball burst two thousand feet over the ground and in
the combined explosion, shock wave, and firestorm that
followed, two-thirds of the city either vaporized or was
burned to ashes. About one hundred thousand Japanese died.

News of the stupendous new weapon reached Moscow
the same day, and twenty-four hours later Stalin launched
the Soviet Union on a crash program to catch up and, if
somehow possible, overtake the Americans. A second atomic
bomb devastated Nagasaki and, within the next week, Japan
capitulated. The collapse came so quickly that Stalin's long-
planned revenge for the historic humbling of Russia by the

Japanese in the Russo-Japanese War of 1904–1905 almost fell through. Soviet troops had been sent into battle against the Asian aggressors only a few weeks before the two atomic bombs ended the war. That had been enough time to allow Stalin to claim the Kurile Islands and reclaim the southern half of oil-rich Sakhalin Island as war reparations. But it had been a very close thing. The dictator knew that, with its fleets of long-range bombers and naval aircraft carriers operating for months far from home shores, capitalist America could dictate Washington's demands to any other nation in the world, and back them up with the ultimate threat of the atomic bomb. American scientists had put their rulers in an invulnerable position.

So even the Soviet victory over the Nazis was not enough to safeguard the USSR against its adversaries. Warfare had abruptly entered a whole new dimension and the motherland must not be left behind. The task ahead was enormous. But Stalin had the man for the job: secret police chief Lavrenti Beria. Only he commanded enough resources in the country and the vast organizational network that would be needed to build the bomb. For over the years of the Terror, the slave labor system had swallowed up millions of Russians, including thousands of scientists and engineers whose skills would be crucial to the effort.

As early as 1940, Soviet physicists under the leadership of the great theoretician Igor Kurchatov in Leningrad had concluded that a chain reaction could be achieved. But the war intervened and, despite the State Defense Committee's approval of high priority for nuclear weapons research, the Uranium Institute, set up to construct an atomic bomb, never possessed enough high-grade uranium, carbon, and other materials to attempt the feat. Little more than theoretical work had been accomplished by the time of the Hiroshima blast. Now, the slave labor resources of the nation were bent to the effort.

The first Soviet chain reaction went critical on Christmas Day 1946, and an important new date was established: a nuclear explosion in time to celebrate Stalin's seventieth birthday on December 21, 1949. Vast new settlements for the mining, separation, and enrichment of uranium were thrown up in the remote wastes of Central Asia and in the Urals at a place later called Kyshtym. Imprisoned scientists were joined by "contract" physicists who worked in nominally "free" institutes that functioned parallel to the prison institutes. The effort leaped ahead, aided by Moscow's espionage efforts, which now began to pay off. Vital information on plutonium diffusion, trigger mechanics, and other arcane subjects flowed out of the American weapons effort. When expatriate German physicist Klaus Fuchs finally was arrested by British counterspies in 1949, he confessed that he had been passing atomic secrets to the Russians since 1941. A Congressional investigation later estimated that the information may have saved the Soviets eighteen months.

This fevered world of spies and slave labor camps was unknown to Sakharov. His own scientific life was directed at defending his doctoral candidate's thesis (Soviet academic steps are more numerous and the path to full doctorate more complex than in most Western nations). The thesis was accepted in 1947, and a theoretical article, "The Generation of the Hard Component of Cosmic Rays," was published in a Soviet scientific journal. The fact that Sakharov's name was appearing in the relatively public forum of scientific journals is a sign that he had not yet joined the nuclear weapons program. The next year, two more theoretical articles by Sakharov were published: "The Excitation of a Gas-Discharge Plasma" and "The Interaction between Electron and Positron in Pair Production." An outsider could have concluded that this new scientist was making plausible progress in his chosen field of nuclear physics. It was just then that Sakharov went underground.

In mid-1948, his longtime mentor, physicist Igor Tamm, was charged with an entirely new task: he was to leapfrog the atomic bomb project and instead spearhead a visionary and daring attempt to surpass the United States totally by

designing and building a much different kind of weapon—
the hydrogen bomb. Tamm tapped his prodigy, Sakharov,
and some other young Soviet nuclear physicists and plunged
in. Instantly, Sakharov's name disappeared from public view.
He was not to be heard from again for almost a decade.
The cloak of secrecy was profound. Dissident Soviet scientist Boris Altschuler describes some of this in his brief
memoir.*

"Get ready, we'll soon be going away," Tamm tells Sakharov and the others.

"Where and why?"

"I don't know myself," Tamm is said to have replied.

Not every Soviet scientist signed on to the nuclear armaments program. For example, Pyotr Kapitsa, a future
winner of the Nobel Prize in physics, flatly refused to engage
in weapons research. Stalin had him arrested. Kapitsa spent
seven years under house arrest until the dictator died and
then emerged to resume his research into the atom, his
conscience untroubled. For his part, Sakharov has made
clear in *Sakharov Speaks* that he was not assailed by doubts
of any sort when he first joined Tamm's team. "I had no
doubts as to the vital importance of creating a Soviet su-
perweapon—for our country and for the balance of power
throughout the world. Carried away by the immensity of
the task, I worked very strenuously and became the author
or co-author of several key ideas." Sakharov is known in
the West as the father of the Soviet H-bomb, a description
he has rejected on the grounds that the collective nature of
the effort makes it impossible to single out any individual.
But there can be no doubt that it was the young physicist's
ingenious mind that carried the Soviet effort past numerous
problems at a rate that later shocked American analysts who
had calculated that the USSR was several years behind the
United States in thermonuclear research.

On Sakharov, p. 132.

In 1950–51, Sakharov and Tamm took up the question of controlled nuclear fusion and together outlined the principles of achieving a controlled fusion reaction that could duplicate the energy of the stars and supply mankind with unlimited power by using hydrogen as a nuclear fuel. The two physicists proposed the magnetic confinement of superheated gaseous plasma in a doughnut-shaped ring surrounded by powerful electromagnets. Sakharov suggested inducing an electric current into the plasma confined inside this doughnut chamber that would set up another magnetic field and further confine the plasma. He theorized that this eventually would lead to the extreme temperatures required to start and maintain a controlled fusion reaction. The device was called the "tokamak," which means magnetic toroidal (or doughnut-shaped) chamber in Russian. The principles of his proposal were revealed to atomic physicists some years later at a series of international symposiums—and remain today among the most promising lines of research into controlled fusion. In the United States, for example, private and government grants in tokamak research total tens of millions of dollars, with much more to come throughout the 1980s.

The first Soviet atom bomb was exploded in August 1949, in plenty of time for Stalin's seventieth birthday, but this was the last nuclear advance the aging dictator was to see. When he died in March 1953, the hydrogen bomb project had not yet achieved its goal. In fact, America technically had beaten the Russians: on November 1, 1952, a vast fireball rent the southwest Pacific. But the American experiment used a "device" that weighed many tons. For all its immense power, the test did not yet give the United States an operational hydrogen weapon. Meanwhile, the USSR was rapidly closing the gap. On August 12, 1953, the Soviet Union detonated a hydrogen bomb device of its own—a massive and convincing demonstration that Soviet science could outstrip the mighty Americans regardless of the ravages of World War II and the backward state of the

Soviet economy. The visionary dictator had departed the scene but no internal development could deter the thermonuclear weapons effort. Even the protracted and bitter fight for Kremlin supremacy, which lasted more than four years and was not resolved until Khrushchev finally bested the anti-party group in 1957, did not intervene.

The power of the new weapon was far beyond the human imagination. For example, the U.S. bomb exploded at Bikini in 1954 had a force equal to fifteen megatons, or fifteen million tons of TNT. This made it seven hundred fifty times more powerful than "Thin Man," the Hiroshima bomb, which had a force of twenty thousand tons of dynamite. As Khrushchev makes clear in his memoirs, the stupendous size of the H-bomb had a dizzying effect on the Kremlin. "I was overwhelmed by the idea of the bomb. . . . It was a terrifying weapon. It gave us an opportunity to exert moral pressure on those who were conducting aggressive policies against the Soviet Union. We developed and tested the hydrogen bomb not in preparation for an attack, but for defense of our country against those who might attack us."*

By the end of 1953, virtually every award and honor available within the USSR had been showered upon the young physicist who had helped so much to place this weapon in the hands of the leaders. At the age of 32, Sakharov was elected a full member of the Soviet Academy of Sciences, an unprecedented honor (collaborator Tamm, in contrast, had waited twenty years for full membership in the academy, receiving it the same year as Sakharov). He was awarded a coveted degree as a doctor of physical and mathematical sciences, received the Order of Lenin and the Stalin Prize, and was made a Hero of Socialist Labor. There were huge bonuses, and his already privileged status as a physicist became truly exalted. The family was given large new quarters and joined the special group of privileged Soviet citi-

---

*Khrushchev Remembers, The Last Testament, p. 71.

zens. The Sakharovs enjoyed vacations at well-appointed Black Sea spas, received special food parcels and clothing allowances, and had the use of an Academy car. There was a *dacha*, country house, in the exclusive party retreat village of Zhukovka outside Moscow, and access to the best health and medical facilities the country had to offer.

In time, his bonus would amount to more than one hundred twenty thousand rubles—even after long overdue currency reform cut the value of the ruble, it was more money than even senior party members would ever see in their own lifetimes. But, outside of a tiny handful of other weapons physicists and engineers, Sakharov's name was unknown. He was a national defense resource and, as such, spent his life secluded from the rest of the country. Only another scientist with a long memory would have recalled the papers by a promising young physicist that had appeared in the late 1940s and realized that the man somehow had been taken into the arms program.

Because of his vital importance to the country's military strength, extraordinary precautions were taken to safeguard his life. Sakharov was guarded around the clock and seldom allowed out of sight of his guards, even when he swam or skied. For security reasons, he could never speak of his work to anyone who lacked his own ultrahigh security clearance—including his wife. He could never speak with a foreigner and never communicate in any way with anyone outside the territory of the USSR. Beginning about 1960, his family was given a comfortable apartment in Moscow, and moved there. Meanwhile, Sakharov spent most of his time at the weapons laboratories in the Urals or Central Asia.

The effect on Sakharov's personal life was profound: the excitement and challenges of the work remained beyond the reach of his immediate family and relatives. His reserved manner deepened into one of remote silence that shielded a gentle, almost childlike personality. He adored sweets, disliked pomposity, cared little for the privileges of his new status. He forgot things, delighted in stargazing, dreamed about achieving new insights into the formation of the universe itself. He enjoyed games and theories of games and probability and, like many scientists, spent much spare time devising number games. Despite the work and the separation, he retained a special air that others as unlike him as Khrushchev understood to be humanitarian and compassionate. In 1949, when Sakharov's wife gave birth to a second child and second daughter, they chose a name that bore unmistakably wistful connotations for a man engaged in devising the most powerful weapons mankind has ever known. Her name was Lyubov, the Russian word for "love."

Russia was stunned when Khrushchev denounced Stalin's crimes during his famous Secret Speech in 1956. Rehabilitation of political victims, which had begun slowly after Stalin's death, quickened, giving substance to the new leader's move. Dismemberment of the Gulag where millions had died ushered in a remarkable era of Soviet history. It didn't matter that Khrushchev had plotted the new policy as a way of consolidating his power and eliminating political enemies. The thaw that ever afterward would bear his name enveloped the country; the ferment that suddenly bubbled up within Moscow's intelligentsia also spread quickly to other intellectual centers, including those of the secret world of nuclear weapons development.

For Sakharov, the winds of change mirrored changes that were occurring within his view of his very special world and its morality. Over the years of his weapons work, Sakharov has said, he saw virtually every aspect of the program. As time passed, he became increasingly disturbed by the immense resources devoted to nuclear armaments; here was the kind of internal migration that had beset J. Robert Oppenheimer, the American physicist who perhaps most resembles Sakharov in doubting the very weapons he helped perfect. "I noticed that the control levers were in the hands of people who, though talented in their own way, were cynical," Sakharov wrote in his introduction to *Sakharov Speaks*. As his doubts grew, so did his striving for understanding of the world beyond the invisible empire of the atom.

In 1955, Sakharov obliquely raised his concerns with Soviet marshal M. I. Nedelin, a crusty former World War II artillery commander whom Khrushchev had chosen to build the country's strategic rocket forces. The young physicist suggested to the senior officer that it would be a catastrophe if thermonuclear weapons were ever used. Nedelin, who five years later was killed when an experimental rocket he wanted to observe blew up on the test pad, told Sakharov that the country's leaders could make up their own minds when it came to nuclear weapons. This was Sakharov's first known attempt to modify the regime's enthusiasm for the new arsenal it was amassing. Despite the rebuff, he continued working with the weapons program and in 1956 received a second award as a Hero of Socialist Labor and won a Lenin Prize—the highest distinction in the country. The next year, a son, named Dmitri after Sakharov's father, was born. The physicist authored an article on the dangers of nuclear testing that was published in a propaganda magazine, *The Soviet Union*, and reprinted in a number of foreign journals.

This kind of propaganda was useful to the state, but it also indicated Sakharov's strengthening resolve to speak his mind. He has written that in 1957 he became strongly influenced by the work of Linus Pauling, Albert Schweitzer, and other disarmament advocates, and that he felt himself "responsible for the problem of radioactive contamination from nuclear explosions."*

The Western scientists' concerns dated from the so-called "Bravo" hydrogen bomb test of 1954 at Bikini. The bomb detonated with a greater force than the scientists had cal-

---

Sakharov Speaks, p. 32.

culated, and wind shifts that had not been predicted carried the fallout beyond the quarantine area. A Japanese fishing vessel, *The Lucky Dragon*, sailed unknowingly through the clouds of radioactivity. Shortly thereafter, the crew fell ill, and one eventually died from radiation poisoning.

The mishap helped forge the anti-nuclear movement in the West. The accident was reported in the Soviet press as one more example of American nuclear crime, the bombings of Hiroshima and Nagasaki having been the first. (Soviet school histories of World War II such as our children used in their four years of Moscow public education routinely described the Pacific war as having been ended by great feats of arms by the Soviet forces, while the Americans heinously sneak-attacked defenseless Japanese cities with their atom bombs.) Soviet propagandists knew they could have a field day with the *Lucky Dragon* tragedy because no such incident, if it ever occurred in Moscow's own weapons testing program, would have to be publicly acknowledged.

When the USSR launched its crash nuclear weapons program in the late 1940s, little was known about the hazards of storing the lethally radioactive wastes produced by manufacturing weapons-grade uranium. One of the fabrication facilities for atom bombs was the isolated site called Kyshtym, deep in the Ural Mountains in the vicinity of Sverdlovsk, the city over which Francis Gary Powers would be shot down in his U-2 in May 1960. The Kyshtym complex produced nuclear weapons and nuclear wastes. In late 1957, according to exiled Soviet biologist Zhores Medvedev in *Nuclear Disaster in the Urals*, sloppily stored and long-neglected wastes without warning suddenly heated and detonated, sending tons of intensely radioactive debris high into the air. It had been a heat discharge, somewhat akin to a kettle blowing its top. This was not an atomic explosion. But, within hours, strong winds spread toxic clouds of radioactive material far downwind. A mass evacuation began, but the fallout reached many places before either word of the disaster or rescuers and decontamination forces could get there. Victims of the mysterious catastrophe streamed into area hospitals.

There is no known account of how many Russians may have died of acute radiation poisoning—or even if anyone in fact did expire from the fallout. But anyone who had received more than about four thousand rads (a unit of radiation exposure) was doomed. Within the first few hours of exposure, these victims would be seized by vomiting and diarrhea that could not be controlled by any medicine. Profound mental depression would deepen into falling blood pressure, shock, convulsions, and coma. Within three days, the first Kyshtym disaster deaths would have been counted.

Russians who received between eighteen hundred and thirty-eight hundred rads would take longer to die—about ten days. Radiation fallout would kill the fast-growing cells of these victims' intestinal tracts, making digestion of any nutrients impossible. High fevers, diarrhea and other symptoms of gastric failure, and a reduced response to infection marked the fatal decline. The third group of early fatalities would have been those receiving between two hundred and one thousand rads, enough to destroy the bone marrow's production of red and white blood cells. From the third to the seventh weeks after exposure, they would be in grave danger from infections that their weakened bodies could not repel. Death would have come to some in this aftermath.

In the months and years afterward, many others who had survived the nuclear accident without apparent side effects would experience unaccountable strange maladies. In some cases these could take decades to emerge. Men and women alike might be made sterile by the radiation, sometimes for months, sometimes for the rest of their lives. Years later, there probably would be a higher incidence of blinding eye cataracts than elsewhere in the Soviet Union. The same would be true for leukemia and other forms of cancer. Finally, it was possible that genetic abnormalities and physical deformities would emerge to be passed inexorably from parents to children and their children for centuries. Unlike a flood, a fire, or even a war, this catastrophe would be locked within the genetic material of the cells themselves.

The Soviets have never acknowledged that anything like the Kyshtym accident has ever occurred—hardly a surprise in a nation where airplanes don't crash, trains don't derail, and coal mines don't blow up. Despite the fact that Medvedev's assertions initially were met with skepticism by a number of Western scientists, there is substantial reason to believe he was right. In recent years, some analysts in the West have begun defending him, in part because émigrés during the 1970s brought consistent descriptions of a vast area in the southern Urals that is closed to normal travel and where people are forbidden to live. Numerous other details, such as reports of periodic expeditions into the area by heavily suited squads that sound much like radiation decontamination units, lead to the strong suspicion that Medvedev's critics are wrong.

The Kyshtym disaster, or the probability of it, must be described, however. I believe it had a profound impact on Sakharov's development as a champion of human freedoms. My own belief is that he and other Soviet physicists learned early of the nuclear accident—either by credible gossip from their colleagues within the relatively small group of men engaged in the nuclear arms programs or because, more logically, they were called upon for advice in the storage of atomic wastes so that the accident would never be repeated. Even in the tightly controlled world of police state military research, it is almost inconceivable that Sakharov and other key men in the nuclear programs would not have been consulted in the aftermath of Kyshtym. However elliptical the inquiries might have been, it would never have taken a man with the intellect of Sakharov very long to guess what had happened. At the same time, it is not surprising that Sakharov has never alluded to Kyshtym in his writings and recollections. He has refused to discuss the substance of the Soviet nuclear weapons program in any way that could be construed by the KGB as a violation of national security secrets. "I have never infringed state secrecy, and any talk of this is slander," Sakharov has asserted.* The Soviets many times have accused Sakharov of being duped by the West, plied with favors in return for military secrets; these accusations are secret police fabrications.

Prior to 1957, there is no strong evidence of substantial activism on the part of the Soviet scientific community against the weapons programs and tests. This is easily attributable to the fact that Stalin was alive until 1953 and the Terror went unrepudiated for three more years after his death. In addition, aside from the highly likely event of individual radiation accidents in the manufacture of weapons-grade plutonium and weapons fabrication, it was not until the 1957 Kyshtym incident that Soviet scientists had the kind of wide experience with radiation poisoning that their American contemporaries had had after Hiroshima and Nagasaki—which sharpened fears of nuclear holocaust among U.S. nuclear scientists.

In part, I believe, the Urals disaster helps explain the peculiar vehemence with which Sakharov addresses the dangers of long-term genetic damage from weapons test fallout. The flavor of his anguish comes through most strongly in the introduction to *Sakharov Speaks*:

"As is known, the absorption of the radioactive products of nuclear explosions by the billions of people inhabiting the earth leads to an increase in the incidence of several diseases and birth defects, of so-called subthreshold biological effects—for example, because of damage to DNA molecules, the bearers of heredity. When the radioactive

---

On Sakharov, p. 250.

products of an explosion get into the atmosphere, each megaton of the nuclear explosion means thousands of unknown victims. And each series of tests of a nuclear weapon involves tens of megatons; i.e., tens of thousands of victims."

There is a genuine note of urgency detectable in the way the physicist describes his subsequent attempts—and repeated failures—to persuade the leaders to suspend their testing. He was joined by Tamm and Igor Kurchatov, the senior Soviet scientist who had accompanied Khrushchev to England in 1956 and who delivered a series of papers on nuclear fusion that included Sakharov's tokamak proposals. At one point, Kurchatov flew to Yalta in a fruitless attempt to talk the vacationing Khrushchev out of a new series of H-bomb tests. Although this struggle by the senior nuclear scientists of the USSR mirrored similar struggles in the United States, the conditions surrounding the Soviets' efforts were vastly different. While Western media delved into the question of health issues (much tougher reporting emerged in the post-Vietnam, post-Watergate era) and nuclear opponents spoke out and demonstrated mounting concerns that reflected the apprehensions of many more who were less vocal, ordinary Soviet citizens were told almost nothing about the dangers of nuclear testing, and did not even comprehend that such bombs were being exploded on Soviet soil. The relative ignorance and powerlessness of Russian masses in the face of nuclear testing must have sharpened Sakharov's concern about the consequences for a nation when its leaders starve the populace of information. As his views developed, he spoke out vehemently against the deliberate policies of the regime in keeping information from the masses. Sakharov's craving for cessation of the test series is tinged with rage, a very foreign emotion for so restrained and gentle a man.

The United States and the Soviet Union agreed to a one-year test moratorium in 1958 which actually lasted until

mid-1961. Then, Khrushchev ordered up a massive demonstration of Soviet might to intimidate President Kennedy
during a tense new showdown over the status of West Berlin.
Sakharov desperately tried to head off the test, sending a
note to Khrushchev during a meeting of scientists with
Khrushchev and others in the Kremlin. The exchanges that
followed between the two men and their own recollections
of the dialogue make clear that their differences were ir-
reconcilable. Different ethics, experience, and outlook divided the privileged and idealistic physicist and the
immensely tough Soviet premier whose instincts remained
largely those of a shrewd peasant with his own survival as
a powerful leader uppermost in mind.

"To resume tests after a three-year moratorium would
undermine the talks on banning tests and on disarmament,
and would lead to a new round in the armaments race—
especially in the sphere of intercontinental missiles and antimissile defense," Sakharov wrote to Khrushchev.

In his memoirs, Khrushchev recalled: "[Sakharov] was
devoted to the idea that science should bring peace and
prosperity to the world, that it should help preserve and
improve the conditions for human life. He hated the thought
that science might be used to destroy life, to contaminate
the atmosphere, to kill people slowly by radioactive poisoning. However, he went too far in thinking that he had
the right to decide whether the bomb he had developed could
ever be used in the future. . . .

"This conflict between Sakharov and me left a lasting
imprint on us both. I took it as evidence that he didn't fully
understand what was in the best interest of the state, and
therefore from that moment on I was somewhat on my guard
with him."

Khrushchev recollected that a petition was discussed and
rejected and then, in a remarkable passage, he describes the
ensuing gigantic explosion, which equaled fifty-seven million tons of TNT, nearly 15 percent greater than Soviet

scientists had estimated: "The bomb made an immensely powerful blast. The world had never seen such an explosion before. . . . It was colossal, just incredible! Our experts later explained to me that if you took into account the shock wave and the radioactive contamination of the air, then the bomb produced as much destruction as 100 million tons of TNT."

Khrushchev ruefully noted that his advisers made clear to him that such a bomb was too big to be used safely against much of Central Europe because its fallout would poison ally East Germany as well as parts of Western Russia. "However, we would not jeopardize ourselves or our allies if we dropped the bomb on England, Spain, France, or the United States," he wrote.*

One year later, Sakharov attempted to persuade the Ministry of Medium Machine Building to forgo "a routine test explosion that was actually useless from the technical point of view. The explosion was to be powerful, so that the number of anticipated victims was colossal. Realizing the unjustifiable criminal nature of this plan, I made desperate efforts to stop it. This went on for several weeks—weeks that for me were full of tension." The night before the shot, he telephoned the minister and threatened to resign if the test were carried out. The minister was unimpressed. Preparations continued and another attempt to postpone the experiment also failed. "The feeling of impotence and fright that seized me on that day has remained in my memory ever since, and it has worked much change in me as I moved toward my present attitude," Sakharov concluded.

Later that year, he suggested to senior officials that the USSR consider reviving an earlier U.S. proposal for banning tests in the atmosphere, oceans, and space, thus eliminating fallout contamination and allowing for a measure of seismographic monitoring. The partial test ban treaty was agreed

---

Khrushchev Remembers, The Last Testament, p. 71.

to by Kennedy and Khrushchev and signed in 1963 in Moscow. It remains in force today, and Sakharov has said, "It is possible that my initiative was of help in this historic act."†

II

Simultaneous with these efforts, a second and equally remarkable battle was under way within the Soviet scientific community for control of the science of genetics. Although genetics nominally was unrelated to atomic physics, the coming of the nuclear age had forced a close tie between the two disciplines because of the power of radiation to alter genetic structure. Inevitably, the struggle over the future of Soviet genetics involved Sakharov. His influence within the scientific community was so great that it proved decisive.

Ever since genetics emerged in the early nineteenth century as a new discipline, Russians have been among the leaders in studying biological inheritance. As a science that delved into the inherited nature of life on earth, genetics turned out to be especially vulnerable not only to fundamentalist religious attack, but also to political subversion. For a number of reasons, this proved especially true in post-revolutionary Russia. When the Bolsheviks came to power, they brought with them the ideological conviction that, in building a new social order, it also was possible to build a New Soviet Man. Like the know-nothing Red Guards of Mao's China two generations later, the peasant zealots of the new "science" of communism were eager to destroy while making their own indelible mark on human history. Stalin's murderous collectivization had ruined the nation's agriculture and, as output declined and the specter of chronic starvation grew, the search for a miracle recovery grew

---

†*Sakharov Speaks*, p. 34.

frantic. The stage was set for an assault that would shatter classic Russian genetics and send the fledgling Soviet Union firmly back to the dark ages of biological research.

The man who engineered this bizarre feat was a provincial agronomist named Trofim Lysenko, who surfaced in the mid-1930s claiming that his revolutionary methods of handling grain seed had brought enormous harvest yields. Lysenko claimed that some protein-rich but slow-growing wheat varieties could be transformed into fast-growing strains by subjecting them to unusual environmental conditions. He claimed that in one generation, his "vernalization" techniques could induce winter wheat, normally planted in the fall to be harvested the next summer, to mature in a single season. He also said he could change fast-maturing spring wheat into high-protein winter wheat by exposing the seeds to frigid winter conditions. His claims ran directly opposite to Mendelian genetics, but they were backed by falsified harvest figures.

Much like the fraudulent Stakhanovite movement that appeared at about the same time, Lysenkoism swept forward. Lysenko's assertion that a living organism could be dramatically changed by environment independent of inheritance was powerfully seductive to the regime. By the end of the decade, Mendelian genetics was routed and the USSR became a scientific laughingstock to the rest of the world. But in Stalin's Russia, the consequences of failing to agree with the new crackpot orthodoxy could be grim. Biologists who opposed Lysenko were purged from their positions; by the late 1940s, a number of scientists, including one of the world's most influential plant geneticists, Nikolai Vavilov, were imprisoned because they refused to submit to the new theories. In a crowning perversion, Lysenko was made director of the Soviet Genetics Institute in 1940 and showered with awards, including membership in the Academy of Sciences.

When Stalin died, Lysenko managed to ingratiate himself

with Khrushchev and continued riding high. But the atomic age caught up with him in a way that was not lacking in its own grim irony. By the mid-1950s, even the world of Soviet genetics had learned that radiation exposure could alter the cells' genetic codes, creating mutations—a ghastly, instant cause and effect somewhat analogous to Lysenkoist principles. There was an urgent need for the Soviets to probe this genetic danger. Lysenko, who preached that chromosomes were irrelevant to heredity, stood in the way. Sakharov was drawn into the effort to resume rational study of genetics. Because of his prestige, it was relatively easy to get audiences with the senior Kremlin leaders. In 1958, for example, he spoke about the crisis in Soviet biology with Mikhail Suslov, the gaunt, bespectacled party theoretician who was to serve as chief Soviet ideologue for nearly thirty years after the death of Stalin. The results were inconclusive, but Sakharov persisted, haunted by "the complete defenselessness of descendants with regard to our actions."*

The issue came up anew at an election to the Academy of Sciences in the early 1960s, when Academician Lysenko sought to have two colleagues admitted as full members. The two received provisional approval within the biology section of the research institute which Lysenko controlled, and then were blackballed by the full membership of the Academy after Sakharov and some other physicists argued forcefully against Lysenkoism. Khrushchev was infuriated but caught off guard. The next year, when the Academy stubbornly refused again to admit the two Lysenkoists to membership, Khrushchev in retaliation launched a plot to liquidate the Academy of Sciences. But before he could carry it off, he was overthrown. Within a year, Lysenko had disappeared from the scene. Classic Mendelian genetics reappeared as an acceptable science, but the Lysenkoists

---

*On Sakharov, p. 184.

hung on stubbornly through the succeeding decade. Meanwhile, Soviet biological research resumed along lines that the rest of the scientific world could understand.

The fight over Lysenko and his immense power moved Sakharov toward greater awareness of political questions; inevitably, his interest and new sensitivity came to be centered on the nature of a system that gave its leaders absolute power to decree which science was acceptable and which was not. The physicist's evolution as a man of political action with interests far beyond the borders of quantum physics continued.

The arrival of the Brezhnev leadership in October 1964 accelerated this process, for the Kremlin's new team soon made clear that the Khrushchev "Thaw" was over. The regime's crudest opening blow was the arrest of writers Andrei Sinyavsky and Yuli Daniel in 1965 on charges of crimes against the state for having their suppressed works published abroad without official permission. After a kangaroo trial in 1966, Sinyavsky was sentenced to the maximum punishment of seven years in labor camp. Daniel received a five-year sentence.

The vise was given another turn when the state quietly proposed a new law: Article 190-1 of the Russian Federation's criminal code, which set a three-year labor camp sentence for "circulation of fabrications known to be false which defame the Soviet state and social system." "One hundred ninety-prime," as it quickly became known, was intended to take its place beside the earlier and harsher Article 70, anti-Soviet agitation and propaganda, under which Sinyavsky and Daniel had been sentenced. This had proved an embarrassment to the Brezhnev leadership because the state's prosecutors had fumbled Article 70's requirement that it be shown that the writers deliberately intended to undermine Soviet power. If the scientists who had won the Lysenko fight believed that their victory heralded a more lenient, reasonable set of leaders, the promulgation of the new law indicated otherwise. In alarm, Tamm and Sakharov joined with nineteen other prominent scientists and artists to warn the figurehead parliament, the Supreme Soviet, that the new measure violated "socialist democracy." In a sign of what would become the new leaders' policy, the twenty-one intellectuals were ignored.

Sandwiched between the writers' arrests and the adoption of the new measure to expand "legal" methods of dealing with artistic and political dissent came yet another confrontation. This one involved the status of Stalin himself. Having been decimated by the Terror, Moscow's intelligentsia were especially sensitive to whispers of a rehabilitation for the denounced and disgraced dictator. Just such rumors had begun to circulate in the capital before the March 1966 party congress. The 23rd Congress, as the first Brezhnev-run national party conference since he and Premier Alexei Kosygin had come to power, had enhanced symbolic value which would add impact to any restoration of Stalin's place in the Soviet firmament. The smallest change in his status would send shock waves across Russia and throughout the Communist world.

Sakharov, Kapitsa, and Tamm, joining with a group of liberal-minded artists, attacked the rumored rehabilitation as a blow that would damage the party and the country. Most Western Communists would be repelled by any rehabilitation. Brezhnev backed down: Stalin remained interred at the foot of the Kremlin wall instead of being returned to the Lenin Mausoleum from which Khrushchev had had him removed at the beginning of the decade. But a stone bust atop a pedestal appeared at the Stalin grave site, an appropriate sign of the careful way the new leaders would seek throughout the Brezhnev era to improve the dictator's image, yet avoid a serious fight with the disaffected intelligentsia.

In looking back later on these formative months of the mid-1960s, Sakharov singled out his opposition to "one hundred ninety-prime" as of special significance: "Thus, for the first time my own fate became intertwined with the fate of that group of people—a group that was small but very weighty on the moral (and, I daresay, the historical) plane—who subsequently came to be called 'dissenters.'"

Early in 1967, Sakharov and a Soviet journalist named Ernst Henri prepared an article on the role of scientists in society. They aimed to have it published by *Literaturnaya Gazeta*, the well-read literary weekly, in hopes of sparking the nation's intelligentsia to begin a serious discussion about reducing the threat of thermonuclear war. The Central Committee refused to authorize publication. In the exchange, Sakharov told Henri that the partial test ban treaty of 1963 came about in part because of efforts by Western as well as Soviet scientists. "This was an undeniable confirmation of the effectiveness of scientists and intellectuals in trying to solve the most important political problems," Sakharov declared.*

While much of the conversation was devoted to the destabilizing disadvantages of an anti-ballistic missile system (later banned by the Salt I treaty), Sakharov bluntly clarified for Henri the two subjects that haunt him—nuclear devastation and the individual's overwhelming moral responsibility to prevent it.

"If Clausewitz's formula were applied across the board in our day and age (i.e., war), we would be dealing not with the 'continuation of politics by other means' but with the total self-destruction of civilization. . . . The destruction of hundreds of millions of people, the genetic deformation of future generations, the destruction of cities and industry, transport, communication, agriculture, and the educational system, the outbreak of famine and epidemics, the rise of a savage and uncontrollable hatred of scientists and 'intellectuals' on the part of civilization's surviving victims, rampant superstition, ferocious nationalism, and the de-

Sakharov Speaks, p. 36.

struction of the material and informational basis of civilization—all this would throw humanity centuries back, to the age of barbarism, and bring it to the brink of self-destruction. This is a gloomy prognosis, but we can't just brush the facts aside."

The two men talked of what American scientists could do to help extricate their country from the Vietnam War. "The historic responsibility of American scientists and intellectuals at this critical juncture in world history is very great," Sakharov said in a typical passage that sounded patronizing but in fact was a way to talk indirectly to Soviet scientists through *Literaturnaya*'s columns. "If they deny their active or passive support to the war machine, if they can help explain to the American people how much more important the preservation of peace is than any or all American domestic problems, the war machine will begin to lose its power and more favorable circumstances will emerge. ... The role of scientists and progressive intellectuals, their ways of thinking and acting, will be enormously enhanced throughout the world. ... Scientists ... must become aware of their power as one of the most important bulwarks of the idea of peaceful coexistence."†

Although never officially published, this exchange quickly turned up in the pages of one of the most unique samizdat journals of the period, Roy Medvedev's *Political Diary*. Sakharov has disclaimed any role in getting the article into samizdat, but it was a milestone in the steady and now irreversible course the physicist was to take over the next decade. *Political Diary* apparently was circulated to no more than a handful of senior party apparatchiks and disaffected Moscow intellectuals. But the underground journal was vivid, authoritative, and wide-ranging. Despite the Brezhnev chill and its own almost invisible circulation, the contents of

---

†Stephen F. Cohen (ed.), *An End to Silence*, pp. 228–34.

Political Diary available to the West provide a very special insight into the nature and range of debate under way within Russia after Khrushchev departed from power. Stalin's crimes, socialist morality, guilt, and retribution all figured in the journal. Although Sakharov and Roy and Zhores Medvedev (identical twins) later would have a philosophical falling out over political reform questions, the brothers were crucial to his emergence as a human rights activist.

While his scientific work continued (three articles published in 1967 with such titles as "Quark-Muon Currents and the Violation of CP Invariance" and "Vacuum Quantum Fluctuations in Curved Space and the Theory of Gravitation"), Sakharov at the age of 46 had become a social and political thinker with an increasingly trenchant voice. From the moment that senior Soviet scientists became concerned about fallout dangers from atomic weapons tests, Sakharov's steady metamorphosis may have been inevitable. But as the Brezhnev era unfolded, with its mounting pressure on dissent, most other scientists, as celebrated and privileged as Sakharov, fell silent. Only he remained courageous enough to speak out—and suffer the consequences.

In May 1968, Moscow's flourishing network of typescript samizdat publishing suddenly caught fire when a new series of twelve linked essays began circulating under Sakharov's authorship.

"Progress, Coexistence, and Intellectual Freedom"* dealt with world ills: the threat of nuclear war, hunger, racism and overpopulation, environmental pollution, totalitarianism. Sakharov blamed the Americans for instigating the Vietnam War, and he blamed the Soviets for the Arab–Israeli confrontation. He called for a fundamental, extra-national dedication to the cause of peace.

"International affairs must be completely permeated with

---

*Published as a book in the U.S. in 1968.

scientific methodology and a democratic spirit, with a fearless weighing of all facts, views, and theories, with maximum publicity of ultimate and intermediate goals, and with a consistency of principles."

The work combined general principles of international conduct—"All people have the right to decide their own fate with a free expression of will"—and toughly worded denunciations of unacceptable aspects of the Soviet system—"The crippling censorship of Soviet artistic and political literature has again been intensified. . . . Wide indignation has been aroused by the recent decree . . . amending the Criminal Code in direct contravention of the civil rights proclaimed by our Constitution." He declared it "imperative, of course" that the state make public all evidence of Stalin era crimes "including the archives of the NKVD, and conduct nationwide investigations" that would identify all the criminals and, inevitably, lead to their punishment.

At the conclusion, he proposed a four-part "plan for cooperation" that depended for success on a series of international developments which, if they occurred, could not fail to transform the world. He optimistically foresaw by 1980 the demise of one-party communism and its replacement by multi-party systems, and a parellel "victory of the leftist reformist wing of the bourgeoisie, which will begin to implement a program of rapprochement with socialism, i.e., social progress, peaceful coexistence, and collaboration with socialism on a world scale and changes in the structure of ownership." These changes would bring the two superpowers together to "solve the problem of saving the poorer half of the world." A world government would come into existence by the year 2000.

Some years later in a rueful retrospective, Sakharov found the essay's ideas neither original nor profound. "Nonetheless, its basic ideas are dear to me. In it I clearly formulated the theses . . . that the rapprochement of the socialist and

capitalist systems, accompanied by democratization, de-
militarization, and social and technological progress, is the
only alternative to the ruin of mankind."*

Within a few weeks, "Progress, Coexistence, and Intellectual Freedom" had been smuggled to the West, where it
became a sensation. Soviet reaction was swift: the next
month, Sakharov's top-secret clearance was revoked and he
was permanently banned from weapons work and reassigned
to the Lebedev Physics Institute. But from the state's point
of view, the damage had already been done. By mid-1969,
millions of copies of "Progress" were in circulation abroad
in more than a score of foreign languages. Renegade Sakharov had become a world figure.

The transformation from carefully concealed scientist to
controversial social critic and defender of the downtrodden
permanently overturned Sakharov's life. The framework of
privilege remained—the limousine, dacha, special vaca-
tion, and health care facilities. But access was cut off to
the inner world of the state, where powerful technocrats and
their advisers advanced their ideas through the Central Committee maze to the interior chambers of the Politburo. Like
an angel who had fallen, Sakharov was shunned and ostracized.

These rapid changes in his status took place at a time of
intense private strain, for his wife of two decades, Klavdia,
was gravely ill with cancer. Her death in 1968 left him a
widower with two daughters—Tatiana, 24, and Lyubov, just
20—and a young son, Dmitri, born in 1957. The oldest
daughter had married the year before, and now Sakharov
was a grandfather with a granddaughter named Marina.
However, father and offspring were not close. The children
had hardly known him when they were young; when his
moral migration began in the early 1960s, they had not
participated. Now, with their mother dead and their father

Sakharov Speaks, p. 37.

deeply immersed in the troubling political problems of perfect strangers, family cohesion crumbled, never to be restored. After his second marriage, these offspring faded from his life. The emotional center for him shifted to his new wife and her children, whom he came to consider his own.

ELENA BONNER'S COMPLAINT

© *Courtesy of Khronika Press*

ON SEPTEMBER 26 I SUBMITTED A COMPLAINT TO the People's Court of Moscow's Kiev District[1] concerning the defense of my honor and dignity. The complaint is based on Article 7 of the Russian Republic's Civil Code.[2] My suit was accepted by Judge Kuzmina.

Two months later I had received neither notification of trial nor a reasoned rejection of my suit. On November 30 I applied to the court once again. This time Leonid Sobolev, chairman of the Kiev District Court, refused to accept the complaint which I had submitted on September 26. He declined to provide written reasons for the rejection, as required by law.

Deprived of the protection of the court, I feel obliged to make my complaint public, together with a further statement by me and a notarized deposition by my husband Andrei Sakharov.

Moscow. December 1, 1983   Elena Bonner

Elena Bonner's complaint submitted on September 26, 1983, to the People's Court asking that Nikolai Yakovlev (and the magazine *Smena*)[3] print a retraction of libelous allegations which have defamed her honor and dignity.

COMPLAINT

Nikolai Yakovlev's article "The Path Down" was published in the magazine *Smena* (no. 14, July 1983). The article defames me. In my complaint, I do not concern myself with the general tenor of the article which contains distorted and defamatory information about my husband, about my children, and about other individuals who have been close to me in the past. I direct the attention of the court solely to certain specific allegations of the author.

I quote the following passages from the *Smena* article.

(1) "It is a story as old as the world. A stepmother entered the Sakharov home and tossed out the children . . . Bonner vowed eternal love to the Academician and for a start pushed Tanya, Lyuba, and Dima out of the family nest and installed her own children Tatiana and Alexei . . ."

(2) "Bonner long ago appropriated all Sakharov's money in the USSR . . ."

(3) "fortified with false documents, she managed to enroll in a medical institute in Moscow . . . and led a merry life . . ."

(4) "The spoiled young lady became quite professional in seducing and then fleecing elderly men of substance. This is a familiar matter, but complications arise from the fact that men of advanced years tend to have a female companion, usually a wife. She must be eliminated. How? Our 'heroine' acted directly—she won over the husband of her ill girlfriend and then brought on that friend's death by blackmail and obscene telephone calls. She got what she wanted. She almost became the wife of the poet Vsevolod Bagritsky. Disappointment. He perished in the war.

"Our maiden, however, never limited herself to a single game. She was highly enterprising. She had simultaneously begun an affair with the successful engineer Moisei Zlotnik. But again an irritating encumbrance—a wife! The engineer got rid of her by the simple expedient of killing her and wound up in prison for many years. This notorious case inspired the noted criminologist and author Lev Sheinin's story "Disappeared," in which Zlotnik's mistress was called Lucy B. It was wartime and for understandable reasons, the frightened but wily Lucy B. went into hiding as an orderly on a hospital train."

(5) "Bonner has developed the habit of beating her husband with whatever comes to hand in order to convince him to do what she wants."

All these citations fall under Article 7 of the RSFSR Civil Code since they defame my honor and dignity. They are all fabrications of the article's author, with no basis in fact.

I ask the court to make plain what really happened—the law provides that the burden of proof rests completely on the defendant—and to return a verdict ordering that Mr. N. N. Yakovlev and the magazine *Smena* publish an appropriate retraction.

*   *   *

Elena Bonner's further statement dated September 26, 1983.

In his article Yakovlev gives a distorted account of my life. I therefore feel obliged to provide a brief autobiography.

I was born in 1923.

My father, Gevork Alikhanov, was head of the personnel department of the Comintern. A Bolshevik and a member of the Communist Party from 1917, he was arrested and charged with treason in May 1937. He was posthumously rehabilitated in 1954.

My mother, Ruf G. Bonner, a member of the Communist Party from 1924, was also arrested in 1937 as the wife of a traitor. She was rehabilitated in 1954 and granted a special pension.

I had completed seven grades of school in Moscow when my parents were arrested. My younger brother and I moved to Leningrad where my grandmother lived with my uncle. My uncle was arrested in late October 1937. His wife was banished. Grandmother was left to bring up the three of us:

my brother, my uncle's two-year-old daughter, and me. My
brother and I had arrived in Leningrad without documents.
(We had no birth certificates.) We were sent to the medical
commission of the local school board. The commission decided that I was sixteen (and not fifteen), so in February I
received a passport with my year of birth incorrectly given
as 1922.

I finished secondary school in Leningrad in 1940. While
still a student, I worked as a cleaning woman, and during
two summers as a file clerk at the Telman factory in Moscow.
In 1940 I signed up for evening courses in Russian language
and literature at the Herzen Teachers Institute in Leningrad
and worked days as a Pioneer[4] leader in a Leningrad school.

I never believed either as a child or as an adult that my
parents could be enemies of the motherland. Their ideals
and their internationalism served as a guide for me. Their
ideals inspired me to enlist in the army as a nurse when the
war began, volunteering with all my heart (if such words
can be taken seriously and not ironically).

On October 26, 1941, I suffered severe wounds and a
concussion near Vala Station on the Volkhov Front. I was
treated in hospitals in Vologda and Sverdlovsk. In late 1941
I was discharged in Sverdlovsk and assigned as a nurse to
hospital train 122. In 1943 I was promoted to senior nurse
and received the rank of junior lieutenant in the medical
corps. In 1945 I was promoted to lieutenant. In May 1945
I was assigned to the White Sea Military District as deputy
chief of the medical unit attached to a battalion of engineers.
I was discharged in August 1945. I was classified as having
a moderate (class 2) disability: the concussion had caused
almost complete loss of vision in my right eye and progressive blindness in my left eye. I spent the next two years
fighting to save my sight. (I recall with gratitude the doctors
in Leningrad who aided me in that struggle: Dr. Fridlan-
skaya; Professor Tron; Professor Pollak; Professor Chir-
kovsky; and Dr. Sukonshikova. Later on, I was admitted

twice to a hospital in Odessa where my doctors were Professor Vladimir Filatov and his wife Dr. Skorodinskaya.) In 1947 my condition was finally stabilized, although I have been classified ever since as either mildly (class 3) or moderately (class 2) disabled depending on my sight. In 1970 I was designated a moderately disabled (class 2) lifetime invalid of the Great Patriotic War.

I enrolled as a student at the First Leningrad Medical Institute in 1947. I completed the six-year course in 1953. From that time until I reached retirement age, I always worked except for an interval of a little more than a year in 1961–62 when my son was very ill. I was a district doctor, a pediatrician in a maternity hospital, and a lecturer on childhood diseases in a medical school. I worked in Iraq on assignment for the Ministry of Health. My professional work was often combined with writing. I have published in the magazines *Neva* and *Yunost*, in the *Literary Gazette*, and in the *Medical Worker*. I wrote for All-Union radio. I was a contributor to the book *Actors Who Died on the Front Lines of the Great Patriotic War* and served as one of the editors for the book *Vsevolod Bagritsky: Diaries, Letters, Poems*. I was a part-time advisor for the Writers' Union Consultation Bureau, and was employed for a while as an editor by the Leningrad branch of the Medical Publishing House. I have been designated a Distinguished Health Worker.

I joined the Komsomol in 1938. During the war I served as the Komsomol organizer on the hospital train, and later I was the union organizer for my class at the Medical Institute.

I never deemed it possible—psychologically—to join the Communist Party while my parents were considered traitors or, to use the phrase current at the time, "enemies of the people." After the 20th and especially after the 22nd Party Congresses, I decided to join the Communist Party. I became a candidate member in 1964, and a full member in

1965. After the fall of 1968 I came to realize that I had made a mistake, and in 1972 I resigned from the Party as a matter of conscience.

I have two children. My daughter Tatiana was born in 1950 and my son Alexei in 1956. Their father, Ivan V. Semenov, was a fellow student at the First Leningrad Medical Institute, and he still works there. We separated in 1965. Tatiana enrolled in Moscow University in 1967. She was expelled in the fall of 1972 for participating in a demonstration at the Lebanese embassy protesting an act of terrorism: the murder of Israeli athletes at the Munich Olympics. In 1974 she was reinstated, and in 1975 successfully completed her studies, graduating "with distinction." Alexei graduated from secondary school with excellent marks, and also did well while majoring in mathematics at Moscow's Lenin Teachers Institute. He was expelled during his senior year under the pretext that he had not passed his military training (a subject not included in the institute's curriculum). My son-in-law Efrem Yankelevich completed the Moscow Institute of Telecommunications.

My complaint lists five points. My husband deals with three of them in his deposition. I shall cover the remaining two items, points (3) and (4).

[Translator's summary.

In response to (3), Mrs. Sakharov states that she matriculated in a Leningrad—not a Moscow—medical school, after submitting her high school diploma and successfully passing an entrance exam. She used no false documents.

(4) Moisei Zlotnik murdered his wife Elena Dolenko, a former schoolmate of Mrs. Sakharov, in October 1944. The last time Mrs. Sakharov had seen Elena was in 1942, before she married Zlotnik. Mrs. Sakharov was acquainted with Zlotnik, who was the

cousin of her friend Regina Etinger. Mrs. Sakharov was questioned, about her knowledge of the victim and the murderer during the investigation. In Sheinin's fictional story based on this case, Lucy B. is portrayed as an innocent victim of Zlotnik, and not an instigator of murder.

Vsevolod Bagritsky was neither old nor rich since he was born in 1922 and killed in 1942 before his twentieth birthday. Mrs. Sakharov and Vsevolod Bagritsky grew up together in Moscow and were childhood sweethearts. They went together to deliver food parcels for their mothers who had been arrested in 1937 and were both confined in Moscow's Butyrka Prison. In the fall of 1940, when Bagritsky was eighteen, he impulsively married Marina Filatova, but they separated within a month and were divorced. Mrs. Sakharov never met and never spoke to Marina Filatova.]

That completes the factual portion of my submission to the court. But why does Yakovlev need my biography in the particular way he has presented it? Because in the tragic conditions of our life, someone hopes that this nasty "literary" concoction will cause the death of two elderly and very sick people and addle the brains of millions of trusting readers. Articles in the style of Goebbels are suited to the purpose. The thousands of furious, spiteful letters we are receiving prove this. They recommend that Sakharov "repent," "divorce the Jewess," "speak his own mind and not Bonner's." The pogrom arranged for me on the Gorky–Moscow train proves this, as do the rowdy encounters which greet Sakharov and me on the streets of Gorky, and the threats of violence and even murder.

In 1983 a series of articles by Yakovlev entitled "The CIA vs. the Country of Soviets" appeared in the mass circulation (8,700,000 copies) magazine *Chelovek i Zakon* (Man and the Law). In Yakovlev's book *The CIA vs. the USSR*

and in the *Smena* article, the Jewish-Zionist theme had
appeared in somewhat muted form, depending on the selection of names and on references to anonymous and
mythical students of Sakharov. In the *Chelovek i Zakon*
article, however, it has become absolutely plain and open.
I quote from the section entitled "The Firm of E. Bonner
and Children."

> In their attempts to subvert the Soviet system from
> inside, the CIA has resorted extensively to the services
> of international Zionism... They use not only the spy
> networks of the American, Israeli, and Zionist special
> services and the Jewish-Masonic agency B'nai B'rith
> associated with them, but also elements susceptible to
> Zionist propaganda. Academician A. D. Sakharov be-
> came one of the victims of the CIA's Zionist network.
> Whatever angry words may be directed at Sakharov
> (and they are fully warranted), still one must feel pity
> for him in human terms... Making use of the special
> nature of his personal life over roughly the past fifteen
> years (more on this later), provocateurs from subver-
> sive agencies have pushed and are continuing to push
> this unbalanced man into behavior which contradicts
> the image of Sakharov the scientist. It is a story as old
> as the world: a stepmother entered the Sakharov home
> after his wife's death... That dreadful woman foisted
> herself on the widower Sakharov.

I ask your pardon for this long quotation which in part
repeats the *Smena* article, but it is clear from the context
that *I* am the provocateur from the subversive Masonic,
Zionist, and CIA services, that *I* am responsible for all
Sakharov's activity in defense of peace and human rights.
He is a victim, a mentally unbalanced person. The anti-
Semitic content of Yakovlev's article printed in a popular
law magazine is an incitement of national hatred. It is strik-

ingly reminiscent of the 1953 case (instigated by Lydia Timashuk) of the "doctor-murderers,"[5] one of the most shameful pages in our country's history. Yakovlev's readers may have forgotten that affair, but he is a professor and a historian—he should remember it.

What does Yakovlev want from me? For me to betray my husband? I have never betrayed anyone. To put me in fear of a trial for treason (with a possible death sentence)? I have never been a part of any intelligence service, not American, Masonic, or Zionist. All of Yakovlev's countless publications have been prompted by the simple fact that I am Sakharov's wife. Moreover, I am a Jew, which makes his task easier. But I hope to end my days true to the Russian culture and environment which have shaped my life, and to my Jewish-Armenian nationality.

I am proud that it has been my difficult lot but also my good fortune to be the wife and friend of Academician Andrei Sakharov.

*   *   *

Deposition made by Andrei Sakharov in Gorky on November 19, 1983

I wish to make the following deposition in connection with my wife Elena G. Bonner's complaint concerning the injury to her honor and dignity caused by Nikolai N. Yakovlev's book *The CIA vs. the USSR* (3rd edition, Moscow, 1983) and article "The Road Down" (*Smena*, no. 14, July 1983).

1. The following statement made by Yakovlev in his *Smena* article (page 21) is a lie.

In the late 1960's, Bonner finally went after big game—the widower A. D. Sakharov. But alas, he has three children: Tatiana, Lyuba, and Dima. Bonner

vowed eternal love to the Academician and for a start
pushed Tanya, Lyuba, and Dima out of the family nest
and installed her own children Tatiana and Alexei.

No one has the right to describe a stranger's private life
in the vulgar and mendacious terms used by Yakovlev in
this quotation and in many other passages. In an article
which has just been published in *Chelovek i zakon* (Man
and the Law, no. 10, 1983), Yakovlev makes the insinuation
still more pointed: "That dreadful woman foisted herself
upon the widower Sakharov."

Elena did not "foist herself" upon me. Neither did she
"vow eternal love." I asked her to become my wife. From
that time on, she has selflessly borne her difficult and tragic
lot. It is *our* fate, *our* joys and sorrows. I ask protection
from the mean and vulgar meddling of Yakovlev.

As to matters of fact, the two younger children of my
first marriage, my daughter Lyubov Sakharov (born in 1949)
and my son Dmitri Sakharov (born in 1957), lived with me
until my second marriage in a three-room, 610-square-foot
apartment on Marshal Novikov Street. They have continued
to live there to this day without interruption. My wife Elena
and her children Tatiana (born in 1950) and Alexei (born
in 1956 and not in 1955 as reported by Yakovlev) have
never lived for a single day in that apartment. After my
marriage, I moved into the two-room apartment of my
mother-in-law where five people besides myself were
crowded into 365 square feet.

My elder daughter Tatiana Sakharov (born in 1945) married and moved out of our home in 1967 while my first wife
Klavdia Vikhireva was still alive.[6] I made a down payment
on a cooperative apartment for Tatiana through the Academy
of Sciences, and in 1972 she moved into a three-room apartment located on the Rostov Embankment in the center of
Moscow. She is still living there with her husband and
daughter.

These facts can be verified by the relevant housing registers and by the statements of witnesses. I ask you to summon as witnesses: Alexander A. Bobylev; Yakov B. Zeldovich; Yury A. Romanov; and Evgeny L. Feinberg.[7] (Yakovlev, by the way, has deliberately employed diminutive names for my children and normal names for my wife's children in order to create the impression that small children were "pushed out" onto the street.)

2. It is a lie that my wife Elena "appropriated" my savings. In 1969 I donated 139,000 rubles to the State Fund (for the Red Cross and for the construction of a Cancer Center). From 1971 to 1973 I gave more than 500 rubles monthly to the children of my first marriage and to my brother Georgi Sakharov. In 1973 I transferred 14,400 rubles, half of my remaining savings, to my children. In 1972, I gave my ZIM car to my elder daughter Tatiana. From 1973 to 1977, I paid my son Dmitri a monthly allowance of 150 rubles, and I have given him money on occasion since then. I have also continued to assist my brother financially. I have made these disbursements since 1971 with the knowledge and approval of my wife, and sometimes at her initiative.

3. Yakovlev has written a deliberate falsehood when he describes my son-in-law Efrem Yankelevich as a dropout and a loafer. Efrem successfully completed his studies at the Moscow Institute of Telecommunications in 1972. He now lives in the United States where he is performing complicated and responsible duties as my representative abroad with power of attorney. Yakovlev describes Alexei Semenov and Tatiana Semenova Yankelevich as lazy good-for-nothings. That is a deliberate libel which can easily be refuted by documentary evidence.

4. Yakovlev writes:

> With the change in his family situation, Sakharov's interests shifted. The theoretician branched out. He took up politics. He began to meet with people who came to be called "human rights activists."

Yakovlev's implication is false. I met my future wife Elena Bonner in the autumn of 1970. (Yakovlev has deliberately altered the date to the late 1960s.) I had become seriously interested in social and political issues by the mid-1950s. I played a role in the conclusion of the 1963 Moscow Limited Test Ban Treaty. This can be confirmed by calling as witness Efim Slavsky, Minister of Medium Machine Building and a member of the Central Committee.[8] My book *Progress, Coexistence, and Intellectual Freedom* was published in 1968, more than two years before I met Elena Bonner. My later statements have primarily elaborated the ideas on society which were outlined in that essay. I made the acquaintance of many noted human rights activists during the first half of 1970 before meeting Elena Bonner.

5. Yakovlev falsely describes the circumstances of the hunger strike conducted by my wife and myself in order to obtain permission for our daughter-in-law Liza Alexeyeva (who had become a hostage for my public activity) to join her husband in America. Our decision to conduct a hunger strike was a mutual one. Each of us recognized the necessity for this step and its gravity. We *both* fasted (see *Izvestia*, December 4, 1981). On the thirteenth day of our hunger strike, we were removed by force from our apartment, separated, and confined in different hospitals. We ended our hunger strike on the seventeenth day after the authorities assured us that our demand would be satisfied.

6. Yakovlev writes:

> Bonner has developed the habit of beating her husband with whatever comes to hand in order to convince him to do what she wants.

Yakovlev quotes with approval an article which appeared in the New York Russian-language newspaper *Russky golos* (Russian Voice):

Sakharov has apparently become a hostage of the Zionists who dictate their terms using the capricious and unbalanced Bonner as go-between.

Yakovlev writes further:

... the testimonial was awarded to Sakharov by those who knew how to enlist him objectively in the service of imperialism. How? To understand that we must penetrate Sakharov's private life. It is a story as old as the world. A stepmother entered the Sakharov home...

Regular aberrations in his mood have been noted. Calm when Bonner leaves him and stays in Moscow, depressed when she returns from the capital... Next comes the collective composition by the couple of some libelous squib, interrupted on occasion by a stormy scene and blows... Keep this in mind when studying the frequent "revelations" broadcast *in Sakharov's name* by Western radio voices.[9]

All Yakovlev's assertions which I have quoted are conscious lies and malicious provocations. Yakovlev does not produce and cannot produce any evidence that my wife beats me and thereby influences my actions and statements. Yakovlev's allegation which defames the honor and dignity of my wife and of myself is absolutely false.

Yakovlev's allegation about aberrations in my moods— as if my wife's presence depresses me—lacks any foundation and is equally false.

All my articles, books, and appeals, published in the West or circulated in the Soviet Union, express my own opinions which have evolved over the course of my life. Yakovlev makes me out to be a fool, an overgrown child controlled by a willful, treacherous, mercenary woman. Yakovlev writes that I am mentally unwell. Anatoly Alexandrov, president of the Academy of Sciences, recently made a similar insinuation. They are trying to discredit my public statements by implying that these have been instigated by others and are not my own idea. They are also pursuing a second and possibly more important aim: they want to paralyze my public activity by placing my wife in a dangerous, unbearable situation and by damaging her health. Insinuations about my wife's personal life and imaginary past crimes and slurs on her moral qualities reinforce the attacks. Her nationality is emphasized, pandering to popular prejudice.

I am profoundly grateful to my wife for her self-sacrifice and determination in the face of our tragic existence, for encouraging the humanistic side of my public activity. But I declare unequivocally that the full personal responsibility for all my public activity and for the content and form of my statements is mine and mine alone. I categorically deny Yakovlev's allegations that my statements have been distorted by pressure from my wife or anyone else. I believe that my statements serve the interests of peace, progress, freedom, and human rights, of a humane and open society. I deny Yakovlev's charge that my ideas have an antipopular, proimperialist bias.

I am the author of every one of the statements attributed to me (provided the texts have been authenticated by my wife or by Efrem Yankelevich, my representative abroad). Yakovlev's use of the phrase "revelations broadcast *in Sakharov's name*" is tantamount to a malicious lie. It seems advisable in this connection, however, to declare formally that I cannot be held responsible for any statements made in my name which may be published in the Soviet Union or abroad unless the texts have been personally confirmed by me, by my wife Elena Bonner, or by Efrem Yankelevich. (I am not aware of any counterfeit statements in circulation at this time.) My declaration covers articles, books, memoirs, statements, appeals, interviews, and all publications including scientific articles.

My current circumstances oblige me to announce that, in the event of my death, I have bequeathed to my wife Elena Bonner my author's rights in all my written works, published and unpublished. I appoint her the sole executor and heir of my literary estate. In the event of my wife's death, I appoint Tatiana (Semenova) Yankelevich the sole executor and heir of my literary estate. My wishes in this regard as well as a number of other dispositions have been recorded in a notarized will. The original will has been deposited at the Prioksky District Notary's Office in Gorky.

*   *   *

Translator's Notes

[1]Mrs. Sakharov filed her complaint in Moscow where she is still registered at 48B Chkalov Street, apt. 68, Moscow B-120, her mother's apartment which is mentioned in Dr. Sakharov's deposition.

[2]Article 57 of the Soviet Constitution states:

Citizens of the USSR have the right to protection by the courts against encroachments on their honor and reputation, life and health, and personal freedom and property.

Article 7 of the Fundamentals of Civil Legislation is entitled "Protection of Honor and Dignity" and states:

Citizens and organizations shall have the right to sue at law for retraction of statements defamatory to their honor and dignity, where the person circulating such statements fails to prove that they are true.

Where such statements are circulated through the press, they must, if found untrue, be retracted also in the press. The manner of retraction in other cases shall be established by the court.

Where the court judgment has not been carried out, the court may impose a fine on the wrongdoer which shall be collected for the benefit of the state. Payment of fine does not relieve the wrongdoer from the duty to perform the act prescribed by the court judgment.

[3]Nikolai Yakovlev is a historian with a law degree who has written extensively on Soviet–American relations and Soviet history. An article by Alexander Solzhenitsyn's first wife Natalia Reshetovskaya attacking Yakovlev's depiction of Solzhenitsyn in *The CIA vs. the USSR* was published in *Russia*, no. 2, New York, 1981.

Smena is a popular semimonthly magazine for young people published by the Komsomol (Communist youth organization).

[4]Members of the Soviet organization for schoolchildren are called Pioneers.

[5]Wide publicity was given in January 1953 to the arrest of leading Soviet doctors, almost all Jewish, who were accused of poisoning prominent Soviet citizens. Popular anti-Semitism was aroused, and there has been speculation that Stalin was preparing to deport all Soviet Jews to Siberia. Those of the doctors who survived their imprisonment were cleared of all charges and released immediately after Stalin's death in March 1953. Lydia Timashuk, a doctor herself, played a major role in orchestrating the campaign.

[6]Klavdia Vikhireva died of cancer in 1969.

[7]Alexander Bobylev is a relative of Dr. Sakharov's first wife Klavdia. Zeldovich and Feinberg are physicists and colleagues of Dr. Sakharov.

[8]The Ministry of Medium Machine Building is responsible for the testing and production of nuclear weapons.

[9]The quotations are from the *Chelovek i Zakon* article.

TWO STORIES

by Edward Teller

WHEN, IN ABOUT 1975, I MET ALEKSANDR
Solzhenitsyn, he immediately asked, "Do you know Sakharov?" "No," I answered. "Neither have I corresponded
with him." Solzhenitsyn replied, "This is a remarkable and
terrible world."

I assumed that Solzhenitsyn's regret was that colleagues
involved in parallel scientific work had not met. Since that
time, I have read most of Sakharov's published political
works, and I now suspect his comment had another basis.

Sakharov and I were born thirteen years and about a
thousand miles apart, to families that valued and practiced
learning, music, and courtesy. We both became theoretical
physicists, both applied our knowledge to weapons development, and both of us have acquired the misnomer "the
father of the hydrogen bomb," a description that, as Sakharov says, "reflects very inaccurately the real (and complex) situation of collective invention."

The similarities between Andrei Sakharov and myself do
not stop here, but the points of divergence within these
common experiences are so great that the stories lose all
semblance of a parallel nature. When a country loses its
freedoms, the tragedy reverberates destructively through individual lives and throughout this remarkable and terrible
world.

Sakharov entered the university in Moscow, his home-
town, in 1938. By the time Hitler attacked Russia in 1941,
Sakharov's abilities were recognized as exceptional. He was

deferred from military service to finish his undergraduate studies. A year later, he entered defense work, designing quality control devices. In 1945, in a victorious but sorely damaged nation, he began his graduate studies in Moscow under Professor Igor Tamm, an eminent physicist, and completed them three years later. Then he began another phase of his life.

> A few months after defending my dissertation for the degree of Candidate of Doctor of Science, roughly equivalent to an American Ph.D., which occurred in the spring of 1948, I was included in a research group working on the problem of a thermonuclear weapon. I had no doubts as to the vital importance of creating a Soviet superweapon—for our country and for the balance of power throughout the world.[1]

He was at that time twenty-seven years old.

When I was twenty-seven years old, I arrived in the United States. I suspect that, while I may have been through more upheavals, I had enjoyed greater pleasures and much greater safety. Between the ages of six and eleven, I lived in a nation at war, but I was close to its violence only briefly, and my only clear memories are of the hunger of that period. The real tragedy of the First World War was that it killed the infant democratization that had begun in both Russia and Hungary.

At eighteen, I left Hungary, where anti-Semitism closed off most opportunities for me, to study in Germany. There I entered a community of scholars saturated with the discoveries of the early part of the century, concepts that changed our outlook on the universe in a profound way. I joined in the adventure of freely exploring ideas of all sorts. Finding a spiritual home is considerable compensation for the great shock that arises when one has to leave one's family and country.

I completed my doctoral work under Werner Heisenberg, a brilliant physicist and a wonderful human being. At twenty-three, I became a research associate at Göttingen, enjoying the company of a wide circle of friends from many nations, both there and in Leipzig. The next year, 1933, the political situation in Germany sent me to Denmark, and the following year to England, and the next year to the United States. Although by then I had lost a great deal—my native land, contact with my family and old friends, even the continent I had known—my new friends in the scientific community in the United States, together with several fellow émigrés, were considerable consolation.

My first years in the United States were happy years connected with a steady increase in pure knowledge and the opportunity to share it. But in 1939, I became peripherally involved in what later became the Manhattan Project. The next year, after the invasion of Belgium and Holland, I made a commitment to working on weapons for the defense of freedom. In 1942, I recognized that a fission bomb made the possibility of a thermonuclear weapon likely. In April 1943, I joined the research group at Los Alamos.

Sakharov's experience in his early weapons work was so different from my own that when I read his account, I could hardly appreciate its ramifications. I knew he had begun work on the hydrogen bomb in 1948 under Stalin, and that in 1977, he had described Stalin as "one of the greatest criminals of the sorely tried twentieth century."[2] This in itself would be a terrible burden to bear.

However, Sakharov's immediate discoveries must have been almost overwhelming.

In 1950 our research group became part of a special institute. ... Until the summer of 1953, the chief of the atomic project was Beria, who ruled over millions of slave-prisoners. Almost all the construction was done with their labor.[1]

I remember how annoyed most of us at Los Alamos were with General Groves, the military commander of the Manhattan Project, and how much time we gave to petty complaints about his security measures. The contrast between Sakharov's environment and mine is so great that I am hardly able to comprehend it. I can only point out that the Soviet nuclear research program—from its initiation in 1948, through its successful production of a fission weapon in 1949, to shortly before the successful test of a fusion device in August 1953—was directed by the head of the secret police, a Russian* who, perhaps, killed more of his fellow Russians than anyone in history.

How could a man like Sakharov have worked for this criminal? I doubt that in 1948 Sakharov thought of anything except his country's terrible recent experiences and the prevention of any recurrence. I doubt that Sakharov knew, as he entered the program, that Pyotr Kapitsa had been placed under house arrest for refusing to work on the concurrent Russian atomic bomb project. And his mentor, a considerably older and more experienced man, Nobel Laureate Igor Tamm, went with seeming willingness into the weapons project. Having just completed his doctoral studies in theoretical physics, it is most unlikely that Sakharov had given much thought to the internal politics of the Soviet Union.

My first serious attempt to understand and participate in political affairs came in late June 1945, when I was thirty-seven years old. At the instigation of my friend and fellow Hungarian-American Leo Szilard, I first began to think seriously about how the atomic bomb should be used. Szilard had asked me to circulate a petition—asking that the atomic bomb be demonstrated to the Japanese before it was used—among the scientists at Los Alamos. I decided to do so, and went to the director of the laboratory, J. Robert Oppenhei-

---

*Laurenti Beria and Joseph Stalin were Georgians. Therefore, the word Soviet would be more appropriate here.—Ed.

mer, for permission. Oppenheimer pointed out that Szilard and I were physicists, unacquainted with political affairs which were far better left to foreign policy experts. I withdrew my request.

A few months later I learned that Oppenheimer had not only squelched Szilard's petition at Los Alamos, but also had advised the government to forgo prior demonstration of the bomb, an opposite recommendation to Szilard's. I never again have been silent on an issue I considered important and on which I had some special knowledge.

At the end of the war, I was desperately anxious about the fact that the existence of the atomic bomb made the feasibility of a thermonuclear weapon extremely probable. For five years, I talked with everyone in sight about the urgent need for research. This was the beginning of a rift between the majority of my friends in the scientific community and myself, and it caused me considerable pain. Finally, in 1950, enough support was gathered that President Truman gave the go-ahead for work on the hydrogen bomb. The project in Russia was already more than a year old.

If I was separated from my scientific colleagues by my beliefs, Sakharov was separated by his location after 1950 at the secret laboratory in Turkestan and by his life of extreme material privilege. He had an extraordinary salary equivalent to about twenty-seven thousand dollars a year*, special housing, chauffeurs, and complete access to restricted consumer goods. Honors were heaped upon him. He even became a member of the prestigious Academy of Sciences the same year as his mentor, Professor Tamm, thereby becoming the youngest full member in the long history of the Academy. For some individuals, however, the demands of the human spirit make all this of little importance. Sakharov, writing years later, makes it plain that the

---

*Average salary of a senior Soviet scientist is equivalent to five thousand dollars a year.—Ed.

caste system and the cynicism of the leaders caused him chronic suffering.

In 1961, he began a series of actions that changed his life profoundly. Because history is so quickly forgotten, the preceding events deserve a brief review. Atmospheric testing by both the United States and the Soviet Union had continued for the six years that followed the first H-bomb tests. Then, late in 1958, a "gentlemen's agreement" was established between the Soviet Union and the United States to halt all testing. The United States was convinced that our observation techniques were good enough that any Soviet preparations for a meaningful test would be noticed early enough to allow us to prepare our own. In the summer of 1961, the Soviet and American negotiators were discussing a final treaty banning nuclear tests.

That same summer, Sakharov was called to a meeting between Soviet atomic scientists and Premier Khrushchev. After they had gathered around the conference table,

it turned out that we were to prepare for a series of tests that would bolster up the new policy of the USSR on the German question (the Berlin Wall). I wrote a note to Khrushchev, saying "To resume tests after a three-year moratorium would undermine the talks on banning tests and on disarmament, and would lead to a new round in the armaments race—especially in the sphere of intercontinental missiles and antimissile defense." I passed it up the line. Khrushchev put the note in his breast pocket and invited all present to dine. At the dinner table he made an off-the-cuff speech that I remember for its frankness and that did not reflect merely his personal position. He said more or less the following: Sakharov is a good scientist. But leave it to us, who are specialists in this tricky business, to make foreign policy. Only force—only the disorientation of the enemy. We can't say aloud that we are carrying out our policy from a position of strength, but that's the way it must be. I would be a slob, and not chairman of the Council of Ministers, if I listened to the like of Sakharov.[1]

What must it have felt like as a forty-year-old scientist—a man who had worked diligently for the good of his homeland—to discover that the policies of his government were of this kind? It is one thing to have to deal with an individual of questionable values, but to discover in the middle of your life that your entire government is composed of power-hungry barbarians defies imagination.

The Soviet 1961 test series took the United States totally by surprise. Announced by Khrushchev the day before it began, the series involved ten multimegaton devices, including one explosive of approximately sixty megatons, the largest ever produced. The United States, having assumed that weapons testing had ended, had no plans ready. We conducted a hastily assembled test series the following spring.

Understanding the intensity of Sakharov's feeling about the 1961 Soviet tests, which involved well over one hundred megatons of explosives, requires a little knowledge of the nature of thermonuclear weapons. Making a multimegaton explosive requires less sophistication than making a smaller explosive. Because large-sized weapons produce an indiscriminate and militarily worthless amount of damage, the size of U.S. weapons steadily decreased after 1954. By 1961 the Soviets had tested several weapons of smaller size but chose to continue detonating the much larger variety, perhaps for the purpose of intimidation.

The text of Sakharov's Nobel Peace Prize speech addressed the ramifications of this policy clearly.

This cooperation (between the Western states, the socialist nations, and the developing countries) must be based on mutual trust between open societies, or—to put it another way—with an open mind, on the basis of genuine equality and not on the basis of the dem-

ocratic countries' fear of their totalitarian neighbors.
If that were the case, cooperation would merely in-
volve an attempt at ingratiating oneself with a formidable neighbor. But such a policy would merely
postpone the evil day, soon to arrive anyway and, then,
ten times worse. This is simply another version of
Munich.[3]

Sakharov echoed similar advice in a recent open letter to a
physicist who supports the U.S. freeze movement.

Precisely because an all-out nuclear war means collective suicide, we can imagine that a potential aggressor might count on a lack of resolve on the part
of the country under attack to take the step leading to
that suicide, i.e., it could count on its victim capitulating for the sake of saving what could be saved...
Take the next logical step—while nuclear weapons
exist it is also necessary to have strategic parity in
relation to those variants of limited or regional nuclear
warfare which a potential enemy could impose... If
the probability of such an outcome (an all-out nuclear
war) could be reduced at the cost of another ten or
fifteen years of the arms race, then perhaps that price
must be paid....[3]

Sakharov has made an incredible sacrifice in order to share
his expertise and understanding with the defenders of peace
and freedom. Unfortunately, in some instances, his message
seems not to receive much notice.

While breach of faith formed the substance of Sakharov's
plea in 1961, he states that the motivation for his act lay
elsewhere and began four years earlier.

Beginning in 1957 (not without the influence of statements on this subject made throughout the world by
such people as Albert Schweitzer, Linus Pauling, and

others) I felt myself responsible for the problem of radioactive contamination from nuclear explosions. As is known, the absorption of radioactive products of nuclear explosions by the billions of people inhabiting the earth leads to an increase in the incidence of several diseases and birth defects, of so-called subthreshold biological effects . . . Each series of tests of a nuclear weapon . . . involves tens of megatons; i.e., tens of thousands of victims.[1]

While there was a great deal of speculation about possible low-level radiation hazards in the late 1950s and early 1960s, the substantiating evidence of damage—although intensively sought—never appeared.

How could a scientist of Sakharov's ability confuse popular exaggeration with fact? How did he come to place so much emphasis on statements made by Schweitzer and Pauling, and make so cursory an investigation himself? How could a scientist arrive at a decision when all the evidence was still missing? How does an honorable and loyal person deal with the demands of his country and of humanity if they conflict? Surely, no person of any experience can believe that this is accomplished in an easy or a purely logical manner.

My teacher and friend, Werner Heisenberg, faced a similar dilemma during the Second World War. Heisenberg was the director of the German atomic bomb project under Hitler. From a technical point of view, there could have been no better choice. However, Heisenberg disliked the Nazis. He was appalled at the widespread imprisonment and went out of his way to save its victims whenever possible. One pertinent example was Fritz Houtermans, a talented German physicist with leanings toward communism.

After Hitler came to power, Houtermans went to Russia. The years between 1930 and 1939 were very terrible years in Russia. The famine that resulted from the breakneck speed with which Stalin forced collectivization of farms killed millions of people, and during these same years about ten million people, many of them communists, were sent to forced labor camps where they died.

Houtermans, during one of Stalin's purges, was sent to prison, but after the 1939 Hitler–Stalin pact, he was shipped back to Nazi Germany, headed for a concentration camp there. Heisenberg rescued him by insisting that he needed Houtermans to work on the atomic energy project. That, surprisingly enough, is just exactly what Houtermans did. At one point Houtermans suggested that bombarding uranium with neutrons would produce a new element (now called plutonium) which could serve as an atomic explosive.

Heisenberg was too loyal to his country to accept escape when it was offered. When, in 1938, he was urged by his many friends and colleagues in democratic nations to do so, he asked, "Do you desert your brother because he stole a silver spoon?" Unfortunately, the crime turned out to be incomparably greater.

Heisenberg almost succeeded in building a nuclear reactor, but he could not understand the validity of Houtermans' suggestion. How could this have happened to this brilliant physicist? Heisenberg, like Sakharov, cannot be blamed. Finding any solution to the situation in which they were placed required much more than simple logic.

The means by which Sakharov came to his decision to act are far less remarkable than that he reached that decision. The decision took independent judgment, real intelligence, and a truly extraordinary amount of courage. I sometimes wonder how many parallels there may be in the history of the world for this kind of spiritual evolution. We have plenty of wonderful stories about sudden conversions. A slow, thoughtful, and consistent change of opinion, made in the face of immense personal loss, is a rarity. It is not something that can be supported on a wave of emotion or by enthusiasm. It requires the determination and the character of a man with quite unusual integrity.

As I said, Sakharov and I have never met. We might

have met at the second Atoms for Peace Conference. Sakharov is proud that some of his ideas about peaceful fusion energy generation were presented at that time on his behalf. I was there, happy to present information that demonstrated a decrease in my government's secrecy about scientific matters. Sakharov has written extensively about third-world energy needs and technology's role in offering these peoples a more hopeful future. We might have met at a conference related to the development of the third world. However, we have never met. As Solzhenitsyn said, this is a remarkable and terrible world.

I am now more than three-quarters of a century old. Sakharov is an ailing prisoner of one of the most heartless regimes in a century of regimes that have demonstrated man's inhumanity to man in new and ingenious fashions. I am afraid we never shall meet but I shall still hope that such an event might occur. If it does, I am sure that we would disagree on many points within the surprisingly wide but nevertheless strict limits that are set by reason for all thinking men. But I am also sure that I would find great harmony with a man who, lacking all direct experience with living in freedom, can write:

I am convinced that international trust, mutual understanding, disarmament, and international security are inconceivable without an open society with freedom of information, freedom of conscience, the right to publish, and the right to travel and choose the country in which one wishes to live.[4]

Sakharov has unified the opinion of scientists in every part of the world where opinions can be freely expressed. By publicizing his story and those of his friends, he has clarified current issues in a manner that could have occurred in no other way. Since Galileo, no other scientist has been honored as Sakharov is. In my opinion, Sakharov is far more deserving of this respect than the great Italian. He has suffered far more, and, once he clarified his thoughts, he has never recanted.

Citations

[1]Sakharov, Andrei D., *Sakharov Speaks* (Knopf, New York, 1974), pp. 30, 31, 33, 32.

[2] ———, *Den Drieden retten!* (trans. Cornelia Gersten-maier, Burg Verlag, Stuttgart/Bonn, 1983), p. 84. (*"Fraglos ist Stalin einer der groessten Verbrecher unseres schwer geprüften Jahrhunderts..."*)

[3] ———, *Alarm and Hope* (Knopf, New York, 1978), pp. 10, 5.

[4] ———, "The Danger of Thermonuclear War: An Open Letter to Dr. Sidney Drell," *Foreign Affairs*, Summer 1983, p. 1010.

———

THE SAKHAROVS IN GORKY

by Natalya Hesse

NOTE: Natalya Viktorovna Hesse, an old and trusted friend of Nobel prize winner Andrei Sakharov and his family, arrived in Vienna from the Soviet Union on February 5, 1984. Hesse, who is now seventy, has known Elena Georgievna Bonner, Sakharov's wife, for more than thirty years and Sakharov himself since 1970. This friendship, as well as her own views, was not approved of by the Soviet regime. Of her decision to emigrate to the United States to join her son and his family Hesse said:

> The pressure against me was intensified. My apartment was searched, I was interrogated, I was called to the KGB many times for all kinds of talks.... But this was not the reason for my leaving the country. I was never afraid of them [the Soviet authorities], and I would have been able to resist them further.... But there was a change in my personal circumstances, and I decided to leave. And the KGB provided all kinds of "assistance."

The purpose of this "assistance" is quite clear. According to Hesse, the KGB is determined to isolate the Sakharovs completely and to deprive them of any help from their friends.

Before her departure from the Soviet Union, Natalya

Hesse met privately with Sakharov in Gorky and visited Elena Bonner in Moscow. She has brought alarming news of the deterioration of Sakharov's health and of a new heart seizure suffered in January by Elena Bonner, who had still not completely recovered from the previous one. Upon her arrival in Vienna, Hesse was interviewed by Vladimir Tolz, a former dissident who is now a research analyst for Radio Liberty in Munich. The following is a translation of parts of the interview, which was recorded in Russian by Radio Liberty.

TOLZ: Please tell us about your meeting with Andrei Dmitrievich Sakharov.

HESSE: This was our seventh meeting over the past few years since his forced exile to Gorky. In this case, as also in the case of the six other meetings (I will talk about the first one separately), the meeting took place on the street, at a prearranged place and a prearranged hour. We didn't have much time. I already knew that I would be going away and I came to say good-bye to him. He has aged much, he is full of worries concerning the health of his wife, Elena Georgievna. . . . But he is not broken, he is not bending; he is full of worry and he is physically weak, but he is strong in spirit as always. . . .

Between incoherent and hurried exchanges—because we had only a few hours at our disposal—between trivia and important topics—which we touched upon sometimes in more detail, sometimes with laughter or with sorrow—between questions about the life of our dear ones—who had been arrested, whose homes have been searched—we recalled Orwell, and I think this was not incidental. We have lived to see the year predicted by Orwell—1984. And it may seem strange to a Western person, it may seem that Orwell has nothing to do with real life, that his terrible utopia still remains a utopia or maybe an anti-utopia. How-

ever, the Soviet authorities—our dear KGB—have over-
taken Orwell by four whole years. In 1980, Andrei
Dmitrievich Sakharov and Elena Georgievna Bonner were
plunged into a world that surpassed Orwell's nightmarish
fantasies.

I will try to explain concretely what I mean. In 1980, I
had some luck. I arrived in Gorky on January 25, immediately after the seizure and forced transportation of Andrei
Dmitrievich to Gorky. His routine at that time had not yet
been set; the authorities didn't know how to organize it,
and I was able to stay with them for a month. Their entire
apartment is bugged, there isn't a corner where each sigh,
each cough, each footstep, not to speak of conversations,
can't be overheard. Only thoughts can remain secret, if they
haven't been put down on paper, because if the Sakharovs
go to the bakery or to the post office to mail a letter, the
KGB agents will search the place. They will either photograph or steal the written thought.

Andrei Dmitrievich, with his weak heart, his inability to
walk up even five or seven steps without pausing for breath
and trying to quiet his heartbeat, is forced to carry a bag
that I, for example, can't lift. When once we went into a
shop, he asked me to watch over this bag, but I wanted to
see what was on a shelf, and I had to drag the bag after
me. I just could not lift it. In this bag Andrei Dmitrievich
carries a radio receiver, because it would be damaged if left
at home, all his manuscripts—both scientific and public
ones—diaries, photos, personal notes. He has to carry all
this around with him. I think all this must weigh no less
than thirty pounds. And this man with a bad heart—suffering from acute hypertension—is forced to carry this bag
every time he leaves home, even if it is only for ten minutes.

There is in the apartment a special generator that creates
additional interference over and above the interferences
caused by conventional jammers in all cities of the Soviet
Union. This produces a terrible growl that drowns even the
jammer's noise. In order to hear at least some free world

voice, one has to go away from the house. It would be better to go out of town, but Andrei Dmitrievich cannot take even one step beyond the city limit, cannot go past the sign with the word "Gorky" on it. He is immediately turned back, he is denied such a possibility, although there is no published verdict condemning him to such isolation.

This is complete lawlessness on the part of the so-called competent bodies. It is very interesting that the recent law on citizenship uses this term, "competent bodies," without any explanation. This is one example of the extent of illegality in our state. There cannot exist a judicial term that is not and cannot be explained. However, the law states that some cases must be reviewed by the MVD, while in some other instances, as prescribed by other articles, the same cases are supposed to be dealt with by "competent bodies." It is not clear who these "competent bodies" are. When the term is used in the press, one can only guess who and what they are. But when this is not explained in the text of the law, one may only make a helpless gesture and just wonder.

TOLZ: Natalya Viktorovna, you were going to tell us about your first visit to Gorky in greater detail.

HESSE: Yes. At that time I managed to stay there for a month, together with Sakharov and Elena Georgievna, who, however, often traveled to Moscow in an effort to do something there to make Andrei Dmitrievich's life easier. A lot of interesting things were going on. There was a stream of letters, vast numbers of them, ten and occasionally a hundred a day. After a few days I began to sort them out—having decided to take a look—because there were all kinds of letters: some greeting and supporting him, some bewildered, some neutral ones in which people asked him to explain his position—asking whether what the Soviet papers wrote about him was true.

But some of the letters were abusive—there were curses, there were threats. Some letters were, I would say, of an extreme nature. One letter was, in my view, very funny. We all laughed terribly hard when it arrived: "We, second-grade pupils, sternly condemn the position of Academician Sakharov, who wants to unleash an atomic war between the Soviet Union's peaceful democracy and the rotten Western world. Shame on Academician Sakharov! Second-grade pupils." Such a letter was obviously dictated by an illiterate teacher.

Another extreme letter was also very interesting and somehow simply touched one's heartstrings. It began with some swear words, but not obscene, no. Then it said: "I am seventy-four years old. I am a construction engineer. I live well and have a separate room in a hotel. The water pump is about three hundred yards from where I live, and I have to carry firewood from the woods, but still I am a patriot. And your studies were paid for by Soviet money, but you have now betrayed your homeland." This letter was from a woman who represents one of the most terrible types of Soviet patriot. When a person exists at the bottom level of human life and does not realize it—imagining that he lives well—this is very frightening.

After about a week I said: "Listen, these letters must be sorted out, so that we can see the result. There are already many hundreds of them. I'll review them and make an assessment, and then we'll see what they add up to." When all this was done, I loudly announced: "Well, this is terribly interesting: 70 percent are messages of greeting, 17 percent are neutral or expressing bewilderment, and only 13 percent are abusive ones." The result of this careless remark—made aloud—was very unexpected. Letters with greetings and voicing approval simply ceased to arrive. From the very next day we began to receive only abusive letters. This was evidence of very attentive and well-organized monitoring and careful analysis of all conversations within the apartment.

The second incident happened after I had left. I heard about it from Elena Georgievna. She had walked to the

window and, looking at the joyless, empty lot covered with
trash and at the highway beyond with roaring trucks passing
by, said: "From the window in Moscow one can see Red
Square, but from this window, only a bit of the street, trash,
and all kinds of shit. It is better not to look out the window."
And then turning to Andrei Dmitrievich, who was standing
beside her, she said: "You know, Andrei, I think I'll photograph this, take a picture and send it to the West. Let them
look at this wonderful landscape." The next day three trucks
arrived and soldiers collected all the trash on the empty lot
in front of the windows. Commenting on this, Elena Georgievna used to say jokingly: "Thus I'll bring order to Gorky."

I have said that Sakharov was not allowed to leave Gorky's city limits, to step beyond the sign that read "Gorky."
Butt the house itself, although within the city limits, is
located near the borderline. Then there is a ravine—also
still within the city limits; it is a sort of empty lot with a
thick aspen grove. Andrei Dmitrievich and Elena Georgievna once decided to take a walk along a narrow path
and—in accordance with the rules—two persons in civilian
clothes tagged after them. The Sakharovs exchanged some
glances and, having gone separately in different directions
away from the path, hid in the thick bushes. Having lost
sight of them, the agents began running to and fro. Within
three minutes a helicopter arrived on the spot, descended
to about five meters above the ground, and KGB agents
with scared, fierce faces stared out of all the windows, trying
to locate the Sakharovs. Thus it is impossible to hide from
the KGB's "almighty eye" anywhere—even in thick aspen
bushes.

TOLZ: Natalya Viktorovna, a defamation campaign against
Sakharov has become especially intense recently in the Soviet press, as well as in some books—one by Nikolai Yakovlev in particular. Please, tell us in greater detail about
this stage of Sakharov's persecution, which began, I think,
about a year ago.

HESSE: First of all, I will tell you about the Yakovlev episode. Yakovlev has expressed himself in the most shocking manner. His writing cannot be called anything but slop. His book *CIA Against the USSR* [which included attacks on both Sakharov and his wife] was published, I think, in a first edition of 200,000 copies and was later reprinted several times with some changes (one should remember that with changes amounting to 20 percent of the original text, one can collect new royalties).[1] He published this in the magazine *Smena*, which has a circulation of more than a million copies, and, finally, having reworked it and having added a good dose of anti-Semitism, he published it in *Chelovek i Zakon* ["Man and the Law"]. This sounds even more paradoxical, since this periodical has a circulation of more than eight million. So, altogether his ideas have a circulation of about ten million.

Well, during our last meeting, Andrei Dmitrievich told me in detail about his encounter with Yakovlev, who, strangely enough, was allowed to come to Gorky. Sakharov was very elaborate in his narration, laughing and at the same time expressing horror at the extent to which a man can debase himself.

His doorbell rang. Elena Georgievna was in Moscow at the time. Sakharov was alone and was very much surprised. He decided that it must be a telegram. He opened the door. There was an unfamiliar man standing there with a woman— a man advanced in years ("Of my own age," Andrei Dmitrievich said). Andrei Dmitrievich let them in, and the woman immediately asked whether she could smoke in the apartment. Being an extremely well-brought-up person, Andrei Dmitrievich showed them to the largest room, right across from the entrance, said, "Please go in," and hurried into

---

[1] *CIA Target—The USSR* was published in English by Progress Publishers (Moscow, 1982).

the kitchen to get an ashtray, since he himself does not smoke.

When he returned, his guests were already seated. He only had time to think: "Maybe some physicians have finally come from the Academy of Sciences in order to have me hospitalized." He thought so because a few months earlier some physicians had come and had concluded that he was urgently in need of hospitalization. But these two were no medical doctors. The visitor by this time had already managed to display a pile of books, and said: "I am Nikolai Nikolaievich Yakovlev. As you know, I am a writer. Or maybe you don't know this. But I brought you my books as a present and, if you agree, I will autograph them for you."

Andrei Dmitrievich was somewhat taken aback by this extreme impudence and said: "I don't need your presents." He waved his hand, and one of the books fell to the floor. Nobody picked it up—neither Yakovlev nor Andrei Dmitrievich. But Yakovlev continued: "Well, I have published, you know, some articles. And so we have received many inquiries, and I am unable to answer them all. Therefore, I came here to ask you some questions and to get answers that we could relate to our readers."

Andrei Dmitrievich replied that he refused to talk to Yakovlev until the latter apologized in writing for slandering Sakharov's wife—Elena Georgievna Bonner—and her and his own—Andrei Dmitrievich's—family, as well as Andrei Dmitrievich himself. After this he grabbed the book, *CIA Against the USSR*, which was lying nearby and feverishly began turning the pages. "How could you write such slander, such horrible slander? How could you have called our children 'dropouts' when they all have university education...?" To which Yakovlev replied, unperturbed, "Yes, I know."

To most of Andrei Dmitrievich's angry questions, Yakovlev replied that he was aware of this or that. And only when asked, "How did you dare to write that my wife beats me?" Yakovlev said, "Well, so I was told in the prosecutor's office."[2] This man [Yakovlev] is so cynical and so morally degraded that he has no idea of either conscience or shame.

They talked for a few more minutes. Yakovlev said: "I am not going to write an apology. If you think this is slander, you can refer the matter to court. And, generally speaking, try to understand that we are defending you." Andrei Dmitrievich said: "I don't need your defense, and I am not going to go to court—I will just slap your face now." (It was at this point in the narration that I shuddered. I told Andrei Dmitrievich that this was terrible—that it was a frightful moment. And he said he felt the same way.)

Upon hearing this, Yakovlev, who was sitting at the table, covered his cheek with his hand. This is the utmost level of degradation, when a person cannot even face up to a slap honorably, openly, like a man. He covered part of his face with one hand, but Andrei Dmitrievich, who is ambidextrous and so has equal command of both hands, slapped him on the unprotected cheek. At that point Yakovlev and his companion ran away from the apartment—in the exact sense of the term: they jumped up, overturning their chairs, and escaped.

Having finished the story about slapping Yakovlev's face, Andrei Dmitrievich said to me: "You know, I have seen many different people in my life, including many bad ones. But this is something out of Dostoevsky, this is Smerdyakov. One cannot sink any further."

Yakovlev is an expert on America, and they say that his books on historical topics are not bad at all. But those who know him also say that he is cynical in the extreme, that his motto is that the Soviet regime is so abominable that

---

[2]*Interviewer's note*: At another point Hesse said she had been told that the editor who had allegedly been working on Yakovlev's books asked him once, "Nikolai Nikolaievich, where do you get material for your abominable articles?" And Yakovlev said, "Does one need any sources for this?"

one can and must be a scoundrel, that everybody must become a scoundrel. Such is Yakovlev's position, and he practices it in real life perfectly well.

TOLZ: Natalya Viktorovna, could you say something concerning the reaction of Soviet citizens—in Gorky, in particular—to the defamation campaign against Sakharov and his wife, which has now been intensified?

HESSE: Yes. The letter written by four Academy members against Andrei Dmitrievich has played a certain role, although not a very big one, within the context of the campaign of defamation and slander that has been unleashed against him and particularly against Elena Georgievna. I think that the West is of the opinion that it was the letter from these four academicians that played the principal part. (However, even among Academy members one can find people who would burden their conscience with heavy sins for the sake of their careers. And these four academicians, in particular, are known for being go-getters ready to do anything.)

But in Gorky itself the campaign—it was unleashed mainly in Gorky—was provoked not by the letter, which was published somewhere in the corner of a newspaper, but by the fact that the Gorky papers reprinted all of Yakovlev's insinuations concerning Elena Georgievna and, furthermore, added their own commentaries. Since then, at somebody's command, an extremely vicious campaign has been organized. The Sakharovs were even afraid to go to the bakery because they would be insulted. People would holler at them: "Your Yid-wife must be killed."

A neighbor in the Sakharovs' house had been helped by Elena Georgievna, who is a pediatrician (a very good pediatrician, an excellent physician), when the neighbor's child was suffering from an allergy which physicians in Gorky were unable to cure. Elena Georgievna did help the child with her advice, and the child was cured. And this same neighbor used to cry: "It would have been better for my child to rot than to be touched by your dirty hands."

The Sakharovs' car would be covered with graffiti: "Warmonger, get away from here, away from our town!" This seemed to them (and I have discussed this at length with both of them) to be a spontaneous wave of wrath on the part of the people. But whenever I asked Elena Georgievna to describe each incident in detail, her story would always expose some "stage director" who was behind each particular horrible act.

It is very easy to arouse indignation in our country. Indignation is fostered by the hardships of everyday life, by the lines in front of the stores, by the whole drabness and oppressiveness of Soviet reality, which is very hard. Therefore it is sufficient to make just a little hole, to open up the valve just a bit, and one can direct the stream of hate and bitterness any way one wants to. When people are standing in a line, it is enough for someone to shout: "It's not his turn!" or "Don't give him two kilos instead of one!" and the crowd will release its anger upon the unfortunate victim. Thus it is a very simple task to orchestrate something like that.

TOLZ: Natalya Viktorovna, it is known that Elena Georgievna Bonner does not stay in Gorky with her husband all the time and that she is obliged to come regularly to Moscow. What is her situation there? What is her general situation now?

HESSE: The conditions at their apartment in Moscow became quite terrible after Andropov took over all the positions and jobs that he assumed. Now, in addition to two policemen posted at the entrance to the apartment itself (and it must be noted that whereas in Gorky they are ordinary policemen, in Moscow either senior lieutenants or captains are on duty at the entrance to the apartment upstairs), there is also a police car with flashing lights guarding the downstairs entrance, and the man in charge has the rank of major at least.

It is amusing that these policemen in turn are watched over by KGB agents in civilian clothes who make sure that the policemen dutifully carry out their mission. They all have portable radio sets on their shoulders, and they communicate with each other. All visitors are checked against a special list. If a stranger tries to pass through and his name is not on the list, he must show his documents, and if he does not have any, he is simply not allowed in. No foreigners and no journalists are allowed to visit the apartment.

The telephone at the Moscow apartment has been disconnected ever since Andrei Dmitrievich's illegal exile to Gorky, and whenever Elena Georgievna comes to Moscow they disconnect even the public telephone in the booth downstairs so that in order to call someone she has to walk almost a kilometer up a very steep hill, which is practically impossible because of her heart condition. All in all, Elena Georgievna's health is in a terrible state. She has not yet recovered from her first heart seizure; she takes up to forty nitroglycerine pills; her lips and fingernails are of a dark blue color. It is upsetting to look at her.

When she came to Moscow the last time, she wanted to come to Leningrad to see me off, but I went to Moscow myself instead because I learned from friends about the state of her health, and it was clear that no farewell parties were possible. It was at this time that she suffered her second heart seizure, not having been completely cured after the first one.

In general, both of them are denied medical help. Andrei Dmitrievich himself also has been in need of a medical checkup and treatment for a long time, and this was admitted by the physicians from the Academy of Sciences who visited Sakharov in Gorky that one and only time. We had some hope then that things would improve; but, like all our hopes, this one was also destroyed. Neither she nor he has been admitted to a hospital, although both are seriously ill and in desperate need of medical treatment.

And they cannot allow themselves to be treated by physicians in Gorky. These physicians displayed their true nature sufficiently during the Sakharovs' hunger strike. Other physicians at the Arsenal Hospital in Leningrad—it's a prison hospital—once proudly said that they are first and foremost "Checkists"[3] and physicians only afterward. Well, those Gorky doctors, not being professional Chekists, nevertheless behaved as if they were, and it is therefore impossible to trust them and to be treated by them.

Once Andrei Dmitrievich was forced to go to a dentist because he had a toothache (and in such a case a person is willing to go anywhere), and the head of the dental clinic deceived him. She ordered him to leave his briefcase with his precious documents and manuscripts, and then personally turned the briefcase over to KGB agents. I think this incident is known in the West, but it may not be known that she then denied him medical treatment, claiming that he had insulted her—both as a woman and as a citizen. It was naturally very strange to hear such words coming from this particular physician.

As I have already mentioned, Elena Georgievna is being denied proper medical assistance in Moscow. A young woman who recently graduated from a medical institute visits her at home. I've been present during many of her visits. She respectfully and, I would even say, piously listens to advice from Elena Georgievna, who is a physician herself. Elena Georgievna writes her own prescriptions and decides her own treatment. Nevertheless, she urgently needs hospitalization because her condition is becoming even more serious and her strength is leaving her—the strength that seemed to be inexhaustible. "Constant dripping of water wears away the stone," as we say in Russia. But in this case there were not drops but heavy blows on the stone and

---

[3]Members of the Cheka, as the secret police was formerly called.

it has begun to break. During our last meeting Andrei Dmitrievich said: "The first thing to be done, the most important
thing, is to force the authorities to allow Elena Georgievna
to travel abroad for medical treatment. Tell the people you'll
meet in the West that her death would be the end of me
also. And being an eyewitness to all that has been happening, I can state that she is on the verge of dying, this is the
truth."

We must do everything possible. I don't know, maybe
the general public in the West must appeal to their elected
deputies so that they, in turn, would raise the question in
their respective parliaments. This is very important, especially now that we have a new ruler. He might show his
goodwill and prove to the world that the Soviet Union is
really ready to do good and not evil.

TOLZ: Natalya Viktorovna, the campaign against Sakharov
has been continuing for a long time, but it was especially
intensified during the period that has now come to an end—
the "Andropov era." Tell me, in your opinion, in the opinion
of a person who left the Soviet Union only days ago—did
the situation in the country change during the Andropov
period?

HESSE: The regime became extremely harsh. It began with
mass roundups of people in the streets, and in every city
indignant people were told by agitators at meetings that these
were only excesses on the local level. But the same thing
was going on all over the Soviet Union, just as it was during
collectivization. And, in general, the whole moral and spiritual climate in the country became much harsher. It seems
that it is difficult to breathe—just as it was in Stalin's time.
This is a frightening feeling and it affects a person's whole
being. The food situation in large cities has improved but
the provinces remain hungry. In the large cities—in Leningrad, in particular—one can get meat, not always the
kind one wants, of course, but we became accustomed to

this long ago. Sometimes one can get butter without standing in line. . . . So, it is somewhat better in this sense. But, on the other hand, there is complete suppression of everything, and not a gleam of democracy.

ANDREI DMITRIEVICH SAKHAROV

by Vladimir Voinovich

I "DECLASSIFIED" SAKHAROV BEFORE THE SOVIET authorities did, and this is how it happened.

In 1964 (I believe it was) I was sitting in the editorial offices of a Moscow magazine; and while waiting for an editor who had gone off somewhere, I leafed through a reference book on the USSR Academy of Sciences that was lying on his desk. All members of the Academy (and perhaps associate members) were listed in that book, which gave the last name, first name and patronymic, position, address and telephone number, both home and office. I remember being surprised when I learned that Academician Sholokhov had two addresses, one at the village of Veshenskaya and the other in Moscow, the latter not listed, for example, in the Writers Union handbook. Strictly out of curiosity, I began to look for names known to me; and I suddenly noticed that not all the academicians had their addresses and telephone numbers listed in the reference book. For example, following the name Mikulin there was no address and no telephone number, only the mysterious letters OTN. That was all. Since I had once served in the air force and knew that Mikulin was a well-known aircraft designer, I figured that probably he was so highly classified because he had something to do with rocket engines, and that consequently the most highly classified academicians were those for whom no address or telephone number was given. By way of checking I found Korolev[1] (everybody knew that he was the most highly classified), and his name was followed by those same three mysterious letters. Aha! I said to myself. Now we'll count the most highly classified ones. (Apparently I missed my calling as a pretty good intelligence agent.) I began to leaf further through the handbook and came across a name unknown to me: "Sakharov, Andrei Dmitrievich—OYaF." OYaF struck me as an even more mysterious abbreviation than OTN—perhaps because Sakharov himself struck me as more mysterious than the others.

Therefore, when I met up with a physicist I knew, I asked him who Sakharov was. The physicist told me that Sakharov had invented the hydrogen bomb; that he was a genius; and that, like all geniuses, he was a bit eccentric. For example, he went to the store for milk himself. That is, not entirely by himself, because he was always accompanied by several "secretaries" (special jargon for bodyguards) who kept their hands in their pockets, and in those hands clutched pistols with the safety catch off. It would have been easier on those "secretaries" if they had gone for the milk themselves. But why shouldn't a genius who created the hydrogen bomb behave a bit eccentrically? That is, within the limits allowed by special instructions. (I hasten to make the reservation that I did not believe that physicist; and I do not vouch for the reliability of the information he gave me.)

In 1968 Sakharov's name became known to the whole world after the appearance of his article "Thoughts on Prog-

---

[1]Sergei Pavlovich Korolev (1907–66), Soviet scientist and space rocket systems designer, designed and directed the development of many ballistic missiles, geophysics rockets, and launch vehicles, among them the Vostok and Voskod manned spacecraft launches.—Trans.

ress, Peaceful Coexistence, and Intellectual Freedom." He aroused the curiosity of many people, including myself.

Five more years passed by, and Sakharov had already become a quite legendary figure. Some of my acquaintances knew him personally. I had not had occasion to meet him; and to go to make his acquaintance specially, so as to "express admiration" or "shake hands," was something I couldn't do. (Nor do I like it when someone comes to me with that aim.) But I had constantly kept track of the social cause that Sakharov has espoused, and I had thought much about him as an individual.

Once at the Taganka Theater they were giving a premiere of something. And, as always at premieres at that theater, there were present a great many of what are called in English "very important people," including a member of the Politburo, Comrade Polyansky.[2] Among the fairly important people was my friend the well-known writer A. (I have deliberately chosen the first letter of the alphabet so that curious people will not torture themselves with vain guesses.) He was standing next to a tall man; and when I came up to him, he said: "Let me introduce you to each other." The tall man and I shook hands. I mumbled my name, and he mumbled his, which I didn't catch. I said a few words about the show, and then walked off.

The performance had taken place in the morning. After that I had some business to attend to, and in the evening I had guests. It was only when I went to bed that I remembered the theater, the people I had met there, the writer A, and the man he had been talking to. There was something about the latter that was strange. In some way he was different from all the others (including Comrade Polyansky). There was something about him...But that, I suddenly realized, was Sakharov!

---

[2]Dmitrii Polyansky (1917–   ), deputy chairman of the USSR Council of Ministers and member of the Politburo 1962–1966. —Trans.

But how did I guess it? I knew, of course, that A was acquainted with Sakharov; but then he knew almost everybody. And Sakharov had said nothing special to me. He had not expressed any great ideas. He had merely mumbled his name, which I didn't catch. Then why did I now realize that it was he?

I will explain: *Because he bore the imprint of a great personality.*

I have had occasion, in my life, to meet several outstanding persons. And I make bold to affirm that among them there was not a single one with an ordinary and hypocritical face. Ordinary and hypocritical faces are found only on ordinary and hypocritical people.

The next day I called A to check on my guess. "Why did you do that?" he asked me reproachfully. "You immediately turned away and walked off. Andrei Dmitrievich was quite astounded."

I felt frightfully awkward. Sakharov's situation was already such that many people were afraid to socialize with him. He must have thought that I was, too. . . .

To put it briefly, I took advantage of the first pretext, called, and began from time to time to visit the famous apartment on Chkalov Street.

I can't say that I became a friend of Sakharov's; and I'm not even convinced that my visits were necessary to him. But all of my new little books that were published abroad (since there were few of them) I first brought to him. Sakharov gave one of them to somebody to read. It was seized during a search at that reader's home, and now—inscribed by me as a gift—is in the files of the KGB.

Earlier I said that in the course of my life I have had occasion to meet several outstanding people. But I have known an even greater number of famous people—sometimes famous throughout the world. I hope it's clear that "famous" and "outstanding" are not always the same thing. I have known outstanding people who were known only to a small circle of acquaintances. And I have known famous people who became so by accident or thanks to their own special capacity for taking advantage of historical or other circumstances and were not ashamed (in the words of Pasternak) "while counting for nothing, to be a parable on people's lips."

Sakharov has made no special efforts to achieve fame. I don't even know who can be compared to him in attempts to minimize his own merits. From his Kremlin tribunal, Academician Aleksandrov says that Sakharov's achievements are exaggerated; and Sakharov himself says they are exaggerated. The Soviet propagandists claim that Sakharov is doing nothing interesting in science; and Sakharov says that, in general, one should work at physics while under the age of thirty. Since he is older than that, you can take his meaning as you will.

And yet one well-known physicist has told me that still today, all the main experiments with a controlled thermonuclear reaction are based on Sakharov's ideas. And it is said that even the academic higher-ups cannot but acknowledge that during recent years, in a crowded apartment, with daily crowds of petitioners, dissidents, and correspondents, while busy with his chief struggle, and constantly harassed, he regularly produced new papers with new ideas. Personally, I can't imagine how he managed to do that.

I have heard people express the opinion that human rights, about which Sakharov talks so much, are a secondary matter; that a national or religious rebirth is much more important. But without human rights there can be no rebirth. Without them there can only be either decay or, in the best (more accurately, in the worse) case, a change of ideology and the rapid movement of the masses from one swamp into another.

It is often said of Sakharov that he is courageous. But that characterization, if it does not contain a moral evaluation, is one that I do not accept. What is courage? Physical valor? Any adventure-seeker may possess that. But Sakharov does not resemble an adventure-seeker. Conscience and a clear understanding of the catastrophe threatening mankind have prompted him to follow a path where courage alone isn't enough.

The late Konstantin Bogatyrev[3] and I once went to visit Sakharov at his dacha. He met us on the platform at the train station. It was getting toward evening, and the sun, big and red, was already dipping under the horizon. "That sun," said Andrei Dmitrievich, "reminds me of the explosion of a hydrogen bomb."

I had imagined such an explosion differently—as a fiery, boiling element. But I was only imagining, whereas he saw. And he conveyed his notion to me. Now a red setting sun always fills me with a feeling of alarm: I see it indifferently hanging above our lifeless planet.

They have expelled Sakharov from Moscow, and sealed his mouth. That is not only cruel to him, but senseless. Wherever he may be, the problems identified by Sakharov (but posed by history rather than by him) will not disappear. And the longer the people holding the fate of mankind in their hands avoid solving them, the more unswervingly will we slide down into the abyss into which he has already peered.

---

[3]Konstantin Bogatyrev, Moscow dissident, poet, and German translator, died under mysterious circumstances in 1976.—Trans.

WHO'S BRAVER—
THE COSMONAUT
OR THE DISSIDENT?

by Vassily Aksyonov

A WELL-KNOWN SOVIET DISSIDENT AND CLOSE friend of academician Andrei Sakharov once told me a story:

"A year before the authorities sent him into exile, my wife and I were vacationing with the Sakharovs on the Black Sea. Outwardly it looked like a regular party of two aging couples enjoying promenades, bathing and the famous Caucasian culinary delights. We were having a fine time and didn't pay any attention to the KGB fussing around us. Meanwhile, the local 'warriors of the invisible war' (a high-flown name for the KGB used in official Soviet literature) were having a hectic time. Dissident No. 1 was in town! A special squad was set up to provide round-the-clock surveillance. We could feel their 'invisibility' wherever we went. But we tried to limit our own observations to the palm trees along the embankment, the sea's horizon in the west and the snowy mountain peaks in the east. One can do this after special training.

"Once we jokingly asked Sakharov's wife Elena about her husband's prime concern. What does he think about while strolling along the waterfront with a tacit smile on his face? We suggested that he was absorbed in the violations of the Helsinki Accords. 'Baloney!' she said, laughing. 'Here, in this romantic setting, he thinks only of me.'

"That evening we were all strolling along the embankment as palm trees rustled and a brightly lit ship approached the harbor. Stars were coming out and starting to twinkle. 'Ask him,' whispered Elena, anticipating her triumph.

"'Andrei,' we cautiously asked, 'what are you thinking about?' Without delay, he answered, 'About radiation in outer space.'"

On the face of it, this response seems odd. While thinking of Andrei Sakharov as a champion of human rights, we often miss the point of his incredible scientific importance. We must remember, however, that he is a scientist of great stature, who has never stopped working and creating. As the well-known Israeli physicist Harry Lipkin told the *Washington Post*: "Sakharov's ideas are always ten years ahead of the times."

It was precisely science that came to be fertile soil for the Russian dissent movement and it yielded richly. Many pioneers of the movement, people of the 1960s, were scientists. Physicist Yuri Orlov, chairman of the Moscow branch of the Helsinki Watch Committee, was sentenced to seven years in labor camps for his human-rights activity in 1978. Andrei Tverdokhlebov, another prominent physicist, met a similar fate in 1976. Many other scientists, such as physicist Valentin Turchin and mathematician Alexander Esenin-Volpin, were forced to emigrate. It is hard to know exactly how many practicing scientists secretly share the ideas of these courageous ones. The moral uprising of the scientists against the Party bureaucracy was a definite sign of the times. Actually, Party bureaucrats are now characters from the past, while the scientist has always been considered a man of the future.

In the late 1950s the so-called "towns of science" were established in the USSR; the best-known of these were Dubna and Obninsk near Moscow and Akademgorodok in the heart of Siberia. According to the authorities, these were to be "fortresses" of scientific productivity set far away from the dissipation of big cities. The authorities never foresaw that these towns would turn into "nests of sedition."

One of the most remarkable of them in this respect was a Siberian town where amidst the vast void of the taiga nonconformist art was encouraged. There were exhibitions of avant-garde art, performances of forbidden jazz and presentations by controversial young poets and balladeers. Young physicists applauded young lyricists. I recall a night there when it was 30 degrees below zero and through the glass wall of the Academic Center I glimpsed abstract carnival canvases. It was an unforgettable sight!

Siberian scientists made the Kremlin hierarchy nervous with unexpected statistical and sociological research, which—in violation of the most sacred of Soviet traditions, secrecy—they tried to make public. These meddlesome Siberians were not willing to understand the essence of Socialist sociology, whose main preoccupation is the glorification of the Party and its wisdom.

There was a famous café, the Integral, where for a short time an independent discussion club was set up. The discussers, jokingly fencing with foils, argued some pretty serious questions, such as the competence—if any—of a one-party system.

Siberian "freedom" reached its zenith when young scientists marched in the official May 1 parade carrying slogans of the various political parties of the Duma, the prerevolutionary Russian parliament. They called it a carnival procession, but no one failed to perceive it as an eloquent reminder of the short period of Russian democracy. The Communist Party, which used to be just one of many parties in the Duma, was infuriated. This one party, a subject of earlier discussions, now turned out to be competent enough to close the Integral Café and stop the discussion club for good.

By the end of the 1960s, the regime, in order to intimidate its domestic dissidents, began staging a series of political trials. Intellectuals responded with unexpected courage in a spontaneous campaign of signing and sending letters of protest, which swept the country. It took the authorities several years to restore "stability" and bring society back to its current state of stagnation.

Images from that first period of Soviet dissent are connected with various fields of advanced science—physics, cybernetics, biology. One could regard the dissidents as Don Quixotes or merely as cranks, but in fact they combined their quest for chivalry with common sense and pragmatic calculations. Common sense looks bizarre in a world of totalitarianism, with its ideological paganism.

I remember one time in Moscow when we were talking about a rather peculiar subject—who is the braver, a cosmonaut or a dissident? It may look childish on the face of it, but we were trying to juxtapose the two kinds of bravery. The question was what is more serious—a loss of gravity in space, or the loss of one man's unity with society and the launching of his body and soul into the dangerous world of discontent and protest.

Who are the genuine heroes of contemporary Russia? There is still no answer, but in a society where until not long ago no questions existed, the Question Mark is probably a weightier award than the Medal of Hero of the USSR.

A GENERATION
THAT FAILED

by Robert Kaiser

TWENTY YEARS AGO THE SOVIET UNION ABAN-
doned the adventurous but erratic course charted by Nikita
S. Khrushchev and began an experiment with steadier, more
conservative rule. The experiment worked for a while, but
now it has faltered. This immense, rich country is in serious
trouble. The engines of the giant Soviet machine are still
turning over, but they are sputtering.

Despite its success in building a military machine worthy
of a second superpower, the post-Khrushchev generation
has failed—failed to develop a modern and efficient economy, failed to find a way for this country to feed itself,
failed to bring along a new generation of leaders, failed to
fulfill Khrushchev's dream of a dynamic Soviet Union that
would surpass the United States and become a model for
the world.

A decade ago, when I was completing a three-year assignment in Moscow, all of these failures seemed possible,
even probable, but they were not inevitable. It was still
conceivable then that the Russians would come to grips with
their shortcomings. But they did not.

After a month's visit now, one is struck by a society that
is coming to grips with its failures. The candor here, even

145

among senior officials, is startling. They openly discuss the need for profound economic changes, the need for a new generation of leaders, and their lack of optimism about the foreseeable future.

But the situation may be even worse than officials acknowledge. There is evidence of social disintegration here— dramatically declining life expectancy for men, rising infant mortality, increasing alcoholism affecting ever-younger age groups, increasing crime, corruption and cynicism.

In a conversation over tea in a typical Moscow kitchen, one is amazed to be told by a knowledgeable Muscovite that most of the clinics where babies are born in this capital city are contaminated with staph infections, which a large percentage of newborns catch, and which Soviet drugs often fail to cure. In another conversation, a recent patient reported that many Moscow hospitals now have virtually no nursing staff, so patients must depend on friends or family for nursing care. An official newspaper reports that a third of patients being treated for alcoholism began drinking before they were 10 years old.

All this is a far cry from the predictions of Marxist-Leninist doctrine, which foresaw by now the final stage of "advanced socialism" on the eve of "real communism," when such mundane encumbrances as money, government, bureaucracy and so on are supposed to disappear. Instead, the country has reached a stage that might be called "exhausted communism," typified by exhausted old leaders and an exhausted economic system.

The aspect of the new mood in Moscow that makes the strongest impression is the absence of any clear sense of the future. A blank horizon lies before this country, one that matches the geographical horizon visible from this great city on the vast Russian plain. Ask a Russian what things might be like here five or 10 years from now, and the response is a shrug, a blank look or a vague comment about the momentum of this behemoth of a nation.

The old promises of communist ideology are no longer taken seriously. The social and economic problems now seem so vivid that many find it difficult to imagine how they will be solved. But no one I met here had a concrete notion of what may lie over that blank horizon.

At the same time, there is no sign of panic or despair. "It works," one official said of the lumbering Soviet system, just after making serious criticisms of it. "So what?" asked another, after acknowledging the gravity of the country's problems. "The country's not going to fall apart—the society won't disintegrate." An outsider cannot dispute this confidence that the system will survive; by all outward indications, it is deeply, firmly entrenched.

A skeptical intellectual who has lived through most of Soviet history observed that "the wheels are still turning, from momentum. But they are beginning to slow down. And rot is setting in. But it will take a long time for anything conclusive to happen. It won't happen in my lifetime."

The largest barrier now blocking everyone's view of the Soviet future is the phalanx of old men running the country, who simply refuse to make way for the next generations. The four key figures in this group—President Konstantin Chernenko[1], Foreign Minister Andrei Gromyko, Defense Minister Dmitri Ustinov[2] and Premier Nikolai Tikhonov—are, in order, 73, 75, 76 and 79 years old. Chernenko, the youngest, seems the least healthy. In his public appearances he looks more like an overinflated balloon from the Macy's Thanksgiving Parade than a man capable of effective leadership of a great country. No Soviet citizen seeing him now

---

[1]Konstantin Chernenko died on March 10, 1985, and was immediately replaced by Mikhail S. Gorbachev.

---

[2]Dmitri Ustinov died in December of 1984.

could think he was a significant factor in shaping the country's future.

Few younger men are given a chance to prepare for their own day in power. The age group responsible for day-to-day management of the country's affairs—those 50 to about 65—are far removed from the old men on top, who lead lives utterly separated from their countrymen and colleagues. Resentment seems to be increasing. Not one of the officials I interviewed during the past month volunteered real praise for Chernenko personally. "He provides stability" was as close as any Russian could get to a compliment.

The officials available to a Western journalist are all members of a special class that is authorized to meet with foreigners—propagandists for the official media, Communist Party officials, academic specialists on the United States, scientific officials. But others with access to different slices of the Soviet elite said the same frustrations with the status quo and eagerness to move ahead with new men and new policies were widespread.

Twenty years ago, when the then-elders of the Communist Party ousted Khrushchev, they had a clear program for overcoming the shortcomings of Khrushchev's unpredictable regime. They were determined to build up the military might of their country so that it would match the United States. They were determined to restore discipline at home, both inside the party and in society at large. And they were determined to rationalize the domestic economy so that it could fulfill Khrushchev's dreams of surpassing the United States—if not by 1980, as Khrushchev once promised, then not long after that.

A generation later we can judge their success. They did match American military power with a steady, deliberate military buildup that increased their defense spending several percent every year. They did restore discipline and have now wiped out the dissidents who appeared unexpectedly in the late 1960s. But their repeated attempts to make the economy more rational and more efficient all failed, leaving the Soviet Union a semideveloped industrial power that lacks basic infrastructure like a network of good roads or a reliable telephone system, and that cannot produce industrial goods to compete in international markets.

So the post-Khrushchev generation failed to accomplish its most fundamental goal: the establishment of a vibrant, growing Soviet Union that would not only shape world events, but would inspire other peoples to emulate the Soviet model. On the contrary, the Soviet Union is visibly ossifying, and no longer provides a model for its own satellites in Eastern Europe, let alone independent nations.

Economic failure now haunts the Soviet system. The existing economic structure does not offer the prospect of turning the backward Soviet Union into a modern industrial power, and it now faces unprecedented internal strains as it struggles merely to maintain forward momentum.

In conversation after conversation, officials expressed the personal view that dealing with the economic crisis is by far the country's most pressing problem. Many also expressed a kind of fatalistic confidence that changes were bound to come, because they *have* to come to get the country back on course. But one senior official was more cautious. "The question," he said, "is whether the [economic] changes will be made deliberately, according to our plan, or only after we have cracked our heads against the wall once or twice."

The economic problems are staggering, and are discussed with increasing candor in the Soviet press. One of the most outspoken critics of the status quo is Abel Aganbegyan, director of the Institute of Economics and Management of the Siberian department of the Soviet Academy of Sciences.

In two surprisingly candid articles in the newspaper *Trud* (Labor), Aganbegyan made these points: In the previous five-year plan (1976–80), 11 million people reached working age, but in the current five-year plan (1981–85), there will be only 3 million new workers, 2.5 million of them residents of Central Asia. In the five-year plan beginning in 1986, "the increase in the working-age population will be still smaller."

In the past, the Soviets might have compensated for such a decline in the growth of the labor force with increased capital investments in new plant and machinery, but Aganbegyan said this is now impossible. Noting that it was once common for each new five-year plan to raise investment by 50 percent over its predecessor, he cited the latest figures: in the 1976–80 period, investment grew by 32 percent; in the 1981–85 period, it will have grown by 10 percent—"That's all!" Aganbegyan wrote.

Raw materials and energy resources, he added, are disappearing from the European part of the country, where most industry is centered. Siberia and the Soviet Far East now account for 88 percent of all raw material and energy resources, he wrote, and these are increasingly difficult to extract. The growth of new discoveries of energy resources and raw materials has declined 400 to 500 percent, he added.

Only radical changes, Aganbegyan argued, can salvage economic performance: "For the economy's normal development, we must accelerate labor productivity growth rates at least 50 percent," while simultaneously forcing enterprises to use fewer raw materials, make better use of investment capital, "and effect a radical improvement in the quality of output."

Aganbegyan, one of the country's leading economists, supports radical reforms that would prevent the central industrial ministries from meddling in the affairs of individual enterprises, while giving enterprises new autonomy and dramatically improved opportunities to reward their employees for more efficient production. Tentative, "experimental" reforms along these lines were launched during the brief reign of Yuri Andropov in a few specific branches of the economy to see if they would be effective. According to Aganbegyan, they are too tentative:

"There has been no breakthrough in production efficiency . . . the return on capital and the efficiency of capital investments have not improved...." Another popular reform idea, the reorganization of workers into teams or "brigades" that share material benefits if they improve their own performance, is also ineffective so far, Aganbegyan said. "In industry, 6 out of every 10 workers already work in a brigade, yet so far no sharp breakthrough in raising the efficiency of production is visible."

What is striking about this commentary is its directness. Aganbegyan's are not peripheral criticisms but frontal challenges. His conclusion is that the current path will not lead to the desired destination. Such direct attacks are most unusual here.

But apparently, many important people believe that Aganbegyan is right. According to persistent rumors from credible academic quarters, Mikhail Gorbachev, the 53-year-old successor to Chernenko, favors a sharp turn in economic policy. Gorbachev has asked economists for briefings on the reforms designed by Pyotr Stolypin, Czar Nicholas II's enlightened prime minister, who encouraged entrepreneurship among the peasants, and on Lenin's New Economic Policy, or "NEP," which revived some forms of free enterprise in the difficult years after the Bolsheviks consolidated their power.

According to some reports, Gorbachev has overseen drafting of a new variant on NEP that he would like to implement now, making room for much more private enterprise in the service sector and in agriculture. Academic economists are tantalized by the thought that a man of Gorbachev's importance—first-ranking member of the party, and the man responsible for Soviet agriculture—would be so interested in major reforms. But according to one academic source, Gorbachev has privately wondered aloud how the vast "middle level"—the administrative bureaucracy in the ministries and enterprises that has always blocked reforms in the past—could ever be persuaded to go along with really significant reforms.

Those interests are also regularly heard from in the

new debate on economic policy. For every reformer like Aganbegyan, there is another author demanding more old-fashioned discipline, more thorough Communist Party guidance of economic affairs right down to the shop floor, and more exhortation of the labor force—the traditional bag of tricks that has failed in the past.

The temptation to stick with past methods is a great national problem. Overall economic performance is poor, but the status quo serves the needs of the bureaucratic class in charge, or so the members of that class obviously believe. A factory director who can satisfy the plan written for him by higher authorities has no personal interest in reform, which he knows will upset his enterprise, make new demands on him and may lead to nothing but trouble. The officials who now draw up the all-important plan targets would lose power if individual enterprises got real autonomy. And workers used to goofing off might really have to work hard under some kinds of reforms. So while the politicians may decide that reform is desirable or even necessary, many of those who can implement it can be counted on to frustrate whatever plans are made.

Meanwhile, the Soviet economy is really hurting. The labor shortage implied by Aganbegyan's statistics is already a vivid fact of life. In Moscow, the authorities cannot provide a full complement of workers for the construction site of the new American Embassy, despite the fact that the United States is paying these workers' wages in coveted hard currency.

After many years of steady decline in the rate of economic growth, the figure is reported to have gone up slightly in the last two years. But there is now widespread suggestion that the figures are so padded as to be meaningless. The official press has carried numerous reports of enterprises, ministries and even national republics faking their economic statistics.

Other outward signs are negative. Technologically the Soviets remain far behind Japan and the West, and they are only now beginning a serious debate about how to try to catch up with the computer revolution. The next five-year plan *may* include ambitious targets for the production of a Soviet personal computer, but even if it does, the Russians will remain decades behind the advanced countries in the basic computerization of their society.

Drunks and 'Hooligans'

There is a new joke circulating in Moscow about two workmen with shovels walking along the edge of a city street, stopping every five yards so that one of them can dig a hole in the dirt. As soon as it is dug, his comrade fills the hole back in. Then they move along another five yards and repeat the exercise.

A Soviet citizen observing this scene loses his temper and stomps up to the two workers. "Comrades!" he shouts, "What kind of craziness is this? You dig a hole, then the other fellow fills it right up. You're accomplishing nothing at all! We're wasting good money paying you!"

"No, no," one of the workers replies, "you don't understand at all. Usually we work with a third lad, Volodya, but he's home drunk today. Volodya plants trees. I dig the hole, he sticks in the tree, and Ivan here fills the hole back in. Just because Volodya's off drunk, does that mean Ivan and I have to stop working?"

In fact, millions of Soviet workers are off drunk every day. According to credible estimates, as many as 85 percent of the workers in ordinary Soviet factories regularly drink too much—not because they are alcoholics, according to a doctor from the industrial city of Gorki, but because getting drunk is a common habit among the working class.

The statistics on Soviet drunkenness are staggering. According to one report published last December in *Selskaya Zhizn* (Rural Life), "the average age of people suffering from alcoholism has fallen five to seven years in the last decade." The same article reported that "according to research on ill patients, 90 percent of them started drinking before the age of 15, and one-third of them started before the age of 10. In most cases, familiarity with alcohol begins with the cooperation of the parents."

Such candid published reports indicating profound social disorders are extremely rare, but many Russians tell stories that convey a similar message. One Russian couple recounted their experience this summer of walking into a village 100 miles from Moscow at about 5 in the afternoon. "Everyone was drunk," the woman said. "The men, the women, the young people, they were all drunk as skunks. Many were laid out on the ground. It was an amazing sight."

Foreigners who only visit Moscow, Leningrad and Kiev never see rural Russia, where about a third of the population still lives. According to Russians who have spent time in the countryside, it remains backward, almost primitive in many areas. Rural drunkenness is obviously endemic, and many report visiting state stores in rural areas that have almost no food or merchandise for sale, but always have plenty of vodka. One Muscovite reported that in the village where he has a cottage not far from Moscow, peasants buy their vodka "by the carton—20 [half-liter] bottles at once."

Of course drunkenness is not a new problem in Russia, but it is evidently getting worse all the time, affecting more women and children as well as men. Western specialists like Prof. Vladimir Treml of Duke University have assembled statistics demonstrating that consumption of alcohol continues to go up steadily.

Another endemic social problem is burglary. Westerners may be used to crime of this kind, but it is something new and alarming for Russians, who used to consider their country immune from such problems. Apartment houses in Moscow have blossomed with new devices to lock the doors to each entryway, to keep "hooligans" from prowling the halls. The new locks open to a three-number code that must be punched into them by residents or guests. Many Muscovites are putting two and three locks on their apartment doors, something never seen a decade ago.

But for the authorities, the bigger crime problem is robbery of "socialist property"—raw materials, finished goods from factories, spare parts and so on. Officials of the Ministry of Internal Affairs, which runs the police force, have said that this is now the biggest crime problem they face.

Not many years ago, the Soviet newspapers rarely reported on crime, and never gave any general statistics on its frequency. That has changed dramatically. Crime reporting is now common. Just last month the minister of internal affairs, Vitali Fedorchuk, gave an interview to a Soviet paper in which he revealed that overall crime was going up, and he gave surprising statistics on the extent of economic crime.

Muscovites report that the amount of stealing has gone up appreciably in recent years. Government chauffeurs and truck drivers regularly sell the gas in the tanks of their state-owned vehicles to private motorists. Owners of cottages (*dachas*) in the countryside around Moscow report that collective farmers regularly show up with truckloads of stolen sand, fertilizer and other useful commodities that they sell at low prices. (Robbery of the contents of country *dachas* has also become big business; one man in Gorki was charged with looting 49 cottages.) Car owners report that overcrowded garages often steal the parts out of cars they have under repair, replacing them with faulty ones. "Everybody steals, all the time, anything they can get their hands on," one discouraged Muscovite said—an exaggeration, no doubt, but one that many Soviet citizens would subscribe to.

The problem of thievery is now a factor in high-level decision-making. For example, according to Communist Party officials, a debate is currently going on about whether to authorize the existence of private repair garages for automobiles. The Soviets have built 10 million cars since 1970, but service facilities for them are woefully inadequate.

A strong argument against private garages, however, is that there aren't enough spare parts available to stock them. "If we have garages but no spare parts, then thievery will go way up," one official said, explaining that the new garages would have to get parts somehow.

Another serious social problem is health care. According to ordinary Russians, it has deteriorated significantly in recent years. One reason for this has been the passing of a generation of nurses, women who came into the hospitals during or just after World War II. "No one wants to work as a nurse now," one Muscovite said, so these people have not been replaced. Instead, family members or friends must nurse a patient in a hospital. "If you don't have someone to help you, you can just die," one woman said. Another reported seeing seriously ill patients in a Moscow hospital bathing each other, despite their disabilities.

Staph infections in nurseries where babies are born have become an enormous problem, even in Moscow, and infant mortality rates are rising. Medicines are in short supply— all but nonexistent in small cities and towns, according to many Russians. Even in the capital, modern antibiotics are rare. One of the most remarkable statistics about modern Soviet life, calculated by American demographers from incomplete Soviet figures, involves the life expectancy of men. It has fallen from a high of 67 years in 1964 to less than 62 in 1980. No other industrial society has ever recorded such a decline.

Who Wants to Work Hard?

Russians joke that their country is "the homeland of elephants," meaning that it is the center of the universe, the home of all things. The elephant metaphor could be used in another way. The Soviet leadership rides astride this giant society as if it were an elephant. The leaders feel the onward motion beneath them, see that they continue to make slow but steady progress in a forward direction, so assume the best about what is going on down below. But the man astride an elephant has a bad vantage point for carefully examining the beast. Physical or psychological disorders below him are not readily identifiable.

But there are disorders, and they are getting worse. This doesn't mean the all-suffering Russian workers and peasants are about to rise in a new revolution; there is no sign of that. It remains true, as Nikita Khrushchev observed many years ago, that "in general, our people are not very demanding." But neither are they necessarily very enthusiastic. Returning here after a 10-year absence brings a sharp reminder of an easily forgettable fact of Soviet life: almost no one here works hard. "On average," one official said, "out of every 10 people in an office or enterprise, three actually work." A scientist gave a harsher estimate: 300 of the 330 people who work in her institute could disappear tomorrow, she said, and no one would notice the difference.

"You know," said a senior Communist Party official, "I think if you put the question to a referendum, and asked our people if they want the current system with some shortages and problems, but also guaranteed access to the necessities of life, or do you want another arrangement in which much more is available, but in which you might get fired if you don't really work hard, I have a feeling that our people would vote to keep things the way they are. Every society has to make a choice, according to its own values.[3]

* * *

"Stalin died 30 years ago," an elderly Muscovite observed recently, "and our hopes soared." He raised his arms in an

---

[3]It should be noted that this is an opinion of a Party official which does not mean that the majority of Soviet people think the same way. On the contrary, by building the enormous KGB and police apparatus of suppression, the Party shows that it greatly fears peoples' aspiration for freedom and economic changes. (Ed)

arc to demonstrate. "For a while things did change, there was excitement and creativity and we dreamed of a better future. But now," he went on, completing the arc he drew in the air so it became a circle, ending where it began, "we're back to here again."

These are glum days for the Soviet Union's gifted intelligentsia, the intellectual class that has given so much to the world's knowledge and culture during the past two centuries. The sour mood of the intellectuals reflects both objective conditions, which are harder for them, and perhaps more importantly, the absence of hope for a better tomorrow.

Many intellectuals here have succumbed to a wave of nostalgia for the late 1950s and early 1960s, when living and working conditions were worse than today's, but expectations were high and rising.

"In the '50s a new generation was bursting into its own," as one member of that generation put it, "and we could feel the earth shaking under our feet. Older people saw it too, and seized on these youngsters as heralds of a new age. But the new age didn't come."

A professor from Leningrad now in his 50s said the survivors of that period had to share responsibility for the failure to make those dreams come true. "We missed our chance," he said, speaking of the liberal-minded intellectuals who interpreted the thaw that followed Nikita Khrushchev's campaign against the horrific excesses of Stalin's dictatorship as an augury of a new Soviet enlightenment, but lived to see that hope dashed.

Today's Moscow intellectuals feel isolated from an outside world that, 10 years ago, they were just beginning to sample. They complain that it is now difficult to listen to Russian-language broadcasts from stations such as the British Broadcasting Corp. and the Voice of America that had kept them in touch with the outside world in the 1970s, when jamming of broadcasts was stopped. (The jamming was resumed in 1980, apparently to block news of the Solidarity movement in Poland from reaching too many Soviet ears, and it is now worse than ever.)

They complain that they rarely get to read the Russian literature now being published in Israel and the West in great quantities. They complain sadly of the many writers and artists who have left the Soviet Union in recent years, depriving them of cultural heroes as well as personal friends. And they complain that the offical bureaucracy that governs all intellectual and cultural life here seems more determined than ever to discourage originality and talent.

Perhaps most significantly, they complain that there is no younger generation coming along, at least not that anyone has heard of—no new poets or playwrights to provide new intellectual electricity.

"Someone once said that the poets are the light cavalry of literature and culture," a Moscow editor said, referring to the special role poets have played in this country for two centuries. "When the poets charge ahead, others follow. But when the army gets bogged down, as it has now, the poets are the first to sink into the swamp."

If there are talented new poets trying to charge ahead, he added, he has not heard their names, or their verse.

Many Moscow intellectuals report that this is a time of introspection, of preoccupation with personal concerns such as health and religion. "It's a time to stay home," said one middle-aged Muscovite who used to try to see every new play and film.

Many see their plight as partly a product of the worsened international situation. The new cold war that is becoming evident here inevitably means tighter restrictions on the very things intellectuals care most about—travel, exchanges of people, books and ideas, local translations or productions of Western works.

At the same time, many intellectuals believe that their country is on the eve of a new era, under new leaders. This allows them to hope that things could change, perhaps quickly and dramatically—but perhaps, as many acknowledge, dramatically for the worse.

"We've seen bad times before, and we know how bad they can get," said one professor.

"You know," a middle-aged editor observed, "I have no idea what may happen. Maybe I'll be visiting you in America in five years. And maybe I'll be shot."

Treatment of Intellectuals

The intelligentsia is a class apart in the Soviet Union, neither representative of the country nor much admired by ordinary citizens or the politicians in charge. By definition, an intellectual is someone who thinks for himself—potentially a dangerous habit in the Soviet Union.

For foreigners the intellectuals traditionally have been the most interesting Russians, largely because of their immense talents, but also because of their independence, and because many of them share values that are familiar to Westerners.

The state of intellectual life at any given moment is a good barometer of other conditions inside the country. The way intellectuals are treated seems to reflect the self-confidence of the leadership. Their enthusiasm, or lack of it, foretells the creative energies likely to appear in the immediate future. The attitudes and ambitions of university-educated young people also can be a revealing social indicator.

Judging from conversations with intellectuals here and the reports of foreigners who recently have seen scientists, scholars, writers, directors, actors and artists in Moscow and Leningrad, the old man who drew that discouraging circle in the air speaks for many, though not for all of them.

There are new hints of a modern version of Stalinism—tough new censorship, for example. Academics report that the most benign books or articles on subjects far removed from politics are now subject to a kind of arbitrary treatment from the censor that appears intended, most of all, as a form of pressure—harassment for its own sake, an old Stalinist tactic.

The censor also has gotten stricter about excising references to situations that conceivably could be taken as descriptions of Soviet reality, even if they describe the "decadent" West. For example, a woman writing about contemporary Italy recently referred to a writer who, intoxicated by dreams of power, was willing to violate his own conscience. The censor cut the reference.

Defense Minister Dimitri Ustinov brought an increasing number of the country's scientific research institutes under military control by requiring that any institute that does research for the military must be subject to military discipline. Scientists working in those institutes now have a great deal of difficulty publishing the results of their research, even if it has nothing to do with secret work.

A new rule requires that any research paper presented to a scientific meeting that might be attended by a foreigner—even a Czechoslovak or a Bulgarian—must be approved in advance by a special commission at the author's institute. Often permission is withheld until the last possible moment, and sometimes it is denied. Travel to foreign scientific meetings has become markedly more difficult.

Similar kinds of harassment are reported by writers, theater and movie directors and actors, although this is not new. Plays fully rehearsed and ready to be put on are banned at the last minute; completed movies are denied distribution; manuscripts are accepted for publication but then never published.

In both scholarly and creative fields, the target of official restrictions often seems to be talent—not politically controversial material, just original, creative work. Writers of known talent are rejected repeatedly by magazines and publishing houses; promising young scholars with budding international reputations are denied access to foreign colleagues.

Even books on nonpolitical subjects sent from abroad to

Soviet scholars are not allowed to reach their intended recipients. The Academy of Sciences now has a form letter notifying scholars that a book addressed to them has been received "and is available for your use in the special depository at the Academy of Sciences library." In other words, the book can be seen only under official supervision.

Perhaps the strongest symbol of the new orthodoxy is the disappearance of the people who came to be known as dissidents. In the late 1960s hundreds of intellectuals were willing to sign petitions protesting against trials of writers, for example. By the 1970s the number willing to join any kind of protest had fallen to a few dozen. Today it has fallen virtually to zero.

The exile and isolation of Andrei Sakharov, the Nobel Peace Prize winner, is the clearest sign that an entire period in Soviet history—an exciting period for the intellectuals, even those who never personally took part—now has ended.

And yet, interesting scholarly and creative works still appear. There are a few provocative movies every year, a few interesting theatrical productions, a few short stories or novels that set the town abuzz. Most of the best work is so rooted in Soviet reality that it does not translate well; foreigners not steeped in Soviet ways cannot fully appreciate it. But people here can, and do.

Moscow's major theaters have been allowed to set up "small stages" where they can do experimental works for audiences of 200 or fewer, and the censorship is less rigorous than for major productions.

Film studios outside Moscow, particularly one in Tbilisi, Georgia, sometimes allow more interesting work. Non-Russian writers like Chingiz Aitmatov and Fasil Iskander also seem to enjoy a license to write more freely than others, at least sometimes, probably because they are symbols of "multinational culture" in the Soviet Union, which the authorities prize.

Individual theater directors, film makers and writers occasionally can exploit personal connections and friendships to overcome the objections of cultural bureaucrats who want to block their work. "It's always a battle, but sometimes we win," one boasted.

The disciplinary system seems inconsistent, sometimes even weak, which may be a sign of the general exhaustion of the system. A Moscow economics institute was the subject of harsh public criticism by the Central Committee of the Communist Party, and friends of people who worked there were nervous about what would happen next. In the end, though, the institute was given new funds to help compensate for the shortcomings identified in the criticism, and no one suffered any punishment.

Just this month the Taganka Theater, Moscow's most popular, was allowed to put on many of the plays staged by Yuri Lyubimov, the internationally famous director of the Taganka who this year decided to stay in Western Europe rather than return to Moscow after guest appearances in Italy.

Traditionally "traitors" of this kind have been punished with a total ban of their work, but in Lyubimov's case the authorities relented, in part because the popular Taganka had no repertory to substitute for the Lyubimov productions. Lapses of traditional discipline of this kind suggest that elastic can still be found in the system.

There have been other inconsistencies. Jews, for example, report the unpredictable enforcement of anti-Semitic policies. No Jewish students were admitted to the chemistry faculty of Moscow State University this year, an informed source reported, but at a Moscow scientific institute, a Jew was appointed deputy director, to the amazement of his colleagues.

Cynical Younger Generation

A 50-year-old Muscovite was asked recently about members of the younger generation—what were they like? He responded by telling a story about a prominent writer who came into Moscow by train recently and was recognized by a young porter in the train station who carried his suitcases.

"Aren't you so-and-so?" the porter asked, and the writer acknowledged that he was. The porter then asked him detailed questions about each of his last two books. While the writer answered, the porter beckoned to a number of his colleagues in the station to join the conversation. Soon something like a literary press conference was under way, with young baggage porters cross-examining the famous writer.

"You find a lot of talented people working as porters these days," the Muscovite said. "They're former dissidents, or poets, or just honest men who can't put up with regular jobs where they have to be dishonest."

The younger generation is a subject of considerable interest in Moscow these days. There is widespread agreement that the current crop of educated young people is less idealistic, more cynical, more interested in building successful careers than its elders were.

"Of course you can't generalize about all of them," one mother of a 22-year-old said. "There are lots of wonderful ones, just as idealistic as we were. But most of them seem to be in it for themselves, for a comfortable life and career."

Twenty years ago it was relatively easy for an educated but still isolated young Muscovite to accept the world view contained in official propaganda. Ignorance of the outside world and the discipline of the system at home both helped keep him in the dark. But today such ignorance is hard to come by. Western popular culture has invaded this country with a vengeance, and cynicism about the Soviet system is rampant, according to many—including officials—who have watched this generation grow up.

Young university graduates here easily can see that a few people enjoy most of the privileges, and that only the elite can travel abroad—the greatest privilege of all. They understand that the government does not trust them—to go abroad, to hear foreign radio broadcasts, to know the truth. They realize how far the Soviet standard of living lags behind that of the West, and even Eastern Europe.

Blue jeans are one metaphor for these realizations. There are now lots of blue jeans here, but the cognoscenti insist that those made in the Soviet Union and East Europe, as most of them are, do not hold a candle to real American jeans, which sell for 300 rubles a pair—more than $350 at the official exchange rate—on the black market, almost two months' salary for the average worker.

Interest in religion is another sign of the times. A decade ago a few young people were beginning to rediscover the Russian Orthodox Church. Now there are many, singing in church choirs, attending services and studying theology in small groups.

Today's young also seem to accept the fact that the communist system is not going to change dramatically, even if they might like it to. A young Soviet official of about 35 told a Yugoslav friend recently that for his generation, the invasion of Czechoslovakia was a traumatic event that left him and his friends deeply discouraged about the prospects for reforms of the kinds the Czechoslovaks attempted.

"But for today's young people," he went on, "what happened in Poland in 1981 was much less important." He referred to the declaration of martial law that crushed the Solidarity union movement, which was accepted here more cynically than the invasion of Czechoslovakia.

Another sign of youthful cynicism was reported by several astounded members of the older generation. For three years, it is said, groups of young people have dressed in Nazi-style clothes and staged prominent demonstrations in honor of Adolf Hitler's birthday.

"This is really frightening," said one scholar who fought against the Nazis in the "Great Patriotic War," as World War II is known here. He described young men wearing brown shirts and black ties, or with swastikas on their arms, or even wearing Hitler mustaches. Several people said they had heard that the young fascists include relatives of powerful Soviet officials.

For Soviet youngsters to revere and mimic this nation's archenemy, the man held responsible for 20 million Soviet dead in the war, amazes many Russians. "It shows how bad things have become," one said.

A great many Soviet young people have dropped out of political concerns and are busy trying to arrange relatively comfortable lives for themselves, relying on personal connections in key areas of the work force.

But good connections cannot resolve a grave new problem facing young men: the draft. Ten years ago college students knew that they could fulfill their military requirement with—at worst—a brief period in the active reserve as an officer. But now the pool of eligible draftees has shrunk, and the pressures on the military to find competent people to man sophisticated new weapons have increased. Most male students now must expect to be taken into the armed services for two years, usually after completing one or two years in an institute or university. And all of them live under a new cloud: the war in Afghanistan.

That war is an eerie presence in Soviet life. The Soviet expeditionary force in Afghanistan is rarely mentioned in the press and never fully described, but its existence is not denied. A radio program featuring letters from young people in the armed services recently included a message to "comrades in Afghanistan," and on another occasion referred to a lieutenant who has "gone to a fraternal socialist country to help its fight against counterrevolutionaries."

When asked about the war, several parents of draft-age youngsters expressed the hope that their sons would be kept out of it because of their academic qualifications. Young people have heard stories of their contemporaries who were killed.

A woman in Leningrad told a European friend about the

son of her "lift lady," whose job is to keep an eye on the comings and goings of the tenants of an apartment building. The young man came back from the war and told his mother that contrary to his officers' promises that he was going to fight Chinese and American mercenaries, he quickly realized that "we're fighting against the people of Afghanistan." His tour of duty in the war left him in a deep depression; once he attempted suicide. After more than a year, he is tentatively returning to something resembling normal life. His mother feels he is permanently scarred.

An elderly Muscovite despaired of the general popular reaction to the war. There is a little grumbling, he said, "but it has no moral dimension whatsoever. No one questions the morality of what our government is doing. It is very discouraging."

No Soviet 'Lost Generation'

It would be wrong to convey the impression of a Soviet "lost generation." People from many walks of life agreed that talented young people are pursuing official careers, often with enthusiasm, though rarely with idealism.

"I see a lot of cynical careerism, and a lot of willingness to accept 'the rules of the game,'" said the father of a 25-year-old. "Our young people believe in nothing," said another parent, "but they join the party because they know it will advance their careers, and they do what they know is expected of them."

There are numerous signs of an impending generation gap. Some say it has already arrived. Today's 20-year-olds were born in the year Khrushchev was ousted; they know absolutely nothing firsthand about the forces that shaped their parents' lives: Stalin's dictatorship, World War II, the Khrushchev era. What will they be like when they begin to take over responsible positions at the turn of the century? No one had a good answer to that question.

The new generation is cynical, but less afraid than their parents were, no doubt because they do not know the terror of Stalinism or the uncertainty of the Khrushchev era. "They take a lot for granted; they won't be pushed around," said a man in his late 30s.

Surrounded by older people now deprived of their hope, living in a system that encourages cynical careerism, the young and educated of Soviet society represent a key to the future. But how will the key fit into the lock? What sort of a lock will it be? Here, too, the horizon is blank.

Foreign Policy

Soviet Foreign Minister Andrei Gromyko, who is famous as the wily, emotionless diplomat, has dealt with nine American presidents, 14 secretaries of state and six Soviet leaders. But Gromyko ought to be famous for more than longevity and cold blood. He also deserves much of the credit for a Kremlin foreign policy that has failed.

When Gromyko moved into the Ministry of Foreign Affairs to stay in 1953, the Soviet Union was still recovering from the devastation of World War II, but it had good prospects: The biggest country in the world, China, recently had become a fraternal—and subservient—communist state. The Soviets were consolidating their control of a new East European empire. Communist parties in Western Europe and other parts of the world offered tantalizing possibilities for the future. The idea of communism still had a grip on the imaginations of millions in many countries.

In the ensuing three decades, Soviet military power grew impressively, allowing the Soviet Union to meddle in the affairs of countries all over the globe. But military power rarely has been translated into real political influence. The Soviet Union today is powerful but isolated. Its "friends" are no longer friendly, China is a fearsome potential enemy on the Soviet border and the empire in Eastern Europe is in disarray, the victim of a systemic crisis that is beyond Moscow's ability to manage. Communism has lost its appeal throughout the industrialized world, and in most of the Third World too.

Now, faced with what it perceives as an inimical and determined American president and surrounded by neighbors whose hostility seems to be growing instead of diminishing, the Soviet Union is back in a defensive crouch. A brief flirtation with a "forward" strategy in the late '70s, culminating with the invasion of Afghanistan, apparently has ended, leaving the Soviets with expensive but generally unproductive Third World commitments. The wagons are circled, and Gromyko and his colleagues in Moscow are looking—so far without success—for a way to break out.

The election of Ronald Reagan and subsequent changes in American policy crystallized the Soviets' diplomatic dilemma. It would be difficult to overstate the dimensions of what the Soviets perceive as their "Reagan problem." They have been devastated by Reagan's rise, and stunned by his ability to revive the American economy while simultaneously mounting an expensive arms buildup. Even more distressing here has been Reagan's success in maintaining the cohesion of the NATO alliance while East-West arms negotiations collapsed and new rockets were deployed in Europe.

Today, the only important question before the Soviet Union's "Americanologists" is whether Reaganism, as they call it, is some kind of temporary aberration, or a fundamental change in American outlook and policy that will last for many years. Answering this question is a formal task that has been set for Soviet students of America, and for now, it would appear, they are inclined to answer it pessimistically. (Many of the same specialists had predicted that Reagan as president would turn out to be similar to Richard Nixon in terms of his willingness to deal with Moscow, so they have a lot to answer for now.)

Vitriolic Propaganda

The well-reported Soviet propaganda campaign against Reagan and the United States has to be experienced firsthand to be appreciated fully. It is vitriolic and incessant; day after day, Soviet papers and television news programs are filled with anti-Reagan venom.

Reagan has been compared here to Adolf Hitler, the arch-villain in the Soviet view of world history. Cartoons depict him as a missile-crazed cowboy ready to launch nuclear war. His joke about outlawing the Soviet Union and launching the bombers to obliterate it was interpreted here as a glimpse of the true Reagan mentality and was used by official propagandists to fuel further an already emotional scare campaign.

It is difficult for an outsider to evaluate this propaganda— to decide how much of it is a reaction to the most outspokenly anti-Soviet American president in modern times, and how much represents genuine fear. One official provided an interesting glimpse of underlying Soviet attitudes in a conversation here last month.

This Russian—a specialist on East-West relations—was discussing the American military buildup in the new vocabulary that is common here: new Pershing II rockets in West Germany are "first strike" weapons; President Reagan is actively pursuing "military superiority"; the United States has hidden from the West Europeans its belief that a war could be fought against the Soviet Union on European soil.

"But seriously," the American journalist to whom he was speaking interrupted, "you don't really think the purpose of Reagan's policy is to start a war? You don't really think that a couple of dozen Pershings and a couple of dozen MX missiles will give the United States significant military superiority?"

"Of course Reagan's program is not war," the Soviet official answered, his voice suddenly emotional. "He is trying to tell us that the Soviet Union cannot be a super-power. He is trying to beat us down, to damage us politically and economically, after we have worked so hard to establish equality. We can't let him get away with that, and we won't."

That flash of anger may have revealed the essence of current Soviet thinking. Today's Soviet leaders—and to-morrow's—have grown up in a defensive crouch. They deeply believe—not without reason, of course—that pow-erful elements in the capitalist world will never accept their country as a preeminent world power, and will never cease to try to undermine their position. Now an American pres-ident has sprung to life—to bigger-than-life, as seen from here—to embody that recurrent nightmare.

. . . Judging from conversations with numerous officials here—none of them members of the Politburo, but many of them familiar with the thinking of their leaders—Soviet suspicion of Reagan's motives is too deep to allow for any sudden change of heart in the face of Reagan's new peace offensive.

Not that they rule out the possibility of better relations with the Americans in a second Reagan term. Certainly, they say, if Reagan would make concrete gestures to prove that he has changed his mind and wants seriously to deal with Moscow, the Soviets will respond. But what sort of gestures? "For example, withdrawing the new missiles from Europe," in the words of one official—and many others said the same thing. But that is a "gesture" that seems inconceivable from an American or West European vantage point. And so far, the Soviets seem disinclined to accept anything less. They may be willing to talk, but that is a long way from being willing to deal.

In private conversation, numerous officials stated a per-sonal belief that nothing constructive can be expected in Soviet-American relations during a second Reagan term. "It's too late," as one senior official put it. Nearly all of the officials interviewed during a month in Moscow agreed that it is indeed too late to do real business with Reagan. Russians reserve for themselves the right to decide when someone is "anti-Soviet," the ultimate epithet in this society. Once they have attached that label to someone, they almost never remove it.

"Anti-Soviet" is not the same as "anticommunist." Nixon, Soviet officials like to recall, was a notorious anticommunist, but he was prepared to make room for the Soviet Union as a global power, and to respect Moscow's security concerns. But Reagan has persuaded the Soviets that he will never grant them even that much. His name-calling, his joke, his repeated references to changing the political status quo in Eastern Europe all feed the Soviet conviction that Reagan is not just their rival, but their determined enemy.

The official Soviet response to Reagan's challenge has been emotional, clumsy and ultimately counterproductive.

"Maybe we should have used more intimidating tactics to try to block the deployment of the new NATO missiles," one Soviet official said. "We might have succeeded. Who knows? But it is difficult to play a game of bluff with nuclear weapons."

Yes it is, and this is now the Soviets' ultimate frustration. They achieved superpower status militarily, and now they cannot use it, or so it seems to many of them. Their attempts to exert their influence have put them into a classic *tupik*, as the Russians call a dead end.

In other words, the wily, experienced Gromyko has presided over a policy that simply has not worked. The Soviets' position in Eastern Europe remains difficult; with the lone exception of Czechoslovakia, their allies all look west for crucial economic assistance and markets. Events in Poland demonstrate the Soviets' inability to provide prosperity and stability in that key country; East Germany shows more and more independence; Hungary is off on its own track to a considerable degree.

With the West, the Soviets now have a new cold war. This is not without some benefit. A tense international atmosphere, fanned by domestic propaganda, justifies disciplines and hardships at home and further sacrifices to compete in a renewed arms race. But Soviet officials insist—and logic would seem to confirm—that a new arms race does not serve their fundamental interests. They desperately need time and money to deal with the huge problems they face at home and inside their empire.

At first blush the Soviets' discomfort with Reagan might appear to Westerners to be useful, but this is far from clear. As the Soviets seem to see it, Reagan is trying to undermine the very basis of their existence as a world power. He has frontally challenged the legitimacy of the Soviet system and empire. He has boasted that a Western policy based on an arms buildup and tough bargaining tactics will succeed in making the Soviets more reasonable.

Such confrontational tactics do not appear to leave the Soviets any real room for maneuver. How, many officials asked in recent conversations here, could a Soviet government bargain constructively with Reagan without acknowledging to the world that the Reagan method for dealing with them is effective? How could they make deals with him and maintain their global and domestic pretensions?

"Our problem," one Soviet official observed, "is that we have no model for good Soviet-American relations." He suggested a cycle in which one superpower achieves a sense of relative well-being, only to discover that the same circumstances make the other one feel nervous and insecure. This is a plausible description of East-West relations since the early '70s. In the afterglow of detente, the Soviets began to feel better about their global position, began to throw their weight around, and ended up terrifying the United States. Now the Americans have responded with policies that terrify the Soviet Union.

A more creative, more flexible leadership in Moscow might find—with help from a more flexible American government—a path out of this dilemma, but the old men in charge now do not seem up to that challenge. Of course a new leader in the Kremlin will have a chance to start afresh, but he will not be able to ignore recent history. It seems likely—not inevitable, but probable—that a second Reagan administration would bring four more years of bad relations, with little progress in negotiations.

Furthermore, as the Russians repeat to an American visitor, they will survive. "The last four years have demonstrated that we can get along without you," as one put it. Soviet officials take comfort from their ideological view of the West, which convinces them that big economic crises are on the horizon that could disable their capitalist adversaries. At the same time, they seem incapable of acknowledging that their own behavior—the invasion of Afghanistan, the deployment of hundreds of SS20 missiles in Europe, their crushing of Solidarity in Poland, and more—had much to do with the deterioration of East-West relations. They are convinced that it is all the West's fault.

"The problem," said one senior Soviet official, "involves the size of the planet. It is too small. You Americans think you can be secure at our expense. That is impossible. We both can only be secure when we both feel secure."

AN AUTOBIOGRAPHICAL NOTE

by Andrei Sakharov

I WAS BORN ON MAY 21, 1921, IN MOSCOW. MY father was a well-known physics teacher and the author of textbooks and popular science books. My childhood was spent in a large communal apartment most of whose rooms were occupied by our relatives, with only a few outsiders mixed in. Our home preserved the traditional atmosphere of a numerous and close-knit family—respect for hard work and ability, mutual aid, love for literature and science. My father played the piano well; his favorites were Chopin, Grieg, Beethoven, and Scriabin. During the Civil War he earned a living by playing the piano in a silent movie theater. I recall with particular fondness Maria Petrovna, my grandmother and the soul of our family, who died before World War II at the age of seventy-nine. Family influences were especially strong in my case, because I received my early schooling at home and then had difficulty relating to my own age group.

After graduating from high school with honors in 1938, I enrolled in the Physics Department of Moscow University. When war began, our classes were evacuated to Ashkhabad, where I graduated with honors in 1942. That summer I was assigned work for several weeks in Kovrov, and then I was employed on a logging operation in a remote settlement near

175

Melekess. My first vivid impression of the life of workers and peasants dates from that difficult summer of 1942. In September I was sent to a large arms factory on the Volga, where I worked as an engineer until 1945.

I developed several inventions to improve quality-control procedures at that factory. (In my university years I did not manage to engage in original scientific work.) While still at the factory in 1944, I wrote several articles on theoretical physics, which I sent to Moscow for review. Those first articles have never been published, but they gave me the confidence in my powers which is essential for a scientist.

In 1945 I became a graduate student at the Lebedev Physical Institute. My adviser, the outstanding theoretical physicist Igor Tamm, who later became a member of the Academy of Sciences and a Nobel laureate, greatly influenced my career. In 1948 I was included in Tamm's research group, which developed a thermonuclear weapon. I spent the next twenty years continuously working in conditions of extraordinary tension and secrecy, at first in Moscow and then in a special research center. We were all convinced of the vital importance of our work for establishing a worldwide military equilibrium, and we were attracted by its scope.

In 1950 I collaborated with Igor Tamm in some of the first research on controlled thermonuclear reactions. We proposed principles for the magnetic thermal isolation of plasma. I also suggested as an immediate technical objective the use of a thermonuclear reactor to produce fissionable materials as fuel for atomic power plants. Research on controlled thermonuclear reactions is now receiving priority everywhere. The tokamak system, which is under intensive study in many countries, is most closely related to our early ideas.

In 1952 I initiated experimental work on magnetic-explosive generators (devices to transform the energy of a chemical or nuclear explosion into the energy of a magnetic field). A record magnetic field of 25 million gauss was achieved during these experiments in 1964.

In 1953 I was elected a member of the USSR Academy of Sciences.

My social and political views underwent a major evolution over the fifteen years from 1953 to 1968. In particular, my role in the development of thermonuclear weapons from 1953 to 1962, and in the preparation and execution of thermonuclear tests, led to an increased awareness of the moral problems engendered by such activities. In the late 1950s I began a campaign to halt or to limit the testing of nuclear weapons. This brought me into conflict first with Nikita Khrushchev in 1961, and then with the Minister of Medium Machine Building,[1] Efim Slavsky, in 1962. I helped to promote the 1963 Moscow treaty banning nuclear weapon tests in the atmosphere, in outer space, and under water. From 1964, when I spoke out on problems of biology,[2] and especially from 1967, I have been interested in an ever-expanding circle of questions. In 1967 I joined the Committee for Lake Baikal.[3] My first appeals for victims of repression date from 1966–67.

The time came in 1968 for the more detailed, public, and candid statement of my views contained in the essay "Thoughts on Progress, Peaceful Coexistence, and Intel-

---

[1]The Ministry of Medium Machine Building is responsible for nuclear weapons and industry in the USSR.—Trans.

---

[2]In 1964 Sakharov spoke out at the Academy of Sciences against political interference with biology and the persecution of geneticists during a debate on the election of one of Trofim Lysenko's associates.—Trans.

---

[3]The Committee for Lake Baikal was organized to protect Lake Baikal from industrial pollution; it was apparently sponsored by or at least tolerated by the authorities.—Trans.

lectual Freedom."[4] These same ideas were echoed seven years later in the title of my Nobel lecture: "Peace, Progress, and Human Rights." I consider these themes of fundamental importance and closely interconnected. My 1968 essay was a turning point in my life. It quickly gained worldwide publicity. The Soviet press was silent for some time, and then began to refer to the essay very negatively. Many critics, even sympathetic ones, considered my ideas naive and impractical. But it seems to me, thirteen years later, that these ideas foreshadowed important new directions in world and Soviet politics.

After 1970, the defense of human rights and of victims of political repression became my first concern. My collaboration with Valery Chalidze and Andrei Tverdokhlebov,[5] and later with Igor Shafarevich[6] and Grigorii Podyapolsky,[7] on the Moscow Human Rights Committee was one expression of that concern. (Podyapolsky's untimely death in March 1976 was a tragedy.)

After my essay was published abroad in July 1968, I was barred from secret work and excommunicated from many privileges of the Soviet establishment. The pressure on me, my family, and my friends increased in 1972, but as I came to learn more about the spreading repressions, I felt obliged

---

[4]Sakharov's essay was first published in English by the *New York Times* (as "Progress, Coexistence, and Intellectual Freedom") and has been republished in *Sakharov Speaks* (New York: Knopf, 1974); an autobiographical note written by Sakharov in 1973 was published as an introduction to that volume.

---

[5]Valery Chalidze and Andrei Tverdokhlebov are physicists who have left the USSR under pressure from the authorities.—Trans.

---

[6]Igor Shafarevich is a Moscow mathematician who is a corresponding member of the Academy of Sciences.—Trans.

---

[7]Grigorii Podyapolsky was a geophysicist.—Trans.

to speak out almost daily in defense of one victim or another. In recent years I have continued to speak out as well on peace and disarmament, on freedom of association, movement, information, and opinion, against capital punishment, on protection of the environment, and on nuclear power plants.

In 1975 I was awarded the Nobel Peace Prize. This was a great honor for me, as well as recognition for the entire human rights movement in the USSR. In January 1980 I was deprived of all my official Soviet awards (the Order of Lenin, three times Hero of Socialist Labor, the Lenin Prize, the State Prize) and banished to Gorky, where I am virtually isolated and watched day and night by a policeman at my door. The regime's action lacks any legal basis. It is one more example of the intensified political repression that has gripped our country in recent years.

Since the summer of 1969 I have been a senior scientist at the Academy of Sciences' Institute of Physics. My current scientific interests are elementary particles, gravitation, and cosmology.

I am not a professional politician. Perhaps that is why I am always bothered by questions concerning the usefulness and eventual results of my actions. I am inclined to believe that moral criteria in combination with unrestricted inquiry provide the only possible compass for these complex and contradictory problems. I shall refrain from predictions, but today as always I believe in the power of reason and the human spirit.

ANDREI SAKHAROV

Gorky, March 24, 1981

SAKHAROV'S CONTRIBUTIONS TO SCIENCE

by Andrew M. Sessler
and Yvonne Howell

EVERYONE KNOWS THAT SAKHAROV IS CREDITED with being the father of the Soviet hydrogen bomb, which he and Igor Tamm and their fellow scientists successfully developed in 1954. It is perhaps less well known that Sakharov has made very significant contributions to plasma physics, elementary particle physics, and cosmology. In fact, the depth of his insight and the significance of his work mark him as one of the outstanding physicists of our time. His ideas have been years ahead of those of other physicists. As a result, his contributions have not had the impact they should have had. We will concentrate here on sketching out Sakharov's major achievements in three areas of physics, details of which can be found in his collected works.

A. Plasma Physics

Sakharov has made numerous fundamental contributions to plasma physics. He was the first within the Soviet Union to suggest the use of a laser to initiate a controlled thermonuclear reaction (1960–1961). And he was the first (1951) to suggest that the neutrons from a fusion reactor could be used to breed fissionable materials for use in a fission reactor—the so-called hybrid.

In 1948 he conceived of mu-meson catalysis of cold deuterium-tritium mixtures to obtain fusion of the DT. Because the "molecule" of a mu-meson circulating about the two centers D and T is quite small, DT fusion will occur before the mu-meson can decay. This effect was observed eight years later; and although the energy balance of this reaction does not lead to a net energy-production reactor, it may be that a mu-catalyzed hybrid reactor is an economically attractive concept.

Sakharov also proposed (1951–1952) that superstrong magnetic fields could be obtained by using the energy of an explosion around a good conductor. It is hardly necessary to remark that by now there is a whole discipline devoted to obtaining megagauss fields in this manner.

And there is the tokamak, invented by Sakharov in 1950. At this very early date, Sakharov realized that simple toroidal magnetic confinement devices would create particle "drifts" that would lead to unacceptable plasma loss. He proposed two solutions: levitated rings (which are of considerable physics interest but probably not suitable for a reactor) and current induced directly in the plasma (which is a tokamak, now the "main line" of fusion energy research).

Sakharov's contributions to this field, some of the most significant concepts in plasma physics, are truly astounding. If this were his only achievement in physics, that alone would make him a giant; but in fact he has added in a fundamental way to other branches of physics.

B. Elementary Particle Physics

Sakharov has made two very significant contributions to particle physics. The first relates to the quark structure of matter; in particular he deduced the masses of various "el-

ementary" particles from their quark structure. He wrote
with Zel'dovich the fundamental paper on this subject in
1966. (The same work was done independently by Feder-
man, Rubinstein, and Talmi in Israel.)

Over the years Sakharov has maintained an interest in
this subject and has been able to extend his ideas to include
charmed quarks and to take into account chromomagnetic
forces as well as chromoelectric forces (1980). This latter
achievement is remarkable, for it shows that even in Gorky,
Sakharov has somehow been able to keep informed of recent
experimental and theoretical results.

The second highly significant contribution to particle
physics is perhaps Sakharov's most important piece of work.
Namely, he was the first person to put forward a rational
explanation—which may in fact be the correct explanation—of the baryon asymmetry in the universe, that is, of
the fact that the universe appears to contain only matter, not
antimatter. The early work (1966–1967) was not truly appreciated until the late 1970s.

Sakharov's explanation, now the basis of much theoretical and experimental work, is based upon CP violation,
discovered in 1964 by Fitch and Cronin, and the big-bang
universe, rapidly accepted after the 1965 discovery of the
$3K$ background radiation. Sakharov looked at very early
times in the universe—$t = 10 \exp(-43)$s, when the temperature was about $10 \exp(19)$—and assumed that the universe was out of thermal equilibrium, that baryon number
is not conserved, and hence that CP violation would lead
to an excess of baryons over antibaryons. He postulated a
new very weak interaction, via a very heavy boson [$10
\exp(14)$ GeV], that could turn the quarks in the proton into
electrons and neutrinos. In this way he was able to explain
the existence of matter (rather than antimatter) in the universe. Of course there is not very much matter—for every
baryon there are $10 \exp(9)$ photons—which is why a small
effect could be responsible for the baryon asymmetry and
why the explanation is very subtle indeed.

C. Cosmology

About one-third of Sakharov's published papers are in cosmology. One of these is on the initial stages of an expanding universe and the appearance of a nonuniform distribution of matter. Another considers a multisheet model of the universe (one that pulsates rather than a one-time universe). This work involves time reversal and the consequences of negative spatial curvature and nonzero cosmological constant. A paper devoted to extensions of this multisheet model was submitted to the Soviet journal *JETP*— and was accepted by them—in May 1982, two years after Sakharov was exiled to Gorky!

But without doubt Sakharov's most interesting contribution (1967, 1970) is the formulation of an alternate theory of gravitation. The basic idea is that Einstein's general relativity is not a fundamental interaction at all but is an *effective* interaction, a consequence of the quantum fluctuations of matter fields (a topic later studied independently by Weinberg, Zel'dovich, and Adler). He attempts to deduce general relativity as a long-wavelength consequence of "normal" physics at short wavelengths, thus avoiding the intractable problem of quantizing general relativity. Recent work on grand unified theories makes this suggestion more acceptable and allows specific calculations along the lines first proposed by Sakharov.

POLICE DICTATORSHIPS*

by Andrei Sakharov

© *Courtesy of Alfred A. Knopf, Inc.*

AN EXTREME REFLECTION OF THE DANGERS confronting modern social development is the growth of racism, nationalism, and militarism and, in particular, the rise of demagogic, hypocritical, and monstrously cruel dictatorial police regimes. Foremost are the regimes of Stalin, Hitler, and Mao Tse-tung, and a number of extremely reactionary regimes in small countries....

These tragic developments have always derived from the struggle of egotistical and group interests, the struggle for unlimited power, suppression of intellectual freedom, a spread of intellectually simplified, narrow-minded mass myths (the myth of race, of land and blood, the myth about the Jewish danger, anti-intellectualism, the concept of *lebensraum* in Germany, the myth about the sharpening of the class struggle and proletarian infallibility bolstered by the cult of Stalin and by exaggeration of the contradictions with capitalism in the Soviet Union, the myth about Mao Tse-tung, extreme Chinese nationalism and the resurrection of the *lebensraum* concept, of anti-intellectualism, extreme

---

*From the essay "Progress, Coexistence, and Intellectual Freedom."

anti-humanism, and certain prejudices of peasant socialism in China).

The usual practice is the use of demagogy, storm troopers, and Red Guards in the first stage and terrorist bureaucracy with reliable cadres of the type of Eichmann, Himmler, Yezhov, and Beria at the summit of deification and unlimited power.

The world will never forget the burning of books in the squares of German cities, the hysterical, cannibalistic speeches of the fascist "führers," and their even more cannibalistic plans for the destruction of entire peoples, including the Russians. Fascism began a partial realization of these plans during the war it unleashed, annihilating prisoners of war and hostages, burning villages, carrying out a criminal policy of genocide (during the war, the main blow of genocide was aimed at the Jews, a policy that apparently was also meant to be provocative, especially in the Ukraine and Poland).

We shall never forget the kilometer-long trenches filled with bodies, the gas chambers, the SS dogs, the fanatical doctors, the piles of women's hair, suitcases with gold teeth, and fertilizer from the factories of death.

Analyzing the causes of Hitler's coming to power, we will never forget the role of German and international monopolist capital. We also will not forget the criminally sectarian and dogmatically narrow policies of Stalin and his associates, setting Socialists and Communists against one another (this has been well related in the famous letter to Ilya Ehrenburg by Ernst Henri).*

---

*Ernst Henri, a German Communist long resident in the Soviet Union, outlined in this letter the role Stalin's policies had played in making possible Hitler's rise—notably his insistence that the German Communist Party view as its chief enemy the German Social Democratic Party rather than Hitler's Nazis. Henri's thesis was that the German Communists and Social Democrats should have formed a united front against Hitler.

Fascism lasted twelve years in Germany. Stalinism lasted twice as long in the Soviet Union. There are many common features but also certain differences. Stalinism exhibited a much more subtle kind of hypocrisy and demagogy, with reliance not on an openly cannibalistic program like Hitler's but on a progressive, scientific, and popular socialist ideology.

This served as a convenient screen for deceiving the working class, for weakening the vigilance of the intellectuals and other rivals in the struggle for power, with the treacherous and sudden use of the machinery of torture, execution, and informants, intimidating and making fools of millions of people, the majority of whom were neither cowards nor fools. As a consequence of this "specific feature" of Stalinism, it was the Soviet people, its most active, talented, and honest representatives, who suffered the most terrible blow.

At least ten to fifteen million people perished in the torture chambers of the NKVD [secret police] from torture and execution, in camps for exiled kulaks [rich peasants] and so-called semi-kulaks and members of their families and in camps "without the right of correspondence" (which were in fact the prototypes of the fascist death camps, where, for example, thousands of prisoners were machine-gunned because of "overcrowding" or as a result of "special orders").

People perished in the mines of Norilsk and Vorkuta from freezing, starvation, and exhausting labor, at countless construction projects, in timber-cutting, building of canals, or simply during transportation in prison trains, in the overcrowded holds of "death ships" in the Sea of Okhotsk, and during the resettlement of entire peoples, the Crimean Tatars, the Volga Germans, the Kalmyks, and other Caucasus peoples. Readers of the literary journal *Novy Mir* recently could read for themselves a description of the "road of death" between Norilsk and Igarka [in northern Siberia].

Temporary masters were replaced (Yagoda, Molotov, Yezhov, Zhdanov, Malenkov, Beria), but the anti-people's regime of Stalin remained equally cruel and at the same time dogmatically narrow and blind in its cruelty. The killing of military and engineering officials before the war, the blind faith in the "reasonableness" of the colleague in crime, Hitler, and the other reasons for the national tragedy of 1941 have been well described in the book by Nekrich, in the notes of Maj. Gen. Grigorenko, and other publications — these are far from the only examples of the combination of crime, narrow-mindedness, and short-sightedness.*

Stalinist dogmatism and isolation from real life was demonstrated particularly in the countryside, in the policy of unlimited exploitation and the predatory forced deliveries at "symbolic" prices, in almost serflike enslavement of the peasantry, the depriving of peasants of the simplest means of mechanization, and the appointment of collective-farm chairmen on the basis of their cunning and obsequiousness. The results are evident — a profound and hard-to-correct destruction of the economy and way of life in the countryside, which, by the law of interconnected vessels, damaged industry as well.

The inhuman character of Stalinism was demonstrated by the repressions of prisoners of war who survived fascist camps and then were thrown into Stalinist camps, the anti-worker "decrees," the criminal exile of entire peoples condemned to slow death, the unenlightened zoological kind of anti-Semitism that was characteristic of Stalin bureaucracy and the NKVD (and Stalin personally), the Ukrainophobia characteristic of Stalin, and the draconian laws for the protection of socialist property (five years' imprisonment for stealing some grain from the fields and so forth) that

---

*A. M. Nekrich, a distinguished Soviet historian, was expelled from the Soviet Communist Party after publishing a study of Stalin's errors and unpreparedness for the Nazi attack on June 1941. Maj. Gen. Pyotr G. Grigorenko, author of a long memorandum supporting Nekrich and a leading Soviet dissident, has been confined as punishment in Soviet mental hospitals.

served mainly as a means of fulfilling the demands of the "slave market."

A profound analysis of the origin and development of Stalinism is contained in the thousand-page monograph of Roy Medvedev.* This was written from a socialist, Marxist point of view and is a successful work, but unfortunately it has not yet been published. The present author is not likely to receive such a compliment from Comrade Medvedev, who finds elements of "Westernism" in his views. Well, there is nothing like controversy! Actually the views of the present author are profoundly socialist, and he hopes that the attentive reader will understand this.

The author is quite aware of the monstrous relations in human and international affairs brought forth by the egotistical principle of capital when it is not under pressure from socialist and progressive forces. He also thinks, however, that progressives in the West understand this better than he does and are waging a struggle against these manifestations. The author is concentrating his attention on what is before his eyes and on what is obstructing, from his point of view, a worldwide overcoming of estrangement, obstructing the struggle for democracy, social progress, and intellectual freedom.

Our country has started on the path of cleansing away the foulness of Stalinism. "We are squeezing the slave out of ourselves drop by drop" (an expression of Anton Chekhov). We are learning to express our opinions, without taking the lead from the bosses and without fearing for our lives.

The beginning of this arduous and far from straight path evidently dates from the report of Nikita S. Khrushchev to the Twentieth Congress of the Soviet Communist Party. This bold speech, which came as a surprise to Stalin's accom-

---

*Medvedev's study was published in the United States and Britain in 1972 under the title *Let History Judge*.

plices in crime, and a number of associated measures—the release of hundreds of thousands of political prisoners and their rehabilitation, steps toward a revival of the principles of peaceful coexistence and toward a revival of democracy—oblige us to value highly the historic role of Khrushchev despite his regrettable mistakes of a voluntarist character in subsequent years and despite the fact that Khrushchev, while Stalin was alive, was one of his collaborators in crime, occupying a number of influential posts.

The exposure of Stalinism in our country still has a long way to go. It is imperative, of course, that we publish all authentic documents, including the archives of the NKVD, and conduct nationwide investigations. It would be highly useful for the international authority of the Soviet Communist Party and the ideals of socialism if, as was planned in 1964 but never carried out, the party were to announce the "symbolic" expulsion of Stalin, murderer of millions of Party members, and at the same time the political rehabilitation of the victims of Stalinism.

From 1936 to 1939 more than 1.2 million Party members, half of the total membership, were arrested. Only fifty thousand regained freedom; the others were tortured during interrogation or were shot (six hundred thousand) or died in camps. Only in isolated cases were the rehabilitated allowed to assume responsible posts; even fewer were permitted to take part in the investigation of crimes of which they had been witnesses or victims.

We are often told lately not to "rub salt into wounds." This is usually being said by people who suffered no wounds. Actually only the most meticulous analysis of the past and of its consequences will now enable us to wash off the blood and dirt that befouled our banner.

It is sometimes suggested in the literature that the political manifestations of Stalinism represented a sort of superstructure over the economic basis of an anti-Leninist pseudosocialism that led to the formation in the Soviet Union of a distinct class—a bureaucratic elite from which all key positions are filled and which is rewarded for its work through open and concealed privileges. I cannot deny that there is some (but not the whole) truth in such an interpretation, which would help explain the vitality of neo-Stalinism, but a full analysis of this issue would go beyond the scope of this essay, which focuses on another aspect of the problem.

It is imperative that we restrict in every possible way the influence of neo-Stalinists in our political life.

THE LIBERAL INTELLIGENTSIA OF THE WEST:

Its Illusions and Responsibilities

by Andrei Sakharov

IN RECENT YEARS I HAVE HAD OCCASION, FOR the first time, to meet people from the West—to verify and supplement my vicarious impressions of that world, which in so many respects forms a contrast with ours but which, in what is deepest and most important, is humanly understandable.

My attitude toward the foreign intelligentsia—toward the people I have come to know personally—is compounded of a deep liking, hope, and a respect bordering almost upon envy. In the best people from the West I see—and value very highly—an inner freedom, a readiness to debate combined with complete respect for the opinions of others, an absence of national prejudices, a realistic and practical cast of mind, and a readiness to undertake good works.

And yet in my opinion there is one characteristic common

to many Western intellectuals that is somewhat disturbing. I refer to what I have called, in my own mind, "leftist-liberal faddishness." In a naïve form it is partially illustrated by a reply made by one American in a conversation with an emigrant from the USSR: "Well, all right. There are lots of things in Russia that you don't like. *You were mistreated there*. I can understand that. But I imagine you don't have any prejudices against China. Aren't you happy with what's going on there now?"

If my analysis and opinions are mistaken, I hope my friends in the West will forgive my lack of information. But if I have hit the mark even partially, then I believe they should take serious note.

I have no doubts as to the altruism and humanity of most of the Western liberal intellectuals—as to their hopes for the welfare of all people, for equal justice for all. But I fear that such things as a lack of information or the opportunity to analyze it critically, faddishness (which is all-powerful in the West), the fear of seeming old-fashioned (especially to one's own children, as many frankly admit), a lack of imagination where the factor of distance is involved, and an inadequate notion of the tragic complexity of real life (in particular, life in the socialist countries)—that these things may lead, and are already leading, to dangerous mistakes both in the intrapolitical life of the Western countries and in evaluating the difficult questions of international relations. Distance can cause one to have doubts about the strange and frightful things that one has learned only from books and stories.*

The liberal intellectuals of the West undoubtedly have

---

*My wife's mother, who spent many years in Stalin's labor camps as a ChSIR (member of a traitor's family), has a close relative who lives in France (and who, incidentally, is a member of the French Communist Party). He once tried to find out from her whether there was "a particle of truth" in what Solzhenitsyn had written. She could only laugh bitterly.

good reasons for being dissatisfied with many aspects of their society. In hundreds of newspapers they read of acts of violence and cruelty, of social and racial discrimination, of the horrors of famine in the underdeveloped countries, and the terrors of war. They not only read these reports but see them with their own eyes, since there is no problem about traveling through their own country, or obtaining visas for Africa or Latin America.

People in the West enjoy a plethora of accessible information, an abundance of different ideas, and the coexistence of competing political groups. Some of these groups pursue very private interests, but all of them profess some brand of politics. In the West, political activity—the circulation and promotion of social ideas—becomes a profession just as easily as any other kind of activity, and is associated with the material interests of groups and individuals.

As is the case with us, many Westerners find themselves unable on their own to evaluate critically the flood of facts, opinions, and ideas that pours down upon them; and faddishness with all its irrational laws comes to the fore. Often it is not the more logical ideas that take precedence but ephemeral notions that are more extravagant and easier to grasp.

"Left-wing faddishness," it seems to me, is now dominant in the West and has achieved that position through the complex interplay of various factors. Two of these are the eternal hankering of youth after the most radical changes and the fear of the more experienced and cautious representatives of the older generation that they may lag behind their own children. In the West, as everywhere else, there exist complex social problems that cannot be solved immediately, within the framework of the existing system. But radical solutions, with their persuasive, surface simplicity, create the illusion that those problems can be quickly solved.

Another important factor in the dominance of leftist faddishness is the fact that over a period of decades the Western world of free competition among ideas has constantly been fed by a small stream of pro-Soviet or pro-Chinese propaganda in which various, basically sound socialist ideas are tendentiously mixed with half-truths and out-and-out lies. This factor is perhaps not terribly important. But it, too, exerts a force; and in many ways it is rather effectively strengthened by the direct and indirect support of certain writers and politicians.

Such, it seems to me, is the soil that has given rise to the dominant stereotype of the leftist liberal intellectual of the West, with all his illusions and mistakes. Basically, however, the majority of such people have an outlook that is high-minded and humane, have real grounds for dissatisfaction with their society and feel good will and an aspiration toward justice and the common weal. And this permits me to hope that in the final analysis the Western intellectual won't let the rest of us down. Totalitarianism, fascism of whatever brand, demagogues, and intriguing politicians—these things are not, I trust, for the likes of him.

With respect to his own country, the Western liberal intellectual supports the full measure of civil liberties and economic and social reforms of the socialist type. These aspirations are in fact in the spirit of the times; and if they are realized cautiously, they will probably promote justice, happiness, and the flourishing of society, and help to eliminate rough spots and societal defects.

It is not by chance that I emphasize caution. I am deeply convinced that the thoughtless, frivolous pursuit of leftist-liberal faddishness is fraught with great dangers. On the international level, one danger is the loss of Western unity and of a clear understanding of the ever-constant global threat posed by the totalitarian nations. The West must not under any circumstances allow the weakening of its stand against totalitarianism. There is an internal danger for each country of slipping into state-capitalist totalitarian socialism. These two threats are of course closely related. And the growth of leftist ideas must not lead to a weakening of the international defense of human rights throughout the world, with the same standards for the Englishman, the Frenchman, the Black from the Republic of South Africa, the Crimean Tatar, the Russian, the Ukrainian, the Italian, and the Vietnamese. In comparison with these problems, many of the day-to-day matters that are disturbing the ordinary man in the West are of slight significance. If he, his children, or his grandchildren ever live under a system even remotely resembling ours or the Chinese, they will understand—it isn't too late.

The late Arkady Belinkov,* who was received with so much coolness and distrust in the West, once wrote to the PEN club:† "Socialism is the kind of thing it's easy to sample but hard to spit out." And indeed, by virtue of its inherent qualities of immanent stability, and the inertia of fear and passivity, totalitarian socialism (which may be called "pseudosocialism") is a kind of historical dead end from which it is troublesome to escape.

Certain Westerners have expressed the opinion that the failures and calamities in the USSR and the other Eastern socialist nations are due to the fact that these are "benighted Asian countries" without democratic traditions and without any history of respect for the rights of the individual. For these nations—for the Russians, the Chinese, the Vietnamese—everything that takes place (terrorism, muddling, dirt in the maternity home, violations of freedoms—I am intentionally citing disparate things) is allegedly customary and even "progressive," since those people have such a strange way of taking a step forward. But, it is alleged, the West, with its democratic traditions, will rise in one upward swoop to the higher level of "socialism with a human face"—

---

*A Soviet literary critic and former political prisoner who defected in 1968 and died in the United States in 1970 after open-heart surgery. [Translator]

---

†An international writers' organization. [Translator]

humane and effective. In particular, such arguments are, I gather, widespread among the Western Communists—especially among the intellectuals and leaders. But for the rank-and-file Communists they employ the simpler methods of distorting and concealing the truth about the lands of victorious socialism.

These typically leftist-liberal arguments (I call them "inverted Slavophilism") are in no way justified by historical experience. To me they represent a dangerous illusion and an immoral use, perhaps in order to appease consciences, of different yardsticks for "our people" and "other people."

Heretofore socialism has always meant a one-party system, power in the hands of a grasping and incompetent bureaucracy, the expropriation of all private property, terrorism on the part of the Cheka or its counterparts, the destruction of productive forces, with their subsequent restoration and expansion at the cost of countless sacrifices by the people, and violence done to free consciences and convictions. So it has been in the USSR, in the people's democracies, in the People's Republic of China, and in Cuba. (The example of Yugoslavia, the nation most independent of Soviet guardianship and the freest and most open of the socialist countries, is especially significant.)

Is all this inevitable? I believe that in principle "socialism with a human face" is possible, and represents a high form of social organization. But it is possible only as a result of extraordinary collective efforts, plus wisdom and selflessness exercised by a great part of the people—something uniformly difficult to achieve for any country, requiring especially favorable domestic and foreign conditions. The total nationalization of all means of production, the one-party system, and the repression of honest convictions—all must be avoided or totalitarianism will prevail.

I would also assume that the totalitarian states stand at an especially great distance from this ideal; that they are farther from it than capitalist states of the West. In 1968, the world witnessed an attempt by the Czechoslovak Communists, supported by the Czech people—especially the intelligentsia and the working class—to purge totalitarian socialism of its monstrosities (it was there that the phrase "socialism with a human face" came into use) and, at the same time, to rid the country of the USSR's humiliating and dangerous guardianship. This attempt achieved certain successes, and elicited admiration throughout the world. But it was precisely the successes that made the USSR, East Germany, and Poland fear them as dangerous examples, and that served as the reason for the shameful intervention. Totalitarianism defended itself with tanks; but in so doing it compromised socialist ideas in the eyes of millions of people for a long time.

The dangers of totalitarianism associated with the socialist, so-called progressive path of development—especially in the specifically modern setting of a divided world—have been repeatedly and glaringly evident in recent times.

As I write, the world is watching Portugal, where the mechanics of falling into totalitarianism are in operation. Although apparently enjoying the support of Moscow, the Portuguese Communist Party was defeated in the April 1975 elections. After the voting it began to shove its rivals around, using the same unceremonious methods of demagogy, provocation, police tyranny, and blackmail that its forerunners employed in the past: in 1917, 1933, and 1948.

The trend toward totalitarianism of the military-socialist type can also be detected in certain non-Communist circles of the "Armed Forces Movement." Especially sinister is the growing influence on society exercised by the secret police: a "state within a state," a twentieth-century *oprichnina*,* like the NKVD in the Stalin Era. Apparently, the Communists play an especially large role in the Portuguese secret

---

*The "private household" or "bodyguard" of Ivan the Terrible. *Inter alia*, Ivan employed this terrorist organization in his campaign against the boyars. [Translator]

police. One would hope that, for all this, the Portuguese people have learned something from the history of other countries and will avoid the fate with which they are threatened. The world community must do everything possible to help them avoid tragedy.†

The manifestations of the leftist position in international relations are no less serious. The illusions commonly entertained by the leftist-liberal intelligentsia as to the nature of society in the USSR and the other socialist countries, as to real domestic and geopolitical aims of the ruling circles in those countries, make it difficult to evaluate the true significance of détente. And sometimes governments of the Western countries are prompted to take false and dangerous positions—to grant unilateral concessions and "gifts" in the course of détente. In the Western nations, the majority opinion has a direct influence on the practical actions of political leaders, who (so it seems to me, looking at them from here) usually pay heed to their constituents, the press, and public opinion.

In particular, the leftist intellectuals are urging their governments toward unilateral disarmament. But such disarmament could lead to a disturbance of the international equilibrium—to weakening the Western position vis-à-vis the totalitarian threat—and could induce stepped-up expansion by the socialist nations, especially in the strategically important focal points of the Third World; e.g., the Indian Ocean.

The domestic socioeconomic problems of the Western countries should be solved by mobilizing resources and by means of temporary economic belt-tightening—not at the cost of weakening their stand toward the threat. Balanced disarmament is extremely important; but this result cannot be achieved from a position of weakness.

---

†Dr. Sakharov wrote these paragraphs about the fluid situation in Portugal in the early summer of 1975. [Publisher's note]

Also important is the political and economic unification of the Western countries, as in the Common Market (of course not by opposing the United States, the leader of the Western world, but in close cooperation with it). I experienced a feeling of relief at the outcome of the 1975 Common Market referendum in Britain, and of Greece's impending adherence to the Council of Europe. In these situations, the immediate economic aspect of the problem must be relegated to a secondary status. It is most important to oppose expansion by the totalitarian countries. So far, the leftist, "progressive" forces have not taken a clear-cut position in all these maters. The "leftist" mistakes in Vietnam have been repeated in other cases as well. The leftist-liberal intellectuals are often ready to support and defend extremist and even terrorist groups in their own countries and throughout the world, if these groups are using a leftist mask, while at the same time the intellectuals are ready to condemn harshly those who do not make common cause with them for being conservative and reactionary. This viewpoint is a tremendous danger to mankind.

THE CARTER
CORRESPONDENCE

© Courtesy of Alfred A. Knopf, Inc.

From his Inaugural Address pledge not to be "indifferent to the fate of freedom elsewhere," the President was committed to a policy course Sakharov had urged during the campaign and welcomed in practice. Washington commentators and even the President's advisers were, however, divided over the wisdom of the Carter human-rights posture and particularly over how it should be implemented. Few wanted to make the Soviet Union either the first target of the campaign or the test of the policy's efficacy. As the material in this chapter shows, events—many of them accidents—brought the question of Soviet human-rights performance to an early prominence. In effect, Sakharov forced the Administration to a quick decision on what was and remains an explosive East-West issue.

Sakharov's efforts began during the Presidential campaign itself with the following appeal to the incumbent, Gerald Ford, and his challenger, Jimmy Carter. It was sent from Moscow on October 11, 1976, and signed "with profound respect and hope, Andrei Sakharov, Nobel Peace Prize Laureate":

NOW THAT THE CANDIDATES ARE CAMPAIGNING for the American Presidency and preparing and presenting to the American people the principles of their future policies, I consider it important once again to express publicly certain positions which I view as having primary significance.

I am convinced that guaranteed political and civil rights for people the world over are also guarantees of international

203

security, economic and social progress, and environmental protection. Freedom of belief and conscience, free exchange of information, freedom of movement, and the freedom to choose one's country of residence—such rights cannot be set apart from the basic problems facing mankind. And in the defense of human rights there can be no place for isolationism or national self-seeking.

By broadening the recognition of these principles, the Helsinki declaration has opened new possibilities for international action. Among them is the campaign for a general, worldwide amnesty for political prisoners. You know that in our country and in other countries of Eastern Europe, in China, and in many countries of the Third World and the West, there are now thousands of prisoners of conscience in prisons, camps, and special psychiatric hospitals, condemned for their participation in the exchange of information, for their beliefs, for religious activity, for an attempt to leave the country. They are undergoing cold, hunger, backbreaking toil, persecutions, and humiliations which are unworthy of the civilized world. I call upon you not to lessen your efforts in the struggle for the freedom to choose one's country of residence. I stress again the exceptional importance of the free international flow of people and information, including unhindered radio broadcasting.

It is my hope that in the spirit of the freedom-loving and humane tradition of the American people, the commitment to advance human rights throughout the world will occupy an ever greater place in U.S. policy.

The day after Jimmy Carter won the election, Sakharov sent him a short but fervent telegram of congratulations:

I welcome your election. Your decisive unambiguous statements in defense of human rights throughout the world are of vast significance. They raise new hopes. I am sure that the USA—full of courage and determination, strong in its democratic and moral traditions, powerful in its economic and military resources, the first country of the West—will carry with honor the burden history has placed upon her citizens and leaders.

On January 21, when a member of Moscow's community of Jewish "refuseniks"—those, like Benjamin Levich, Aleksandr Lerner, and Vladimir Slepak, denied permission to emigrate to Israel—brought an American lawyer, Martin Garbus, and his wife to the Sakharov apartment, the Soviet physicist was in an anxious frame of mind. Twice since a bomb had exploded in the Moscow subway on January 8, he had spoken out forcefully to warn that the KGB might use the explosion as a pretext for new repression against dissidents. But sensationalistic hints that the nonviolent dissenters might be turning in frustration to terrorism were receiving more attention in the West than Sakharov's and others' vigorous denials that any such thing had occurred or could.

Then when Garbus suggested that he could carry a letter from Sakharov to President Carter, Sakharov responded eagerly to the proposal. Garbus had come to Moscow to speak to Soviet officials about the conviction of Amner Zavurov, a young "refusenik" in Uzbekistan caught in a Catch-22 prosecution for not having the internal passport authorities had taken from him when they gave him permission to emigrate. Now Garbus had only an hour or two before his flight back to America. Sakharov normally requires half a dozen or more drafts before writing the final version of any statement. This time, however, he wrote hurriedly, and Garbus' "refusenik" escort produced an equally hasty English translation on the spot. The resulting versions do not always match in paragraph order or even in content. The Russian original, for instance, listed only fifteen names of prisoners on whose behalf Sakharov appealed to the President, but the names of Gabriel Superfin and Vasily Fedorenko appear in the English translation, suggesting the unusual hurry with which the letter was composed.

A week after the Moscow meeting, Garbus gave Sakharov's letter to State Department officials and to reporters for The New York Times *and* Los Angeles Times. *A letter the author had intended as a private communication suddenly became a public event, printed January 29 in a slightly abbreviated version in a major U.S. paper just as Americans were beginning to understand the seriousness and the complexity of Jimmy Carter's commitment to human rights. The letter itself—in an edited text combining the Russian original and the English translation done in Moscow—follows:*

Dear Mr. Carter,

It's very important to defend those who suffer because of their nonviolent struggle for an open society, for justice, for other people whose rights are violated. It is our duty and yours to fight for them. I think that a lot depends on this struggle—trust between peoples, confidence in lofty promises, and, in the final analysis, international security.

Our situation is difficult, almost unbearable—not only in the USSR, but also in all the countries of Eastern Europe. Now, on the eve of the Belgrade Meeting, with the struggle for human rights rising in Eastern Europe and the USSR, the authorities are stepping up their repression and their attempts to discredit dissidents. They are unwilling to make any concessions to the human rights most essential to any society (freedom of belief and information, freedom of conscience, freedom to choose one's country of residence, etc.). They cannot accept the honest competition of ideas. The persecution of the members of the Helsinki Watch Groups in Moscow and the Ukraine, and especially the provocation in the Moscow subway, which we have to compare to the 1933 Reichstag fire and the 1934 murder of Kirov, require emphatic condemnation.

Do you know the truth about the situation of religion in the USSR—the humiliation of official churches and the merciless repression (arrests; fines; religious parents deprived of their children; even murder, as in the case of the

Baptist Biblenko) of those sects—Baptists, Uniates, Pentecostals, the True Orthodox Church, and others—who seek independence of the government. The Vins case is the best-known example. Terror is also used against other groups of dissidents. During the past year we have known of the murders of dissidents—that of the poet and translator Konstantin Bogatyrev is well known—which have not been investigated at all.

It is very important that the President of the United States continue his efforts to obtain the release of those people who are already known to Americans and that those efforts not be in vain. It is very important to continue the struggle for the severely ill and for women political prisoners.

I give you a list of those in need of immediate release, but it is very important to remember that there are many others in equally difficult situations. This is the main list. There are very many others who need the same support, and we haven't got the moral strength to cross out any of the names: Kovalev, Romanyuk, Dzhemilev, Svitlichny, Gluzman, Ruban, Shtern, Yuri Fyodorov, Makarenko, Sergienko, Ogurtsov, Pronyuk, Maria Semyonova, Vins, Moroz, Superfin, Fedorenko. (Fedorenko has been on a hunger strike for two years. He is serving a thirteen-year sentence for high treason since he tried to cross the frontier by hanging to the undercarriage of a train.) Detailed information about each of them is available from Khronika Press; its publisher, Edward Kline, knows all the cases.

I have a serious problem with communications. My telephone to the West is completely blocked. No calls reach me, and it is useless to go to the telephone station [in the post office—Ed.] since I'm always told that the other party doesn't answer. (I'm always closely watched.) This question of communications is basic to my public activity and the entire human-rights movement in this country. I ask you to take steps at the international level in this connection.

I also want to ask especially that you raise your voice in defense of [Yugoslav writer] Mihajlo Mihajlov, the Charter

'77 group in Czechoslovakia, and the Workers' Defense
Committee in Poland. With profound respect,

Andrei Sakharov

On February 2, Sakharov told a Newsweek *interviewer
that he had not meant his letter to President Carter to be
public. The exchange:*

Q: Are you disappointed that your appeal to President
Carter was published? Can the West achieve more through
quiet diplomacy than by public statements?

A: The first and second parts of your question relate to
completely different themes. I attach great importance to
publicity, and I am convinced that the defense of human
rights is impossible unless the world knows about violations
of these rights. As I have already said, however, I do not
think I have the right to give any advice or recommendations
about what specific measures should be taken by officials
in foreign countries.

In regard to my letter to Mr. Carter, it was written during
an American lawyer's visit which lasted less than one hour
because he was rushing to catch his plane. This was not an
appeal which I had intended to be made public. I do not
know why *The New York Times* decided to print it. Yet, if
the publication of this letter helps even one of the seventeen
people mentioned in the letter, then I will be completely
satisfied.

*Interviewed for CBS on February 10, Sakharov urged
Washington to be firm on human rights:*

Q: What do you see as the attitude of the Carter Admin-
istration to you and to other dissidents? Do you think that
Washington policies have an effect? What should the Carter
Administration say or do?

A: The new President's moral, courageous position evokes
my respect and hope. It is not interference in other countries'

internal affairs to conduct a decisive, consistent, and principled defense of human rights throughout the world. On the contrary, such conduct preserves the moral, democratic values of the American people and of mankind as a whole. It is the preservation of a free future for the United States and for the entire world.

I have neither the right nor the opportunity to give advice to the new Administration about how it should act in any particular situation. I can only permit myself to say that any disagreement, uncertainty, or partial retreat will give the Soviet authorities the impression that the new Administration is giving in to blackmail and pressure. I am deeply convinced that will not actually occur, for any appearance of weakness will affect all aspects of East-West relations, including disarmament negotiations. Unfortunately, the recent episode of the statement issued by the State Department after I was called in by the Procuracy did give Soviet authorities just such a misleading impression of the new Administration's weakness or vacillation. Possibly this is one of the reasons for the wave of repressions in recent days, although it is perfectly clear that these repressions were planned before this. I repeat, I am absolutely convinced that the Soviet authorities have a false impression. The most recent declarations by the President and by the Secretary of State support my belief and hope.

I have often spoken of the key importance of the problem of the choice of one's country of residence. Carter's telegram to Vladimir Slepak during the presidential campaign shows that the President shares that opinion. It gives me hope that this issue will remain part of the President's unwavering concern.

The "episode" of a State Department declaration on Sakharov which Secretary of State Cyrus Vance had not cleared for release caused great comment in the Washington press and some real anxiety for Sakharov in Moscow.

The "repressions" referred to were the arrests of Helsinki

*Watchers Mykola Rudenko and Oleksei Tykhy in the Ukraine
and of Aleksandr Ginzburg in Moscow, followed—the day
of the CBS interview—by that of Professor Yuri Orlov,
founder of the Soviet Helsinki Accord monitoring groups.*

*One week after the CBS interview—February 17—Dr.
Sakharov was invited to the U.S. Embassy in Moscow to
receive an answer President Carter wrote him from the
White House, February 5:*

Dear Professor Sakharov:

I received your letter of January 21, and I want to express
my appreciation to you for bringing your thoughts to my
personal attention.

Human rights is a central concern of my administration.
In my inaugural address I stated: "Because we are free, we
can never be indifferent to the fate of freedom elsewhere."
You may rest assured that the American people and our
government will continue our firm commitment to promote
respect for human rights not only in our country but also
abroad.

We shall use our good offices to seek the release of
prisoners of conscience, and we will continue our efforts to
shape a world responsive to human aspirations in which
nations of differing cultures and histories can live side by
side in peace and justice.

I am always glad to hear from you, and I wish you well.

Sincerely,
Jimmy Carter

*Elated, Sakharov released the text of the President's letter
to Western journalists in Moscow and that day wrote out
his reply to Carter:*

Dear Mr. President:

Your letter of February 5, which I received today, is a
great honor for me and support for the unified human-rights

movement in the USSR and the countries of Eastern Europe, of which we consider ourselves a part. In your letter, as earlier in your inaugural speech and other public statements, you have confirmed the adherence of the new American Administration to the principles of human rights throughout the world. Your efforts to assist in freeing prisoners of conscience are particularly significant.

When you were elected, I wrote in a congratulatory telegram of the profound respect which your position evokes in us. Several times I have written and said that the defense of fundamental human rights is not interference in the internal affairs of other countries, but rather one of the most important international concerns, inseparable from the basic problems of peace and progress. Today, having received your letter—and I fully understand its exceptional nature— I can only repeat this once again.

I shall also use this opportunity to mention specific cases, including those prisoners of conscience about whom I wrote you in January. One of them, Sergei Kovalev, has a dangerous tumor. I ask you to intercede for his immediate transfer to the prison hospital in Leningrad. Once again, I stress the arbitrary selection of names. Actually, I do not believe I have the right to make such a choice. The fate of many, many political prisoners requires equal attention.

Four members of the Helsinki Watch Groups were arrested in February—Aleksandr Ginzburg, Mykola Rudenko, Oleksei Tykhy, and group leader Yuri Orlov. Their arrest is a challenge to all the states signatory to the Helsinki Accord. I ask you to appeal for the release on surety or bail of Ginzburg and Rudenko, both of whom are ill. It is essential that heads of all governments which signed the Helsinki Accord take active measures to obtain the release of all members of the group so that it can continue its important work.

From foreign radio broadcasts, I learned that you expressed the desire to meet me if I should come to the USA. I am very grateful for this invitation. Without doubt, such a visit and personal contacts would have special significance for me. Unfortunately, at the present time, I do not foresee any chance of my taking such a trip.

I want to express the hope that the efforts of people of good will, as well as your personal efforts, Mr. President, will promote the realization of those lofty aims of which you wrote me. With deep respect,

Sincerely,
Andrei Sakharov

Dr. Sakharov also added his Moscow address (48B Chkalov Street, Apt. 68) and telephone number (227–27–20) to his signature, and in a February 23 interview with a correspondent of France-Soir, *he analyzed the meaning of his correspondence with the President and the limits of his role in advising the West:*

Q: What has changed for you personally and for the struggle after the Carter letter?

A: Concretely—nothing. For myself, personally—nothing. For the struggle, I imagine that it is a matter of time. Those moral criteria which, as President Carter stated in his letter, will be the basis of the activities of the new Administration are very important not only for the moment, but in the long term. When the President of a great country speaks of it, interest in human rights can only grow, and that is very good.

But I would like to see actual, rapid solutions to those questions where speed is essential. I wrote in reply to the President to ask him to intercede immediately to effect the transfer of Sergei Kovalev, who is gravely ill. But Kovalev is still in Camp 36 and still on a hunger strike. Only an immediate transfer to a hospital can save his life. In my letter, I also asked for help in freeing Aleksandr Ginzburg and Mykola Rudenko on surety or bail. Seven people—among them my wife and I—have asked the Procuracy about this, but have received no reply. I wrote that the four members of the Helsinki Watch Groups in the USSR should be released so that the group could continue its important work. However, all four are in prison. I am certain that these three specific issues can be resolved without affecting the SALT negotiations and must be dealt with as soon as possible.

Unfortunately, since this has not occurred, I cannot say that anything has changed after the President's letter to me.

Q: What can the West do?

A: It seems to me that I cannot give advice—any more than anyone could living in our country or in Eastern Europe. Western leaders, Western public figures, are simply better informed than we are. They don't live under pressure, under the yoke of repressions, without a free press, without postal or telephone connections. We can't give advice. We speak out—and loudly—about what is going on here, and just to speak the truth here is very difficult in itself. By speaking out, we are defending peace and the future. But as to drawing conclusions about what should be done—that the West must decide for itself.

A month later, March 25, an ABC News correspondent asked if the exchange with Carter had been, as many in the West were saying, counterproductive:

Q: Since Carter became President, some dissidents have been arrested and you have been threatened with criminal prosecution yourself. Some say that President Carter's position on human rights has led the Soviet government to put stronger pressure on the dissidents. Do you agree?

A: Categorically—no! Repressions are our daily life. They existed under Nixon, under Ford, and both before and after Helsinki. The latest wave of repressions began during the first days of January—that is, before Carter took office. Of course, by having made public statements on human rights, Carter did assume a certain responsibility.

But if specific actions do not follow general statements, if the public in America and in Europe—legislatures, busi-

214 ANDREI SAKHAROV AND PEACE

ness people, scientific and cultural organizations in charge of contacts, and labor unions—do not support these statements and the principles expressed in them, then not only will these people not be freed, but a further intensification of repression may occur.

Q: Many Soviet commentators say that Carter's letter to you is interference in the internal affairs of the USSR. Do you agree?

A: A personal letter—in which the USSR is not even mentioned—can in no way be interference in its internal affairs.

Dr. Sakharov's estimate of the diplomatic niceties involved in his correspondence with the President was not shared by the Soviet government. The day after the President's letter was released in Moscow, Soviet Ambassador Anatoly Dobrynin called at the State Department to lodge what press accounts called a heated protest. It was followed by others in the Soviet press, including a major commentary in Pravda, the official party organ. In a speech on March 22, Leonid Brezhnev personally denounced "outright attempts by official American agencies to interfere in the internal affairs of the Soviet Union." He said the Soviet Union "will never tolerate interference . . . by any country under any pretext," but especially not under cover of "a clamor being raised about the so-called 'dissidents' and about the 'violation of human rights' in socialist countries."

In Washington the effect of the exchange was both to make the Administration's human-rights policy front-page news and to call the policy's wisdom and execution into public question.

That debate has continued well into the Administration's second year in office, but its outlines were apparent from the first month. Six days after the Inauguration, the State Department issued a statement of concern for the promoters of Charter '77, followed the next day by the "unauthorized" admonition to Moscow that "any attempts . . . to intimidate

Mr. Sakharov... long admired as an outspoken champion of human rights... will conflict with accepted international standards." When the correspondence between the White House and Chkalov Street became public, critics of President Carter were quick to call his policy improvised and to warn against unnecessarily provoking the Kremlin.

Arthur Schlesinger, Jr., wrote in the Wall Street Journal *of March 4 that the President's stance "must be judged thus far... a considerable and very serious success.... His letter to Sakharov obviously expressed real personal concern. It also registered widespread public sentiment in the United States and elsewhere. For human rights is evidently one of those ideas whose day has finally arrived." But the historian and one-time White House adviser quickly cautioned that the letter to Sakharov did not seem to be "part of a thought-out policy," that the policy should not "seem just one more stick with which to beat the Russians" and that "official sermons to the world may encourage us in the delusion that we are morally superior to everybody else."*

James Reston in his New York Times *column of February 19 wrote that the letter to Sakharov "has sent a polite shudder through the entire diplomatic fraternity. The best they can say for [Carter] is that maybe it was an innocent mistake of inexperience." Mr. Reston also reported the statement of National Security adviser Zbigniew Brzezinski that the response to Dr. Sakharov had been "thought through" and was "prudential." Brzezinski viewed the letter as being not as "pointed and provocative" as a public reply, and said it had been necessary to write, since to ignore the Sakharov letter would have been "scarcely reasonable." Admiringly, Reston concluded that even though the exchange "raises some awkward questions," it shows the President's "assumption that if the Soviet Union can be diverted by a letter to Sakharov from trying to get control of the world arms traffic, maybe an arms agreement would not mean all that much."*

More critical, Joseph Kraft commented in the Washington

Post *on February 24 that the President "seems not to have fully assessed . . . the scope [of] the issue of human rights in the Communist world" and was "unprepared for a vigorous response" from the Soviets to his actions and statements. "The human rights factor," Kraft wrote, "is far too important to be handled on a one-shot, tit-for-tat basis without a thorough exploration of effects and side-effects on such issues as arms control. . . . A President is probably better off burnishing the [American] record from time to time on an impersonal basis than being a compulsive talker."*

In short, Sakharov's letter—written in haste and not meant for publication—became the catalyst for a major debate on U.S. foreign policy, an argument which still continues on the role of human-rights advocacy in furthering or impeding East-West relations. In the view of one unnamed State Department official quoted by Robert K. Kaiser in the Washington Post *on February 27, 1977: "The whole thing has grown like Topsy and seems to be feeding on itself." In fact, both Sakharov's initiative and Carter's response appear, in retrospect, to have been the natural, almost inevitable convergence of two human-rights campaigners destined to come together.*

A LETTER FROM EXILE

by Andrei Sakharov

I SHOULD LIKE TO OFFER SOME THOUGHTS ON problems that have been troubling me and discuss the way they appear to me here in Gorky, a city closed to foreigners, in the depths of the Soviet Union, where I now have vigilant surveillance by the KGB.

World Problems

In the 1960s and '70s, the Soviet Union, making use of its growing economic and scientific-technological potential, carried out a fundamental reequipping and expansion of its weaponry. There was a substantial increase in both the quality and quantity of the missiles and nuclear weapons developed earlier, and in other new systems of military technology: transport vehicles for the largest land force in the world, the latest word in tanks and aircraft, combat helicopters, fire-control systems, communications, nuclear submarines, fast hydrofoil craft, and many others.

A major change has occurred in the world balance of forces, and this change is intensifying. It is true, of course, that the development of new technology and the growth in numbers of weapons have not been confined to the Soviet

Translated by Raymond H. Anderson.

Union. This is a mutually stimulating process in virtually all technologically developed countries. In the United States, in particular, such developments have perhaps proceeded on a higher scientific-technological level and this, in turn, caused alarm in the Soviet Union.

But in order to assess the situation properly it is imperative to take note of the particular features of the Soviet Union—a closed totalitarian state with a largely militarized economy and bureaucratically centralized control, all of which make the growing might of such a country even more dangerous. In more democratic societies, every step in the field of armaments is subjected to public budgetary and political scrutiny and is carried out under public control. In the Soviet Union, all decisions of this kind are made behind closed doors and the world learns of them only when confronted by *faits accomplis*. Even more ominous is the fact that this situation applies also to the field of foreign policy, involving issues of war and peace.

At the same time that the changes in the balance of forces was occurring—though not only because of that change—there was both covert and overt Soviet expansion in key strategic and economic regions of the world. Southeast Asia (where Vietnam was used as a proxy) and Angola (with Cuba as the proxy), Ethiopia, and Yemen are only some of the examples. The invasion of Afghanistan may be a new and more dangerous stage in this expansion. The invasion, which occurred against the background of the tragedy in Tehran, and possibly had some concealed connection with it, exacerbated world tensions and obstructed talks on disarmament and the settlement of other conflicts. In particular, the invasion made it impossible, at the present time, for the United States Congress to ratify the SALT II treaty, which is of such crucial importance to the world.

Several months earlier, the Soviet Union had unleashed at home and had instigated abroad a demagogic campaign against plans by the United States and North Atlantic Treaty Organization allies for an urgently needed modernization of their missile forces in Europe—this at a time when the Soviet Union had already completed such a modernization—and had thwarted (I hope only temporarily) talks on limiting medium-range nuclear missiles. The Vienna negotiations on disarmament in Europe are likewise in a deplorable state, which is also mainly the fault of the Soviet Union.

Despite all that has happened, I feel that the questions of war and peace and disarmament are so crucial that they must be given absolute priority even in the most difficult circumstances. It is imperative that all possible means be used to solve these questions and to lay the groundwork for further progress. Most urgent of all are steps to avert a nuclear war, which is the greatest peril confronting the modern world. The goals of all responsible people in the world coincide in this regard, including, I hope and believe, the Soviet leaders—despite their dangerous expansionist policies, despite their cynicism, dogmatic conceptions and lack of self-confidence which often prevent them from conducting more realistic domestic and foreign policies.

Therefore, I hope that when there is some easing of the present crisis in international relations, caused mainly by the Soviet invasion of Afghanistan, there will be a revival of efforts in regard to SALT II, a technologically progressive treaty that provides the essential foundations for SALT III. I hope, too, that there will be new efforts in regard to medium-range nuclear weapons and tactical weapons as well as a reduction in "ordinary" weaponry in Europe.

Negotiations on disarmament are possible only on the basis of strategic parity. The countries of the West must do everything necessary to maintain this parity or, in some categories, to regain it—not allowing themselves to become victims of blackmail and demagogy as in the campaign against American missiles in Europe.

Of equal urgency is a peaceful settlement of "hot" conflicts. The Soviet invasion of Afghanistan was condemned by 104 nations, but the war continues there and no end is in sight. Economic and political sanctions are extremely important; they can help strengthen the hand of the more responsible, nondogmatic members of the Soviet leadership. In particular, the broadest possible boycott of the Moscow Olympics is necessary. Every spectator or athlete who comes to the Olympics will be giving indirect support to Soviet military policies.

It is vital to demand withdrawal of the Soviet troops in Afghanistan. I hope that withdrawal of the troops will become possible—if not now, perhaps later—on the basis of guaranteed neutrality, with stationing in the country of United Nations troops or units from neutral Moslem countries, which should ease Soviet apprehensions.

The Soviet "conditions" that foreign interference be ended are pure demagogy because there is no such interference. In general, Soviet propaganda is conducted now on a crude "military" level. For example, television broadcasts are showing allegedly captured "American" grenades containing nerve gas. Painted on the grenades in large white letters are the words "Made in U.S.A." All this is obviously intended to head off any similar accusations against operations by the Soviet Army.

The Middle East conflict has been dragging on for decades. The main hope for its settlement is development of the Camp David line so that the difficulties and tragedies of the past will not be carried into the future. It is very important that the Palestinians adopt such a position, that they recognize the existence of Israel, renounce terrorist-guerrilla methods of struggle and refuse to be pawns of those who supply them with guns. There is no evidence yet of any movement in this direction.

Israel, it seems to me, should show more restraint, particularly in regard to settlements in the occupied lands. The Middle East crisis can be solved only in the context of general world problems. Therefore, United States mediation seems to me to be of utmost importance.

In November 1979, I wrote to Leonid I. Brezhnev, chairman of the Presidium of the Supreme Soviet of the USSR, urging him to help assure uninterrupted supplies of food to the starving people in Cambodia, where famine is the consequence of the crimes of the deposed Pol Pot regime and the war. This problem, like that of the refugees from Vietnam, Cambodia, Ethiopia and other countries, remains as critical as ever. Now there is the problem of refugees from Afghanistan and Cuba. Saving people must be put ahead of all military and political considerations and national prestige.

At the moment I write this, the world has just learned of the failure of the American attempt to rescue the hostages in Tehran. I feel that this was a brave and noble effort. It was undertaken only after it had become clear that the Iranian authorities would not free the hostages voluntarily, thereby taking upon themselves responsibility for a crime that flouts the standards of international behavior.

I do not understand how so many technical problems could have arisen. These are no doubt being subjected to intensive scrutiny, not only the technical questions but also the possibility of sabotage. Success of the American mission would have saved the world from a nightmare. No one should condemn the United States because the mission failed. And no one should criticize President Carter for the secrecy in which the mission was organized. It would be my guess that the secrecy, if anything, was insufficient rather than excessive. Personal ambitions had no place in this. Overall, the actions of Mr. Carter in these tragic days win only respect from me.

Success of the American rescue mission would have eliminated a need to impose sanctions against Iran, and it would have been in the interest of the Iranian people themselves. It appears now that sanctions have become inevitable, and it is very important to achieve unity of action by the countries of the West. Solution of the hostage problem is a matter for all countries that consider themselves democratic and strive to preserve the norms of international relations. This is not just an American problem but a worldwide one, as was shown by new acts of terrorism: the successfully resolved incidents in Bogotá and London.

World attention should be paid to many other problems whose burden now rests mainly on the United States—economic and technological aid to developing countries, help to refugees and the starving, and general economic, ideological, and military resistance to the expansion of totalitarianism.

Western unity is one of the main conditions for international security, a unity that will promise resistance and ultimately lead to rapprochement and the convergence of world systems, averting thermonuclear catastrophe.

Western Problems

A totalitarian system conducts its policy through control from a single center—diplomacy, information, and disinformation services inside and outside the country, foreign trade, tourism, scientific-technological exchanges, economic and military assistance to liberation (a word that must sometimes be used with quotation marks) movements, foreign policy of satellite countries, and all kinds of clandestine activities—all these are coordinated from a single center. Special attention must be paid here to clandestine activities, since a person is inclined to forget something if it is not waved in front of his eyes. The West and developing countries are filled with citizens who by reason of their positions are able to promote Soviet influence and expansionist goals.

Some of them are motivated by ideas that at least merit discussion. After all, in the Soviet Union, the ideological epicenter, and in China as well, Communist ideology is not a complete fraud, not a total delusion. It arose from a striving for truth and justice, like other religious, ethical, and philosophical systems. Its weakness, its failure, and its degradation—evident from the very beginning—represent a complex historical, scientific, and psychological phenomenon that requires separate analysis.

There are others among such people who conduct themselves in a "progressive" manner because they consider it profitable, prestigious, or fashionable.

A third category consists of naive, poorly informed, or indifferent people who close their eyes and ears to the bitter truth and eagerly swallow any sweet lie.

Finally, there is the fourth group—people who have been "bought" in the most direct sense of the word, not always with money. These include some political figures, businessmen, a great many writers and journalists, government advisers, and heads of the press and television. Overall, they make up a substantial group of influential people.

(I can't resist telling about an incident involving my wife and me. Two leading and influential American scientists, arriving in the Soviet Union to take part in a conference, were given envelopes containing money for personal expenses. Out of politeness and embarrassment they felt they could not decline the money. So, in a state of confusion, they gave it to us and asked that we pass it on to scientists who had lost their jobs. We don't know how many other such incidents there have been.)

Of course, there are many spies, secret agents, and organizers of sabotage. This is true of nations other than the USSR, but a totalitarian system has special opportunities. In particular, one cannot arbitrarily reject allegations by some writers about connections between the KGB and international terrorism. The absence of direct proof regarding such links and concern about a further worsening of tensions make governments of the West reluctant to look too deep into this sensitive question.

Unity of all its forces is one of the advantages of totalitarianism in its world offensive threatening the pluralist West. What can the West do to counter this challenge? Of course, in historical perspective, in conditions of peaceful and orderly development, the pluralist and free systems are more viable and dynamic. Therefore, the future will follow the path of pluralist and converging scientific-technological progress.

But the world is facing very difficult times and cruel cataclysms if the West and the developing countries trying to find their place in the world do not now show the required firmness, unity, and consistency in resisting the totalitarian challenge. This relates to governments, to the intelligentsia, to businessmen, and to all people. It is important that the common danger be fully understood—everything else will then fall into place. In this regard, I believe in Western man. I have faith in his mind, which is practical and efficient and at the same time aspires to great goals. I have faith in his good intentions and his decisiveness.

Recent months have been under the shadow of the events in Afghanistan and Tehran. The reaction in Europe, at least the initial reaction, has not been as consistent and united as, in my opinion, it should have been. One could read assertions in the press of the following type: Let Carter worry about it. He's the one facing the elections. After all, this is a purely American matter. We have our own problems.

I am unable to judge how widespread are such views. In my opinion, they are very harmful. Recently, the West German author Günter Grass and three other writers issued a statement in this spirit. The Soviet press delights in quoting such statements, forgiving the authors all their past "sins." The anti-Americanism of certain representatives of the West European intelligentsia would be merely amusing, given their show of exaggerated sensitivity, if it were not so harmful.

In truth, Europe has much of which it can be proud. But it is inappropriate for Europe to adopt an arrogant attitude. The tragic nature of our time does not permit this. Europe must fight shoulder to shoulder with the transoceanic democracy, which is Europe's creation and Europe's main hope. A certain lack of unity, of course, is the reverse side of the coin of democratic pluralism, the West's major strength. But this disunity is also caused by the systematic Soviet policy of driving "wedges," a policy that the West has not resisted adequately because of carelessness and blindness. Nonetheless, I feel that in the course of recent crises a positive shift has appeared in the stand of the West and of the developing countries. Only the future will show whether I am right.

Among the important events of recent years is a movement toward greater independence by several European Communist parties—though now the French have apparently beaten a quick retreat. There may be profound consequences if the parties continue to reject dogmatism and unquestioning support of Moscow (in such matters as Afghanistan, for example) and if they accept certain pluralist principles. It would be very important if the European Communist parties joined all democratic forces in supporting the struggle for human rights in the Soviet Union and other Communist countries.

One of the causes of the weakening position of the West is its dependence on oil supplies, a "fatal dependency," as an American leader has remarked. The geopolitics of the Soviet Union is aimed precisely at this weak point. In these circumstances, the West cannot afford to deprive itself of nuclear energy, which gives room for diplomatic and economic "maneuvering." Concern about safety and environmental hazards should have no bearing on the principal issue—to build or not to build nuclear stations—but only on how to build them. The price in terms of polluting the environment is greater from coal and oil than from nuclear energy. Of course, other sources of energy must be developed as an alternative to oil, including coal, despite its ecological shortcomings. Strict conservation must be introduced in the use of electricity and heat. Steps must be taken to provide small cars, good public transportation, insulation of homes, integrated heating systems and, especially, introduction of technological processes in industry to conserve electricity. Western voters must demand this from government leaders and not allow demagogues to exploit these problems for their selfish ends.

Internal Problems

Defense of human rights has become a worldwide ideology, uniting on a humane basis peoples of all nationalities and with the most diverse convictions. I have very high regard for them all: for Amnesty International and its struggle for release of prisoners of conscience, against torture and the death penalty; for the International League for Human Rights; and for the rights activists in Eastern Europe, China, and other countries, where they show great bravery in coping with cruel repression.

In the Soviet Union, the movement for human rights emerged in its present form at the end of the '60s with publication of the *Chronicle of Current Events*, an anonymous underground journal that reports cases of violations in the Soviet Union factually and without subjective comment. Despite severe repressions, the journal has continued to appear, a total to date of fifty-four issues. In more recent years, appeals by the Helsinki Group [formed in the Soviet Union to check on compliance with human rights provisions of the 1975 Helsinki agreement on European security] began to appear.

The human rights movement has no political objectives and its participants have no desire to gain political power. Their only weapon is free access to and dissemination of information. It is of vital importance that the movement limit itself to nonviolent methods. Such a position is logical in a country that has passed through the violence of every circle of hell. Calls for new revolutionary upheavals or for intervention would be mad, and a terrible crime in an unstable world only several steps from the thermonuclear abyss.

Participants in the human rights movement speak out

openly for human rights whenever they learn of violations, and they inform the people. They have also set themselves the task of correcting the historical record about a society and individual citizens if the truth has been distorted by official propaganda. They help the families of victims of repression. I am convinced that this is what is needed—a pure moral movement to plant in people's minds a basis for democratic and pluralist transformation. This is crucial to the country and essential to all mankind for the sake of peace on earth.

The consciousness of broad masses of the population has been deformed by a number of factors: Decades of totalitarian terror . . . old and new prejudices . . . the lure of a relatively good life after generations of havoc. (I mean of course a very limited good life, nothing like the well-being and freedom of workers in the West or the privileged elites in the Soviet Union) . . . the constant need to wheel and deal, to scheme and break the law. The ideology of the Soviet philistine (I have in mind the worst people, but they, unfortunately, are rather frequently found among workers and peasants and throughout the intelligentsia) consists of several uncomplicated ideas:

• Cult of the state, involving, in various combinations, submission to authority, a naive belief that life in the West is worse than in the Soviet Union, gratitude to a "benefactor" government, and, at the same time, fear and hypocrisy.

• Egoistic endeavors to ensure a good life for oneself and one's family, to "live like everyone else" with the help of graft, theft ignored by bosses, and ever-present hypocrisy. Yet there is a desire among better people in this category to achieve a good life through their own labor, by their own hands. Nonetheless, it is still necessary to wheel and deal and to play the hypocrite.

• The idea of nationalist superiority, which takes on a dark, hysterical, and pogromlike form among some Russians, and not only among Russians. One often hears exclamations: "We're wasting our money on these black (or yellow) monkeys! We're feeding parasites!" Or one hears: "The Jews are responsible!"—or the "Russians" or the "Georgians" or the "Chuchmeki," a derogatory term for the people of Central Asia.

These are very disturbing symptoms after sixty years of proclaiming "friendship of the peoples."

Officially, Communist ideology is internationalist, but it surreptitiously exploits nationalist prejudices. So far, this has been done with some caution, and I hope that these forces will not be unleashed. After the class hatreds we have suffered, we certainly have no need for a racist-nationalist ideology. I am convinced that this is dangerous and destructive even in its most humane (at first glance) "dissident" manifestations. There are few people who react seriously anymore to slogans about building Communism, although there was a time when, perhaps as a result of a certain misunderstanding, Communist slogans reflected a wish for justice and happiness for all in the world.

But internal propaganda intensively exploits the nation-wide tragedy of World War II and the pride that people feel in their active part in historic events of that time. The irony of life is that it was only during the war that the ordinary person felt his importance and his dignity in an inhuman world of terror and humiliation. There is intensive exploitation of the risk of war and the much decried American military bases around our country. Feelings of suspicion are stirred up about schemes of the "imperialists."

A nation that has suffered the horrible losses, cruelties, and destruction of war yearns above all for peace. This is a broad, profound, powerful, and honest feeling. Today, the leaders of the country do not, and cannot, go against this dominant desire of the people. I want to believe that in this regard, the Soviet leaders are sincere, that when peace is involved they are transformed from robots into people.

But even the people's deep wish for peace is exploited, and this is perhaps the cruelest deception of all. The deep yearning for peace is used to justify all the most negative features in our country—economic disorder, excessive militarization, purportedly "defensive" foreign policy measures (whether in Czechoslovakia or Afghanistan), and lack of freedom in our closed society. And those negative features also include the ecological madness, such as the destruction of Lake Baikal, meadows and fields, and the country's fish resources, and the poisoning of our water and air.

The people of our country submit uncomplainingly to all the shortages of meat, butter, and many other products—though they do grumble at home. They put up with the gross social inequality between the elite and the ordinary citizens. They endure the arbitrary behavior and cruelty of local authorities. They know about the beatings and deaths of people in police stations but as a rule keep quiet. They do not speak out—sometimes they even gloat—about the unjust treatment of dissidents. They are silent about any and all foreign policy actions.

A country living for decades under conditions in which all means of production belong to the state is suffering serious economic and social hardship. It cannot grow enough food for its people. It cannot, without the benefit of détente, keep up with the contemporary levels of science and technology.

From the time I wrote "My Country and the World" [published in 1975], the average salary has risen, but the cost of living has evidently risen even higher, because daily life has not improved. The much acclaimed free medical care steadily gets worse. (It is "free" because the wages of most workers are kept so low and because one must pay for expensive medicines.) The situation in education is not much better, especially in the countryside. It is no longer possible to explain away all these problems as a result of the war or occasional mistakes.

There is an urgent need for economic reforms that would increase the independence of enterprises and allow elements of a mixed economy. There is need for more freedom of information, a free and critical press, freedom for people to travel abroad, freedom of emigration, and a free choice of one's place of residence within the country. In the long run, there should probably be a multiparty system and elimination of Party monopoly over all ideological, political, and economic life.

But all of this, even though obvious to most people, remains for the time being nothing but wishful thinking. The dogmatic bureaucrats and the new people replacing them—anonymous and shrewd cynics, moving in the many "corridors of power" of the departments of the Central Committee, the KGB, the ministries, and the provincial and regional Party committees—are pushing the country toward what they consider to be the safest path but that is in reality a path to suicide.

Everything is as it was under the system created by Stalin. The leaders carry on the arms race, concealing it behind talk of their love of peace. They interfere in troubled areas around the world, from Ethiopia to Afghanistan, in order to increase prestige, to strengthen the nation's power, and to ensure that the guns don't get rusty. They round up dissidents, returning the country to the quiet "pre-dissident" period, as my son-in-law, Efrem Yankelevich, has described the situation.

In the last ten or fifteen years there has been a worsening of the traditional Russian curse, drunkenness. The government has attempted some timid half-measures—more in word than deed—but it is unable to accomplish much. Alcoholism is a worldwide phenomenon, not wholly a result of conditions in our country. But certain specific factors do play a major role.

Expenditures for drinking reduce surplus purchasing power of the population, but the main point is that an alcoholic poses no threat to the government. Also, drinking is the only real freedom available and the authorities are not foolhardy enough to take this away without giving something in return. There are economic, social, and psychological elements in all this. And the result: Instead of dry wine and good-quality old vodka, the authorities flood the market with cheap and poisonous fortified wine, known as *bormotukha*, which swiftly destroys men, women, and youngsters. As the "quiet" tzar, Aleksei Mikhailovich, said three hundred years ago: "Don't drive the hotheads away from the taverns."

The people of our country are to some extent confused and intimidated, of course. But there is also a conscious self-deception and an egoistic escape from difficult problems. The slogan "The People and Party Are One," which hangs from every fifth building, consists not entirely of empty words.

But it was from the ranks of the people that the defenders of human rights emerged, standing up against deceit, hypocrisy, and silence, armed only with pens, ready to make sacrifices, yet lacking the stimulus one derives from the certainty of quick success. They had their say. They will not be forgotten. On their side, they have moral force and the logic of historical development. I am convinced also that their activity will continue in one form or another, whatever the size of the movement. What is important is not the arithmetic but the qualitative fact of breaking through the psychological barrier of silence.

But history develops according to its own slow (and tortuous) laws. We are now living through difficult and troubling times—a worsening of international tensions, Soviet expansionism, shameless anti-American, anti-Western, anti-Israeli, anti-Egyptian, and anti-intellectual propaganda, and threats of still greater tension ahead.

Inside the country, these are times of ever greater repression. It is terrible to think that the most honorable and generous people, who have devoted many years to defending others through public protest, have fallen victim to arbitrary repression.

I feel obligated to tell something about a few of them: Tatyana Velikanova, a mathematician and mother of three children, a grandmother, participant in the struggle for human rights for more than twelve years, from the very beginning to the present. Showing no interest in fame, glory or personal gain, sacrificing much in her personal life, she has always been at the center of the battle, committing herself to the fate of hundreds of victims of injustice, speaking out on their behalf, helping them in every way she could, not caring whether their opinions were close to hers or distant. Her only consideration was whether someone had suffered injustice.

I do not reproach those who could not bear up under the many years of strain, those who quit the struggle, or even those who in some way betrayed themselves. But they demonstrate all the more why we should admire the courage of this woman.

Another is Malva Landa, a geologist, an active member of the Helsinki Group, one of the volunteers in the aid fund helping dissident families, and for many years, for decades in fact, a friend of political prisoners and their families, totally dedicated to the idea of justice.

It is the same with Sergei Kovalev, a talented biologist and a deep and penetrating thinker, kind, patient, and strong. We were all devoted to him when he was free. I was often impressed by the deep respect he received from many of his fellow prisoners during six years in a labor camp.

Another is Victor Nekipelov, who gave his utmost to help others in trouble or subjected to injustice, a sensitive poet, a loving father, a brave man.

All the world knows of Prof. Yuri Orlov, the physicist, a courageous man always in the forefront, founder of the Helsinki Group.

The world also knows of Anatoly Shcharansky, falsely accused of espionage in an attempt to intimidate the Jewish emigration movement.

I have deep respect for the talented writer and World War II invalid Mykola Rudenko; Vyacheslav Bakhmin, the courageous and honorable member of the Working Commission on Psychiatric Abuse; Leonard Ternovsky, a radiologist and member of the same commission and also of the Helsinki Committee in Moscow, a remarkably kind and steadfast man.

Repression has been intensified against religious believers and those who defend their cause. Noteworthy among these are the names of the priests Gleb Yakunin and Dmitri Dudko and of Victor Kapitanchuk, Lev Regelson, Alexander Ogorodnikov, and Vladimir Poresh. Also, the names of the church elder Nikolai Goretoi and of eighty-four-year-old Vladimir Shelkov, who recently died in a camp, should be well known.

Mustafa and Reshat Dzhemilev and Rolan Kadiyev, fighters on behalf of the Crimean Tatars, are once again imprisoned.

As I was writing this article, more tragic news reached me: the arrest of Alexander Lavut, a talented mathematician and one of the veterans of the struggle for freedom of information. I have known Lavut for many years. Modest, serious-minded, and good-natured, he never sought to draw attention to himself. But he worked on behalf of many people. Many of them, including me, will miss his kind words and sound advice. All those I have listed have either been sentenced to long terms or are awaiting an illegal trial. All those who are free have the inescapable duty to speak out on their behalf and on behalf of the many others I have not mentioned.

Some Words About Myself

I live in an apartment guarded day and night by a policeman at the entrance. He allows no one to enter but family members, with a few exceptions. There is an old friend who lives in Gorky; the price he pays for associating with us is a summons to the KGB for a talk after each visit. There is a Gorky physicist who has been denied an emigration visa; he also has to go to the KGB after his visits to us. The only other visitors are people judged suitable by the KGB. There is no telephone in the apartment. I am unable to telephone Moscow or Leningrad even from the public telephone bureau at the post office. The call is immediately disconnected at the orders of the KGB agents who always follow me. I receive very little mail, and that consists mainly of letters "reeducating" me or merely cursing me. Oddly enough, I get the same kind of letters from the West. However, I also get some mail from the West with kind words and I am deeply grateful to the senders.

When I accompanied my mother-in-law to the station on her departure for Moscow, KGB agents, pistols in hand, made a show of preventing me from approaching the coach, making it clear that the order forbidding me from going beyond the city limits was not just empty words. A radio-jamming facility has been set up in the apartment building, just for me. In order to listen to the radio, it is necessary for my wife and me to go for walks at night with a transistor receiver. While we are out walking, the KGB agents are in our apartment damaging the typewriter and tape recorder or searching through our papers. I occupy myself with scientific work, but I suffer from a lack of regular contact with colleagues.

At the end of the third month of my stay in Gorky, on the eve of the arrival in Moscow of Western participants in an unofficial scientific seminar, the KGB allowed my colleagues in the Physical Institute of the Academy of Sciences to visit me. It even recommended that they do so. I am very grateful to those who did come. It had been a long time since I had the opportunity to discuss developments in science. During their stay, the police post was moved away from the door and the jamming facility was turned off. But as soon as my colleagues had left, promising that others would come in time, everything returned to the former state. And there was a resumption of the regular summons to the Ministry of Internal Affairs for registration.

In terms of everday life, my situation is much better than that of my friends sent into exile or, particularly, sentenced to labor camp or prison. But all the measures taken against me have not even a shred of legality. It is part of a harsh, nationwide campaign against dissidents, including the attempt to force me to keep silent and thereby make it easier for repressive action against others.

On January 22, in Moscow, KGB agents forcibly took me to the Deputy Prosecutor General, Aleksandr M. Rekunkov, who informed me that I was being stripped of my awards and would be sent into exile. He produced only the decree of the Supreme Soviet concerning the awards, giving an impression, however, that the decree also called for exile. But that was not so. I still do not know which branch of government or who personally made the decision to have me exiled. All my inquiries meet only with silence. In any event, the decision is illegal and is in violation of the Constitution. In two letters to Rekunkov and in a telegram to the chairman of the KGB, Yuri V. Andropov, I demanded revocation of the illegal exile order and said I was prepared to face an open trial.

In recent months the Soviet press has printed many articles accusing me of "mortal" sins—contempt for the people and their aspirations, slander of the Soviet system, inciting the arms race, groveling before American imperialism, and divulging military secrets. I shall not reply, once again, to those accusations here. In part, this article is my reply. I put forth my position, in very brief form, in my first statement from Gorky. All my activities stem from a desire for a free and worthy destiny for our country and our people and all countries and peoples of the world. I consider the United States the historically determined leader of the movement toward a pluralist and free society, vital to mankind. But I equally respect all peoples for their contributions to our civilization and future society.

In April, the former president of the New York Academy of Sciences, Dr. Joel Lebowitz, visited Moscow. He passed on to the president of the Soviet Academy of Sciences, Anatoly P. Aleksandrov, a petition from American scientists urging that I be freed from exile and be allowed to return to Moscow or, if I should so choose, emigrate to the West. Aleksandrov replied that the exile was for my own welfare because I had been surrounded in Moscow by "dubious characters" through whom there had been a leak of information involving state secrets. That was an outrageous assertion. I have never had dealings with "dubious characters." My friends are honorable and decent people, all of whom are known to the KGB. If state secrets have been betrayed, any guilty persons (including me, first of all) should be put on trial. But the accusation about betrayal of secrets is nothing but slander. The response to the demand that I be allowed to emigrate was also somewhat strange: "We have signed the treaty on nonproliferation of nuclear weapons and we abide by it strictly." As if I were a hydrogen bomb!

I am frequently asked whether I am ready to emigrate. I feel that constant discussion of this matter in the press and many foreign broadcasts is premature, motivated by thirst for sensationalism. I feel that every person has the right to emigrate and, in principle, I do not exclude myself. But I do not regard this as a valid question for me at this time because the decision does not depend upon me anyway.

I regard as just and legal the demands of my foreign colleagues that my exile order be revoked and that I be allowed to return home or go to the West. These are my rights not only as a scientist but also as a human being. I am very grateful for the concern and for the clearly formulated demands.

This article is being taken to Moscow by my wife, my constant helper, who shares my exile and willingly takes upon herself the heavy burdens of traveling back and forth, handling my communications with the outside world, coping with the growing hatred of the KGB. Earlier, she withstood the poison of slander and insinuation, focused more on her than on me. The fact that I am Russian and my wife is half Jewish has proved useful for the internal purposes of the KGB.

Recently, someone appeared at the door of my mother-in-law at 5:30 A.M., describing himself as an officer of the KGB. He warned that if her daughter, meaning my wife, did not stop her trips back and forth from Gorky and stop inciting her husband with anti-Soviet statements, they would take certain measures. Earlier, some of our friends received letters with similar threats against my wife. Every time my wife leaves, I do not know whether she will be allowed to travel without hindrance and to return safely. My wife, although formally not under detention, is in greater danger than I am. I urge those who speak out on my behalf to keep this in mind. It is impossible to foresee what awaits us. Our only protection is the spotlight of public attention on our fate by friends around the world.

May 4, 1980

A MESSAGE FROM GORKY

by Andrei Sakharov

I am grateful and proud to accept this award, named for a remarkable man and scientist, Leo Szilard. I know of Szilard's outstanding scientific merits and of his public activity, which sprang from his innate, acute feeling of personal responsibility for the fate of mankind on our planet, and for the possible consequences of science's great victories.

In the years of Szilard's life and activity it became clearer than ever before how great the responsibility of scientists is to the society. And, to a large extent, it is due to Szilard that this awareness began to spread in the scientific community. Unfortunately, today, almost twenty years after Szilard died, the problems that disturbed him are not less acute or tragic.

Today, as then, the world is politically and ideologically divided into two opposing camps. Both sides are threatening each other with missiles and nuclear weaponry. Destructive capacity increases every year and has already reached a level at which its use would cause the deaths of hundreds of millions of people and cause destruction unprecedented in the history of mankind; create chaos, devastation and suffering; and hurl human society back centuries. The total annihilation of mankind and life on Earth is not out of the question—perhaps even with the existing reserves of nuclear arms—and is even more probable with the further quantitative and qualitative development of the means for mass destruction.

Meanwhile, the confrontations are not static. One glance at the map of the world today and in the first postwar years is enough to realize that the line separating the areas of prevailing influence has been continuously moving in one direction—to the benefit of the socialist camp. One could call this a manifestation of the laws of history; some might say of historical justice. Others might call this a socialist expansion replacing one sort of social and legal problems with others, no less acute and tragic. The most important thing is the objective result, which is a further aggravation of the international situation and an increasing danger of local conflicts growing into a worldwide clash.

The problems of the underdeveloped countries are as acute as they were earlier. There is no doubt that unevenness of development creates enormous suffering for the greater part of mankind and poses a threat to world stability. Maybe that is the main source of danger. To decrease that unevenness is one of the chief tasks of our time, demanding coordinated action by all countries, developed and developing. Unfortunately, the division of the world produces negative results in this matter as well. At present, the Soviet Union provides the developing countries with only very small amounts of technological and economic assistance—and only to those under its influence. Having practically withdrawn from participation in worldwide joint efforts, the Soviets have, however, become a major supplier of arms.

Since the late 1960s international terrorism, a sort of terrorist international of "left" and "right" groups, has become a serious destabilizing factor. Those states that directly or indirectly encourage these destructive forces are undoubtedly causing great harm to the entire world, their own people included.

One of the most tragic and dangerous events of recent years was the Soviet invasion of Afghanistan. Many tens of thousands of Afghanis have died in the three years of war; according to some estimates, the number of victims exceeds 100,000. Many Soviet soldiers have died. Millions of Afghanis have fled the horrors of war and left the country; about one-third of the population have become refugees. The Soviet invasion seriously aggravated the international situation, affected the rate of the arms race and, in particular, the fate of SALT II. If there are no changes for the better in the world, Afghanistan could become the Abyssinia of a new world war!

Today we ask ourselves once again: Does mutual nuclear terror serve as a deterrent against war? For almost 40 years the world has avoided a third world war. And, quite possibly, nuclear deterrence has been, to a considerable extent, the reason for this. But I am convinced that nuclear deterrence is gradually turning into its own antithesis and becoming a dangerous remnant of the past. The equilibrium provided by nuclear deterrence is becoming increasingly unsteady; increasingly real is the danger that mankind will perish if an accident or insanity or uncontrolled escalation draws it into a total thermonuclear war. In light of this it is necessary, gradually and carefully, to shift the functions of deterrence onto conventional armed forces, with all the economic, political and social consequences this entails. It is necessary to strive for nuclear disarmament. Of course, in all the intermediate stages of disarmament and negotiations, international security must be provided for, vis-à-vis any possible move by a potential aggressor. For this in particular one has to be ready to resist, at all the various possible stages in the escalation of a conventional or a nuclear war. No side must feel any temptation to engage in a limited or regional nuclear war.

There are two specific problems. One is that the main

part of the Soviet Union's nuclear potential is concentrated in gigantic land-based missiles. Essentially, this is a first-strike weapon. It is necessary to strive to eliminate these weapons or to reduce their number. There is little chance of this happening before the West has analogous missiles and is ready to eliminate them as well as the other means of nuclear war. The second problem is that the Soviet Union is not likely to eliminate its powerful medium-range missiles, which have upset the nuclear equilibrium in Europe and which threaten China and Japan, before the West deploys analogous missiles.

Certainly the ultimate goals are international security, the elimination and demolition of nuclear weaponry, and rapprochement—convergence by countries with different political systems. In the long run, convergence is the only alternative to global destruction. This goal cannot be achieved without profound political and ideological changes—both in the relations between socialist and Western countries, and within the countries themselves.

In the postwar years Niels Bohr, as well as Szilard and many other like-minded people, dreamed that open societies would provide an important and indispensable guarantee for international security. Since then, Stalin's tyrannical regime with its monstrous mass crimes has become a thing of the past in the Soviet Union. But the key features of the system formed under Stalin have basically survived. They are: the monopoly of the Party and the state in economics and ideology, which is even harsher in the political and military spheres; and the attendant violation of civil rights, which contradicts the principle of the openness of society—violations of freedom of conscience and the free flow of information; of the right to choose one's country of residence and place of residence within the country; the unfounded persecution of dissidents and prisoners of conscience. Of course, the scale of persecution cannot at all be compared to that of Stalin's times. But to persecute people for their convictions, people who have not resorted to violence or advocated it, is in essence inadmissible. I am certain that the plight of the prisoners of conscience—many of whom are sentenced to seven and even fifteen years of deprivation of freedom—cannot help but disturb us. It is very important to fight for each prisoner as an individual. Universal amnesty for prisoners of conscience in the Soviet Union and throughout the world would not only be an act of humanity but an important step on the path of strengthening international trust and security.

I would like once more to remind you of the profound alarm felt by our great predecessors—Einstein, Bohr, Russell, Szilard—for the fate of mankind, and of the ideas they left us. These ideas—about peace, about the danger that threatens mankind, about the importance of mutual understanding and tolerance, about the openness of society, the respect for human rights, the convergence of states with different political systems, the responsibility of scientists— are as important today as when they were expressed for the first time.

THE DANGER OF THERMONUCLEAR WAR

by Andrei Sakharov

© *Courtesy of Foreign Affairs*

An Open Letter to Dr. Sidney Drell*

Dear Friend:

I have read your two splendid lectures—the speech on nuclear weapons at Grace Cathedral, October 23, 1982, and the opening statement to Hearings on the Consequences of Nuclear War before the Subcommittee on Investigations and Oversight. What you say and write about the appalling dangers of nuclear war is very close to my heart and has disturbed me profoundly for many years now. I decided to address an open letter to you, feeling it necessary to take part in the discussion of this problem, one of the most important facing mankind.

In full agreement with your general theses, I will express

---

*Dr. Sidney Drell is deputy director of the Stanford Linear Accelerator Center.

certain considerations of a more specific nature which, I think, need to be taken into account when making decisions. These considerations in part contradict some of your statements and in part supplement and, possibly, amplify them. It seems to me that my opinion communicated here in open discussion can prove of interest in view of my scientific, technological, and psychological experience, acquired in the period when I took part in work on thermonuclear weapons, and also because I am one of the few independent participants in this discussion in the U.S.S.R.

II

I fully agree with your assessment of the danger of nuclear war. In view of the critical importance of this thesis, I will dwell on it in some detail, perhaps repeating what is already well known.

Here, and later on, I use the terms "nuclear war" and "thermonuclear war" nearly interchangeably. Nuclear weapons mean atomic and thermonuclear weapons; conventional weapons mean any weapons with the exception of three types with the capability of mass destruction—nuclear, chemical, and bacteriological weapons.

A large nuclear war would be a calamity of indescribable proportions and absolutely unpredictable consequences, with the uncertainties tending toward the worse.

According to data from United Nations experts, by the end of 1980 the world's overall supply of nuclear weapons consisted of 50,000 nuclear charges.* The total power of these charges (most of which are in the 0.04- to 20-megaton range) amounts to 13,000 megatons according to the ex-

---

*Editor's Note. "Charge" is a standard Soviet term—used frequently in arms control negotiations—embracing warheads on ballistic missiles and also armaments aboard bombers, which may be in bomb or missile form. There is a separate Russian word for warheads.

perts' estimates. The figures you have presented are not in conflict with those estimates. In this regard you mention that the total power of all the explosives used in the Second World War did not exceed six megatons (three megatons, according to the estimates with which I am familiar). However, when making this comparison one must take into account the greater relative efficacy of smaller charges with the same total power, but that does not alter the qualitative conclusions about the colossal destructive power of the nuclear weapons that have been amassed.

You also cite data according to which the U.S.S.R. at the present time (1982) has 8,000 thermonuclear charges deployed and the United States 9,000.† Many of these charges are warheads on ballistic missiles, and many of these are multiple independently-targetable reentry vehicles (MIRVs). It should be noted that the basis of the U.S.S.R.'s arsenal (70 percent, according to statements by TASS) consists of gigantic land-based missiles (in silos) and somewhat smaller intermediate-range missiles, on mobile launchers. Eighty percent of the U.S. arsenal consists of submarine-based nuclear missiles, much smaller but less vulnerable than silo-based missiles, and also of strategic bombers carrying nuclear bombs, some of which are apparently very powerful. It is doubtful whether masses of aircraft could penetrate Soviet territory deeply—but a more precise assessment of their capabilities must take the possibilities of cruise missiles into account; these would probably be able to penetrate the enemy's air defense systems.

Currently, the most powerful American ICBMs (I am not speaking of the planned MX) possess several times less throw-weight than the principal land-based Soviet missiles. The American ones carry fewer MIRVs, and the yield of their warheads is less. (It is assumed that when dividing the

†*Editor's Note.* These totals refer to the number of charges deployed on intercontinental ballistic missiles, submarine-launched ballistic missiles, and intercontinental-range bombers.

throw-weight of a missile among several warheads—let's say ten—the aggregate yield of the multiple warheads is less than the yield of a large single warhead on the same missile. But MIRVs greatly increase the ability of one side to attack compact targets on the other. MIRVs are also highly destructive against targets spread out over a wide area such as large cities. The aggregate yield may be less than that of a large single warhead, but the destructiveness will remain high because of the multiple blasts spread out over the area. I have dwelt on these details since they may prove of substance in further discussion.)

You cite the estimates of the international journal of the Royal Swedish Academy, according to which an attack on the principal cities of the Northern Hemisphere by 5,000 warheads with a total power of 2,000 megatons will kill 750 million people as a result of the shock wave alone.

I would like to add the following to that estimate:

1. The overall number of long-range nuclear weapons possessed by the five nuclear powers is three or four times greater than the figure used in the Swedish estimate and their overall power is six to seven times greater. The accepted average number of casualties per missile—250,000 people—cannot be considered an overestimate if one compares the accepted power of a thermonuclear charge of 400 kilotons with the power of the 17-kiloton explosion at Hiroshima and the number of victims from its shock waves, no fewer than 40,000.

2. An extremely important factor in the destructive capability of nuclear weapons is thermal radiation. The fires at Hiroshima were the cause of a significant portion (up to 50 percent) of the fatalities. With the increase of the charges' power, the relative role of thermal radiation increases. Therefore, this factor significantly increases the number of direct casualties.

3. During an attack on especially dense, compact enemy targets (like silo-based missile launchers, command points, communication centers, government institutions, shelters,

and other of the more important targets) it must be assumed that a significant portion of the explosions will be ground-level or low. In such cases there inevitably will be "traces," bands of dust fallout raised by the explosion from the surface and "impregnated" by the products of uranium fission. Therefore, although the direct radioactive effect of a nuclear charge takes place in a zone where everything alive is, in any case, annihilated by the shock wave and by fire, its indirect effect—through fallout—proves very substantial. The area contaminated by fallout so that the total dose of radiation exceeds the safety limit of 300 roentgens is, for a typical one-megaton nuclear charge, thousands of square kilometers!

During the ground-level test of the Soviet thermonuclear charge in August 1953, tens of thousands of people were evacuated beforehand from the zone where fallout was possible. People were only able to return to the settlement of Kara-aul in the spring of 1954! In war conditions an orderly evacuation is impossible. Hundreds of millions will flee in panic, often from one contaminated zone into another. Hundreds of millions of people will inevitably become the victims of radioactive irradiation, the mass migrations of people will make the chaos, the deterioration of sanitary conditions and the hunger all the greater. The genetic consequences of irradiation will threaten man as a biological species and all animal and plant life on the Earth.

I entirely agree with your basic idea that mankind has *never* encountered anything even remotely resembling a large nuclear war in scale and horror.

No matter how appalling the direct consequences of nuclear explosions, we cannot exclude that the indirect effects will be even more substantial. The indirect effects could be fatal for modern society, which is extraordinarily complex and thus highly vulnerable.

The general ecological consequences are just as danger-ous, although by virtue of the complex nature of ecological interdependencies, forecasts and estimates are extremely difficult here. I will mention some of the problems discussed in the literature (in your talks, in particular) without assessing their seriousness, although I am certain that many of the dangers indicated are entirely real:

1. Continuous forest fires could destroy the greater part of the planet's forests. The smoke involved would destroy the transparency of the atmosphere. A night lasting many weeks would ensue on Earth followed by a lack of oxygen in the atmosphere. As a result, this factor alone, if real, could destroy life on the planet. In less pronounced form, this factor could have important ecological, economic, and psychological consequences.

2. High-altitude wartime nuclear explosions in space (particularly the thermonuclear explosion on ABM missiles and the explosion of attacking missiles whose purpose is to disrupt enemy radar) could possibly destroy or seriously damage the ozone layer protecting Earth from the sun's ultraviolet radiation. Estimates of this danger are very imprecise—if the maximal estimates are true then this factor is sufficient to destroy life.

3. Disruption of transportation and communication could prove critical in the complex modern world.

4. No doubt there will be a (complete or partial) disruption in the production and distribution of food, in water supply and sewage, in fuel and electric service, and in medicine and clothing—all on a continent-wide scale. The public health-care system will be disrupted, sanitary conditions will revert to a medieval level and may become even worse than that. It will be impossible in practice to provide medical assistance to the hundreds of millions who have been wounded, burned, or exposed to radiation.

5. Hunger and epidemics in a context of chaos and devastation could take more lives than the nuclear explosions would take directly. It is also not out of the question that, along with the "ordinary" diseases which will inevitably spread far and wide—influenza, cholera, dysentery, typhus, anthrax, plague, and others—entirely new diseases could

arise as the result of the radiation-caused mutation of viruses as well as especially dangerous forms of the old diseases against which people and animals would have no immunity.

6. It is especially difficult to foresee mankind's maintaining any social stability in conditions of universal chaos. Great gangs will kill and terrorize people and struggle among themselves in keeping with the laws of the criminal world: "You die today, I'll die tomorrow."

Of course, our experience of social upheaval and war demonstrates that mankind possesses unexpected reserves; people's vitality in extreme situations surpasses what could have been imagined a priori. But even if mankind were able to preserve itself as a social body, which seems highly unlikely, the most important social institutions—the foundation of civilization—would be destroyed.

In sum, it should be said that all-out nuclear war would mean the destruction of contemporary civilization, hurl man back centuries, cause the death of hundreds of millions or billions of people, and, with a certain degree of probability, would cause man to be destroyed as a biological species and could even cause the annihilation of life on earth.

Clearly it is meaningless to speak of victory in a large nuclear war which is collective suicide.

I think that basically my point of view coincides with yours as well as with the opinion of a great many people on earth.

III

I am also in complete agreement with your other conclusions. I agree that if the "nuclear threshold" is crossed, i.e., if any country uses a nuclear weapon even on a limited scale, the further course of events would be difficult to control and the most probable result would be swift escalation leading from a nuclear war initially limited in scale or by region to an all-out nuclear war, i.e., to general suicide.

It is relatively unimportant how the "nuclear threshold" is crossed—as a result of a preventive nuclear strike or in the course of a war fought with conventional weapons, when a country is threatened with defeat, or simply as a result of an accident (technical or organizational).

In view of the above, I am convinced that the following basic tenet of yours is true: *Nuclear weapons only make sense as a means of deterring nuclear aggression by a potential enemy*, i.e., a nuclear war cannot be planned with the aim of winning it. Nuclear weapons cannot be viewed as a means of restraining aggression carried out by means of conventional weapons.

Of course you realize that this last statement is in contradiction to the West's actual strategy in the last few decades. For a long time, beginning as far back as the end of the 1940s, the West has not been relying on its "conventional" armed forces as a means sufficient for repelling a potential aggressor and for restraining expansion. There are many reasons for this—the West's lack of political, military, and economic unity; the striving to avoid a peacetime militarization of the economy, society, technology, and science; the low numerical levels of the Western nations' armies. All that at a time when the U.S.S.R. and the other countries of the socialist camp have armies with great numerical strength and are rearming them intensively, sparing no resources. It is possible that for a limited period of time the mutual nuclear terror had a certain restraining effect on the course of world events. But, at the present time, the balance of nuclear terror is a dangerous remnant of the past! In order to avoid aggression with conventional weapons one cannot threaten to use nuclear weapons if their use is inadmissible. One of the conclusions that follows here—and a conclusion you draw—is that it is necessary to restore strategic parity in the field of conventional weapons. This is expressed somewhat differently, and without stressing the point.

Meanwhile this is a very important and non-trivial statement which must be dwelt on in some detail.

The restoration of strategic parity is only possible by investing large resources and by an essential change in the psychological atmosphere in the West. There must be a readiness to make certain limited economic sacrifices and, most important, an understanding of the seriousness of the situation and of the necessity for some restructuring. In the final analysis, this is necessary to prevent nuclear war, and war in general. Will the West's politicians be able to carry out such a restructuring? Will the press, the public, and our fellow scientists help them (and not hinder them as is frequently now the case)? Can they succeed in convincing those who doubt the necessity of such restructuring? A great deal depends on it—the opportunity for the West to conduct a nuclear arms policy that will be conducive to the lessening of the danger of nuclear disaster.

In any case, I am very glad that you (and earlier, in another context, Professor Panofsky) have spoken out in favor of strategic parity in the area of conventional weapons.*

In conclusion, I should stress especially that a restructuring of strategy could of course only be carried out gradually and very carefully in order to prevent a loss of parity in some of the intermediate phases.

IV

As I have understood them, your further thoughts on nuclear weapons per se amount to the following:

It is necessary to conduct a balanced reduction of the nuclear arsenal, and a first stage in this process of nuclear disarmament might be a mutual freeze on the currently existing nuclear arsenals. I will quote you: "Decisions in the

---

Editor's Note. The reference here is to Wolfgang K. H. Panofsky, Professor of Physics at Stanford and Director of the Stanford Linear Accelerator Center. Professor Panofsky notes that the statement accurately reflects his views.

area of nuclear weapons should be based simply on the criterion of achieving a reliable deterrent and not on other additional demands relating to nuclear war since, generally speaking, such demands are not limited by anything and are not realistic." This is one of your central theses.

For talks on nuclear disarmament you propose that one quite simple—and, within the limits of the possible, fair—criterion for assessing nuclear strength be worked out. As that criterion you propose taking the sum total of the number of delivery vehicles and the total number of nuclear charges which can be delivered (probably one should assume the maximal number of certain standard or conventional charges which can be delivered by a given type of missile with a corresponding division of the usable weight).

I will begin by discussing that latter proposal of yours (made jointly with your student, Kent Wisner).* This proposal seems practical to me. Your criterion takes into account delivery vehicles of various throw-weights by assigning them various weight factors. This is very important—the assigning of an equal weight factor to both the small American missiles and the large Soviet missiles was one of the points for which I, at one time, criticized the SALT I Treaty (while in general viewing the very fact of the talks and the concluding of the Treaty in a positive light). Here, in distinction to criteria using the power of the charge, as a rule not published officially, the number of deliverable charges is easy to determine. Your criterion also takes into account the fact that, for example, five missiles each carrying one warhead have a significant tactical advantage over one large missile carrying five warheads. Of course, the criterion you

---

Editor's Note. The proposal was orginally set forth in Sidney D. Drell and Kent F. Wisner, "A New Formula for Nuclear Arms Control," *International Security*, Winter 1980/81, pp. 186–194, and is refined in Dr. Drell's "L+ RV: A Formula for Arms Control," *The Bulletin of the Atomic Scientists*, April 1982, pp. 28–34.

propose does not encompass all the parameters like distance, accuracy, or degree of vulnerability—they will have to be allowed for supplementarily or, in some cases, not taken into account so as to facilitate agreements.

I hope that your (or some analogous) criterion will be accepted as the basis for negotiations both on intercontinental missiles and (independently) on medium-range missiles. In both cases it will be much more difficult than it now is to insist on unfair conditions in the agreements and possible to move from word to deed more swiftly. Most likely, the very acceptance of your (or an analogous) criterion will require a diplomatic and propaganda struggle—but it's worth it.

V

From this relatively specific question I will move to one more general, more complex and controversial. Is it actually possible when making decisions in the area of nuclear weapons to ignore all the considerations and requirements relevant to the possible scenarios for a nuclear war and simply limit oneself to the criterion of achieving a reliable deterrent—when that criterion is understood to mean an arsenal sufficient to deal a devastating blow in response? Your answer to this question—while perhaps formulating it somewhat differently—is positive and you draw far-reaching conclusions.

There is no doubt that at present the United States already possesses a large number of submarine-based missiles and charges carried by strategic bombers which are not vulnerable to the U.S.S.R. and, in addition, has silo-based missiles though they are smaller than the U.S.S.R.'s—all these in such amounts that, were those charges used against the U.S.S.R., nothing, roughly speaking, would be left of it. You maintain that this has *already* created a reliable deterrent—independently of what the U.S.S.R. and the United States have and what they lack! Therefore, you specifically consider the building of the MX missile unnecessary and similarly consider irrelevant the arguments which are advanced in support of developing it—the U.S.S.R.'s substantial arsenal of intercontinental missiles with large throw-weight which the United States does not have; and the fact that Soviet missiles and MX missiles have multiple warheads so that one missile can destroy several enemy silos during a missile duel. Therefore you consider it acceptable (with certain reservations) for the United States to freeze the nuclear arsenals of the United States and the U.S.S.R. at their current numerical levels.*

Your line of reasoning seems to me very strong and convincing. But I think that the concept presented fails to take into account all the complex realities of the opposition that involves two world systems and that there is the necessity (despite your stance) for a more specific and comprehensive unbiased consideration than a simple orientation toward a "reliable deterrent" (in the meaning of the word as formulated above, i.e., the possibility of dealing a devastating retaliatory strike). I will endeavor to explain this statement.

Precisely because an all-out nuclear war means collective suicide, we can imagine that a potential aggressor might count on a lack of resolve on the part of the country under attack to take the step leading to that suicide, i.e., it could count on its victim capitulating for the sake of saving what could be saved. Given that, if the aggressor has a military

---

*Editor's Note. Professor Drell notes that maintaining the U.S. and Soviet nuclear arsenals at their present numerical levels is not the same as the kind of "freeze" usually discussed today—in that it would not preclude changes in the types of weapons within the numerical level. As to a strict "freeze" as usually discussed, Professor Drell's position, stated in his Grace Cathedral speech, is that "the freeze movement has been very helpful in creating... a constituency for arms control. Though I recognize some deficiencies of the freeze as literal policy, I support it and will vote for it as a mandate for arms control...."

advantage in some of the variants of conventional warfare or—which is also possible *in principle*—in some of the variants of partial (limited) nuclear war, he would attempt to use the fear of further escalation to force the enemy to fight the war on his (the aggressor's) own terms. There would be little cause for joy if, ultimately, the aggressor's hopes proved false and the aggressor country perished along with the rest of mankind.

You consider it necessary to achieve a restoration of strategic parity in the field of conventional arms. Now take the next logical step—while nuclear weapons exist it is also necessary to have strategic parity in relation to those variants of limited or regional nuclear warfare which a potential enemy could impose, i.e., it is really *necessary* to examine in detail the various scenarios for both conventional and nuclear war and to analyze the various contingencies. It is of course not possible to analyze fully all these possibilities or to ensure security entirely. But I am attempting to warn of the opposite extreme—"closing one's eyes" and relying on one's potential enemy to be perfectly sensible. As always in life's complex problems, some sort of compromise is needed.

Of course I realize that in attempting not to lag behind a potential enemy in any way, we condemn ourselves to an arms race that is tragic in a world with so many critical problems admitting of no delay. But the main danger is slipping into an all-out nuclear war. *If* the probability of such an outcome could be reduced at the cost of another ten or fifteen years of the arms race, then perhaps that price must be paid while, at the same time, diplomatic, economic, ideological, political, cultural, and social efforts are made to prevent a war.

Of course it would be wiser to agree now to reduce nuclear and conventional weapons and to eliminate nuclear weapons entirely. But is that now possible in a world poisoned with fear and mistrust, a world where the West fears aggression from the U.S.S.R., the U.S.S.R. fears aggression from the West and from China, and where China fears it from the U.S.S.R., and no verbal assurances and treaties can eliminate those dangers entirely?

I know that pacifist sentiments are very strong in the West. I deeply sympathize with people's yearning for peace, for a solution to world problems by peaceful means; I share those aspirations fully. But, at the same time, I am certain that it is absolutely necessary to be mindful of the specific political, military, and strategic realities of the present day and to do so objectively without making any sort of allowances for either side; this also means that one should not proceed from an a priori assumption of any special peace-loving nature in the socialist countries due to their supposed progressiveness or the horrors and losses they have experienced in war. Objective reality is much more complicated and far from anything so simple. People both in the socialist and the Western countries have a passionate inward aspiration for peace. This is an extremely important factor, but, I repeat, itself alone does not exclude the possibility of a tragic outcome.

VI

What is necessary now, I believe, is the enormous practical task of education so that specific, exact, and historically and politically meaningful objective information can be made available to all people, information that will enjoy their trust and not be veiled with dogma and propaganda. Here one must take into account that, in the countries of the West, pro-Soviet propaganda has been conducted for quite a long time and is very goal-oriented and clever, and that pro-Soviet elements have penetrated many key positions, particularly in the mass media.

The history of the pacifist campaigns against the deployment of missiles in Europe is telling in many respects. After all, many of those participating in those campaigns entirely ignore the initial cause of NATO's "dual decision"—the change in strategic parity in the 1970s in favor of the U.S.S.R.—and, when protesting NATO's plans, they have not advanced any demands on the U.S.S.R. Another example: President Carter's attempt to take a minimal step toward achieving balance in the area of conventional arms, i.e., to introduce draft registration, met with stiff resistance. Meanwhile, balance in the area of conventional arms is a necessary prerequisite for reducing nuclear arsenals. For public opinion in the West to assess global problems correctly, in particular the problems of strategic parity both in conventional and in nuclear weapons, a more objective approach, one which takes the real world strategic situation into account, is vitally needed.

A second group of problems in the field of nuclear weapons about which I should make a few supplementary remarks here concerns the talks on nuclear disarmament. For these talks to be successful the West should have something that it can give up! The case of the "Euromissiles" once again demonstrates how difficult it is to negotiate from a position of weakness. Only very recently has the U.S.S.R. apparently ceased to insist on its unsubstantiated thesis that a rough nuclear parity now exists and therefore everything should be left as it is.

Now, the next welcome step would be the reduction of the number of missiles—which must include a fair assessment of the *quality* of missiles and other means of delivery (i.e., the number of charges deliverable by each carrier, its range and accuracy, and its degree of vulnerability—the last being greater for aircraft and less for missiles; most likely, it would be expedient to use your criterion, or analogous ones). And what is absolutely at issue here is not moving the missiles beyond the Urals but *destroying* them. After all, rebasing is too "reversible." Of course, one also must not consider powerful Soviet missiles, with mobile launchers and several warheads, as being equal to the now-existing Pershing I, the British and French missiles, or the bombs on short-range bombers—as the Soviet side sometimes attempts to do for purposes of propaganda.

No less important a problem is that of the powerful silo-based missiles. At present the U.S.S.R. has a great advantage in this area. Perhaps talks about the limitation and reduction of these most destructive missiles could become easier if the United States were to have MX missiles, albeit only potentially (indeed, that would be best of all).

A few words about the military capabilities of powerful missiles: they can be used to deliver the largest thermo-nuclear charges for destroying cities and other major enemy targets—while for exhausting the enemy's ABM systems there will most likely be a simultaneous use of a "rain" of smaller missiles, false targets and so on. (Much is written about the possibility of developing ABM systems using super-powerful lasers, accelerated particle beams, and so forth. But the creation of an effective defense against missiles along these lines seems highly doubtful to me.) We present the following estimates to give an idea of what a powerful missile attack on a city would be like. Assuming that the maximal power of an individual charge carried by a large rocket would be of a magnitude of 15–25 megatons, we find that the area of complete destruction of dwellings would be 250–400 square kilometers, the area affected by thermal radiation would be 300–500 square kilometers, the zone of radioactive traces (in case of a ground-level explosion) would be 500–1000 kilometers long and 50–100 kilometers wide!

Of equal importance is the fact that powerful MIRVed missiles could be used to destroy compact enemy targets, in particular, similar silo-based enemy missiles. Here is a rough estimate of an attack of that type on launch sites. One hundred MX missiles (the number proposed by the Reagan Administration for the first round of deployment) could carry one thousand 600-kiloton warheads.

Considering the ellipse of concentration and the hardness

assumed for the Soviet launch sites, each of the warheads has, according to the data published in the American press, a 60 percent probability of destroying one launch site. During an attack on 500 Soviet launch sites, with two warheads targeted for each site, 16 percent will remain undamaged, i.e., "only" 80 missiles.

A specific danger associated with silo-based missiles is that they can be destroyed relatively easily as a result of enemy attack, as I have just demonstrated. At the same time, they can be used to destroy enemy launch sites in an amount four to five times larger than the number of missiles used for the attack. A country with large numbers of silo-based missiles (at the present time this is primarily the U.S.S.R., but if the United States carries out a major MX program, then it too) could be "tempted" to use such missiles first before the enemy destroys them. In such circumstances the presence of silo-based missiles constitutes a destabilizing factor.

In view of the above, it seems very important to me to strive for the abolition of powerful silo-based missiles at the talks on nuclear disarmament. While the U.S.S.R. is the leader in this field there is very little chance of its easily relinquishing that lead. If it is necessary to spend a few billion dollars on MX missiles to alter this situation, then perhaps this is what the West must do. But, at the same time, if the Soviets, in deed and not just in word, take significant verifiable measures for reducing the number of land-based missiles (more precisely, for destroying them), then the West should not only abolish MX missiles (or not build them!) but carry out other significant disarmament programs as well.

On the whole I am convinced that nuclear disarmament talks are of enormous importance and of the highest priority. They must be conducted continuously—in the brighter periods of international relations but also in the periods when relations are strained—and conducted with persistence, foresight, firmness and, at the same time, with flexibility and initiative. In so doing, political figures should not think of exploiting those talks, and the nuclear problem in general, for their own immediate political gains but only for the long-term interests of their country and the world. And the planning of the talks should be included in one's general nuclear strategy as its most important part—on this point as well I am in agreement with you!

VII

The third group of problems which should be discussed here is political and social in nature. A nuclear war could result from a conventional war, while a conventional war is, as is well known, a result of politics. We all know that the world is not at peace. There are a variety of reasons for this—national, economic, and social reasons, as well as the tyranny of dictators.

Many of the tragic events now occurring have their roots in the distant past. It would absolutely be wrong to see only Moscow's hand everywhere. Still, when examining the general trend of events since 1945 there has been a relentless expansion of the Soviet sphere of influence—objectively, this is nothing but Soviet expansion on a world scale. This process has spread as the U.S.S.R. has grown stronger economically (though that strength is one-sided), and in scientific, technological and military terms, and has today assumed proportions dangerously harmful to international equilibrium. The West has grounds to worry that the world's sea routes, Arab oil, and the uranium, diamonds, and other resources of South Africa are now threatened.

One of the basic problems of this age is the fate of the developing countries, the greater part of mankind. But, in fact, for the U.S.S.R., and to some degree for the West as well, this problem has become exploitable and expendable in the struggle for dominance and strategic interests. Millions of people are dying of hunger every year, hundreds of millions suffer from malnutrition and hopeless poverty. The West provides the developing countries with economic and technological aid, but this remains entirely insufficient due largely to the rising price of crude oil. Aid from the U.S.S.R. and the socialist countries is smaller in scale and, to a greater degree than the West's aid, military in nature and bloc-oriented. And, very importantly, that aid is in no way coordinated with world efforts.

The hot spots of local conflicts are not dying but are rather threatening to grow into global wars. All this is greatly alarming.

The most acutely negative manifestation of Soviet policies was the invasion of Afghanistan which began in December 1979 with the murder of the head of state. Three years of appallingly cruel anti-guerrilla war have brought incalculable suffering to the Afghan people, as attested by the more than four million refugees in Pakistan and Iran.

It was precisely the general upsetting of world equilibrium caused by the invasion of Afghanistan and by other concurrent events which was the fundamental reason that the SALT II agreement was not ratified. I am with you in regretting this but I cannot disregard the reasons I have just described.

Yet another subject closely connected to the problem of peace is the openness of society and human rights. I use the term the "openness of society" to mean precisely what the great Niels Bohr meant by it when introducing it more than 30 years ago.

In 1948, the U.N.'s member states adopted the Universal Declaration of Human Rights and stressed its significance for maintaining peace. In 1975, the relationship of human rights and international security was proclaimed by the Helsinki Final Act, which was signed by 35 countries including the U.S.S.R. and the United States. Among those rights are: the right to freedom of conscience; the right to receive and impart information within a country and across frontiers;

the right to a free choice of one's country of residence and domicile within a country; freedom of religion; and freedom from psychiatric persecution.

Finally, citizens have the right to control their national leaders' decision-making in matters on which the fate of the world depends. But we don't even know how, or by whom, the decision to invade Afghanistan was made! People in our country do not have even a fraction of the information about events in the world and in their own country which the citizens of the West have at their disposal. The opportunity to criticize the policy of one's national leaders in matters of war and peace as you do freely is, in our country, entirely absent. Not only critical statements but those merely factual in nature, made on even much less important questions, often entail arrest and a long sentence of confinement or psychiatric prison.

In keeping with the general nature of this letter, I refrain here from citing many specific examples, but must mention the fate of Anatoly Shcharansky, who is wasting away in Chistopol Prison for the right to be visited by his mother and to write to her, and Yuri Orlov who, now for a third time, has been put for six months in the punishment block of a Perm labor camp, after having been beaten unmercifully in the presence of a warden.

In December 1982 there was an amnesty to honor the U.S.S.R.'s sixtieth anniversary but, just as in 1977 and in the preceding amnesties, there was a point made of excluding prisoners of conscience. So distant is the U.S.S.R. from the principles it proclaims, a country which bears such great responsibility for the fate of the world!

VIII

In conclusion I again stress how important it is that the world realize the absolute inadmissibility of nuclear war, the collective suicide of mankind. It is impossible to win a nuclear war. What is necessary is to strive, systematically though carefully, for complete nuclear disarmament based on strategic parity in conventional weapons. As long as there are nuclear weapons in the world, there must be a strategic parity of nuclear forces so that neither side will venture to embark on a limited or regional nuclear war. Genuine security is possible only when based on a stabilization of international relations, a repudiation of expansionist policies, the strengthening of international trust, openness and pluralization in the socialist societies, the observance of human rights throughout the world, the rapprochement—convergence—of the socialist and capitalist systems, and worldwide coordinated efforts to solve global problems.

February 2, 1983   Andrei Sakharov

WHEN HONOR AND CONSCIENCE ARE LOST

Izvestia *July 3, 1983*

AFTER OPENING AN ISSUE OF THE AMERICAN Magazine *Foreign Affairs* and seeing a long article by Academician Andrei Sakharov in it, we began reading it prepared for anything. We know well that Sakharov tries to besmirch all we hold dear, that he slanders his own nation, presenting it to the external world as some sort of gray, completely uncivilized mass.

Sakharov's creation in *Foreign Affairs* amazed us nevertheless. Pretending to enter into a polemic with Sidney Drell, an American professor at Stanford University who supports a freeze of existing Soviet and American nuclear arsenals, Sakharov urges the U.S. and the West under no circumstances to agree to any limitations on the arms race in general and on nuclear weapons in particular. He directly importunes the leaders in Washington to stick to their militarist course, their course toward confrontation with the Soviet Union and toward military supremacy, arguing that the United States and NATO should not slacken the arms race for another ten to fifteen years at least.

This may seem improbable, but what follows turns black into white. Sakharov warns his addressees against "relying on the enemy to be perfectly sensible." Who is this "enemy"? The Soviet Union, the country where Sakharov lives. He warns America's bosses: Do not believe in the peace-loving nature of the socialist countries. Openly, without embarrassment, Sakharov approves U.S. and NATO plans to deploy American Pershing 2's and cruise missiles in Western Europe, first-strike weapons which will be targeted on our own and other Socialist countries. Sakharov argues that if Washington possesses MX missiles which are also known to be first-strike weapons, then the "United States will find it easier to conduct talks" with the USSR.

We returned several times to these points in Sakharov's article. We experienced a strange sensation: Was it really Sakharov writing all this? We had heard and read it many times before. Secretary of Defense Weinberger makes exactly the same statements. President Reagan speaks like that. It is the language of American generals and political extremists. Sakharov needs only to term the USSR "evil incarnate" and to announce a "crusade" against Communism for them to place him in the Pentagon or the White House.

One other aspect seems unbelievable. Sakharov is a scientist. He knows the facts and is quite well aware of the possible consequences of the actions he urges on the government of a country which has tested weapons of mass destruction on human beings once before. Then the U.S. rained down atomic death on Japanese cities. American leaders wanted to show off their strength to the world and to our country in particular. Sakharov today is really suggesting the use of the monstrous force of nuclear weapons to intimidate the Soviet people again, to compel our country to capitulate before an American ultimatum. And to what country and "civilization" does he belong, and what does he want in the end? Can he really not understand that the build-up of weapons which he advocates threatens not just our country which lost 20,000,000 people in the last war, but every nation without exception and human civilization itself?

And now we begin to think about Sakharov not simply as a scientist. What kind of man is he to fall so low morally, to come to hate his own country and its people? We see in his actions a violation of the norms of humanitarian and decent behavior which we suppose to be obligatory for every civilized person.

We know that Sakharov is very popular with those Americans who would like to wipe our country and socialism off the face of the earth. Such friends are always raising a hullabaloo about "the tragic fate of Sakharov." We do not wish to discuss this boundless hypocrisy right now. No, our government, our people have been more than tolerant toward this man who is living peacefully in Gorky from whence he issues his misanthropic creations.

Here is what comes to mind. Exactly thirty years ago this summer, one of the most unjust and shameful events of the twentieth century took place in the U.S. The American authorities executed the scientists Ethel and Julius Rosenberg. Their execution was based on absurd and foul charges. The "evidence" was fabricated by American secret services. And by the way, in distinction from Sakharov who calls for nuclear blackmail directed against his own country and for making possible a nuclear first-strike against us, the Rosenbergs were not simply innocent persons who fell victim to the pitiless mechanism of American "justice." They had spoken out for the destruction of lethal weapons. And they were completely honest, humane people.

To speak of honesty when a man actually calls for a war against his own country is difficult. Several centuries ago Erasmus said that only those few base persons whose own well-being depends on popular misfortune wage war.

Of course, it is not really Erasmus who is at issue. But even in his time, decent, thinking people were not blinded by hatred, and they did not lose honor and conscience.

Academicians

Anatoly Dorodnitsyn
Alexander Prokhorov
Georgi Skryabin
Andrei Tikhonov

SIDNEY DRELL'S REPLY

September 20, 1983

Dear Andrei,

I was very happy to receive your important open letter to me on the dangers of thermonuclear war. Its publication in *Foreign Affairs* received considerable attention and your message was repeated widely in a number of commentaries as well as in Congressional debate. I was not at all surprised that we are in complete agreement on the fundamental issues. I am writing here to comment to you directly on our specific differences that were identified in your letter.

Repeatedly I have been asked to write publicly about those differences, with particular reference to your qualified endorsement of the MX missile project. I concluded, however, that such a public exchange would not serve a constructive purpose and would instead focus attention even more heavily on just that one topic. As it is, I was unhappy that so much of the attention given by the media to your letter emphasized only the MX question because of its timeliness for the U.S. Congressional vote. Too little of the public commentary addressed the more basic issues that you discussed so beautifully in your essay: the dangers and the scale of disaster of nuclear war, which would be an act of suicide with no winners; the role of nuclear weapons solely to deter *nuclear* aggression; the importance of establishing and maintaining a parity in conventional arms in order not to feel driven to a nuclear "first use" policy; the grave dangers of escalation up the ladder once the nuclear threshold is crossed; the overriding importance of arms negotiations and reductions; your, as always, eloquently stated concerns about human rights and the waste of the world's resources on weapons. I also agree with your judgment of the unlikelihood that a "star wars" ballistic missile defense is practical, and I was pleased to receive your general endorsement of my specific formula for arms control; that is, counting the aggregate total of numbers of warheads plus launchers which is a simple and balanced scheme and provides a practical framework for productive negotiations.

Your open letter to me, translated into English by Efrem and his friend, Richard Lourie, actually arrived just after I had delivered a set of three public lectures on the threat of nuclear weapons at the University of Washington in Seattle. These lectures were published in book form and, with Efrem's permission, I included your important letter in the book in order to emphasize our similar principles, as well as our specific differences. I hope this will be a valuable contribution to public understanding and discussion. These lectures describe more fully some of my views that were contained in the testimony and the Grace Cathedral speech which I left with Elena last December. I hope they will give you a more complete and balanced appreciation of my own views on these issues, especially the freeze and the MX.

What I'm most interested to discuss here are the concerns that you raised about the freeze movement and your discussion of the meaning and requirements of deterrence, which underlie your "qualified" endorsement for the MX missile. Concerning the freeze, as is emphasized in my lectures, to me it represents an important step in creating a public awareness of the grave danger of nuclear weapons, a subject that you and I have both spoken of so frequently. I do not view a freeze literally as practical policy. I do value very much the *form* the freeze movement has taken in the United States thus far. It has contributed to creating an effective public constituency that is now participating constructively in our policy debates and is a force in our elections. I discuss the importance of having such a public constituency in the third chapter in my book. It is in this sense only that I have given the freeze the limited endorsement that I expressed in these and other lectures.

As I view it, a freeze has two specific problems. The first is that, as represented in the American debate, what is properly called for is a mutual, verifiable freeze, and I believe the enormous difficulties of negotiating such a treaty would cause great delays in achieving anything concrete. Therefore, in my own expressions for the freeze, I caution supporters not to view the freeze as a simple and easily achieved *alternative* to the difficult hard-nosed negotiations on arms control that are required if we are fully to meet our national security needs. Secondly, as a proponent of the condition of deterrence with the qualifications described in my lectures (Chapter One in the book), I can support programs for developing new weapons which do not increase destructive power but which do improve the security and survivability of deterrent forces. They can enhance crisis stability and thus help prevent war. So much for my views on the freeze which, to repeat, in the American debate, I believe, has been extraordinarily valuable as a *mandate* for arms control by marshaling public opinion to a degree that has not heretofore existed. I hope you will not be too hard on this view.

Let me next turn to the MX missile and deterrence. I understand the qualified nature of your support for the MX which you view even in its "potential" only as useful for making progress in arms negotiations. This argument has often been given by supporters of the MX in this country and your letter was cited frequently during Congressional debate leading to authorization to build twenty-one MX missiles starting this coming year. Congressional action to appropriate funds for this program is still pending. I think it is important, however, to clarify what helps and what hurts deterrence in considering weapons programs. I won't repeat the discussion of this fully in this letter, but I would ask you to read my first chapter, in particular the sections on "Deterrence" and on "Deterrence and the MX" between pages 11 and 24. I believe that the key point for deterrence, including an appropriate measure of flexible response, is to deploy a retaliatory force that is based securely and survivably. This the MX is not. In fixed silos it is just a vulnerable, first-strike threat. I comment further on this important issue in the Appendix in my response to the Scowcroft Commission recommendations.

Ultimately the MX deployment question is one of *judgment* as to how to make progress in political negotiations. This is not an area in which I consider myself an expert. Also, I well understand that the good fortune, and indeed the luxury, of my own personal circumstances as compared to yours may contribute to my being less, as we say in the U.S., "hard-nosed" on these negotiating matters. It is, indeed, important for the U.S. to negotiate with the Soviet Union with a strong position, but I believe we should do it with weapons and weapons programs that serve a valid purpose to enhance deterrence and not with weapons which, being vulnerably based and at the same time capable of first-strike, are just opposite to the requirements for stable deterrence. The United States is currently in the midst of a broad range of modernization programs, which are much more important than the MX. These include new cruise missiles, bombers, submarines, and SLBM's which will substantially improve the security and deterrent value of our strategic nuclear forces. In this circumstance, I think it would be much more sensible for the U.S. and also, eventually, for the Soviet Union to go ahead only with those military forces that meet our valid military and security objectives for deterrence and to reject political "bargaining chips" that introduce still more dangerous military characteristics. Like you, I would like to see us diminish reliance on vulnerable, big, land-based ICBM's. I do not see the MX as necessary en route to progress.

Since the summer I have had many radio and television interviews, talking about you and Elena, as a result of the letter you sent me. On all those occasions I said how much I look forward to the day when we can sit together once again and when we can discuss these and many other important, and more pleasant, topics in person. I will pursue with unflagging energy my efforts toward that end in all my Russian contacts and statements. Meanwhile, it is a pleasure to be in touch with Tanya, Efrem, Lisa, and Alexei and their children. I hope you and Elena stay well, and I hope to hear from you soon.

Warmest greetings
Sidney Drell

A LETTER TO MY COLLEAGUES

by Andrei Sakharov

November 1983

Dear Friends!

Two years ago your support played a vital role in re-solving the problem of my daughter-in-law Liza Alexeye-va's departure to join her husband. I turn to you once again concerning a matter of critical importance which could have tragic consequences. I ask your help in securing permission for my wife to travel abroad for medical care. (Treatment for her life-threatening cardiac condition is the first priority, but she also needs treatment and an operation for her eyes.) She would like to see her children and grandchildren after a five-year separation. She could visit her mother and possibly bring her back to the Soviet Union.

We believe that medical treatment of my wife in the USSR would be dangerous. Believe me, this is not a case of un-justified "nerves" or of a search for confrontation. My wife has suffered for many years from an unprecedented cam-paign of slander and from intense pressure exerted directly on her as well as on her children and grandchildren. Threats were made to kill her grandchildren. Six years ago we were forced to the decision that it would be better if the children and grandchildren emigrated. This has brought about the tragic separation of our family with an almost complete lack of communication adding to our sorrow. After the departure first of our children and then of Liza Alexeyeva two years ago, my wife Elena Bonner became the sole hostage of my public activity. The whole responsibility for my statements has been shifted onto her. But that is only a part of the problem as I see it. The KGB appraises Elena's role in my life and public activity very highly and seeks to eliminate her moral influence and, I have reasons to fear, her physical presence as well. A unique and unbearable situation has been created. In thinking and speaking about the Sakharov case, you should keep this major complication in mind.

A campaign of slander has been mounted to discredit my wife. Soviet propaganda depicts her as the instigator of all my statements and as a Zionist agent of the CIA. This assertion spiced with scandalous and sophisticated slander about my wife's moral qualities and mythical past crimes was repeated in 1983 by three publications so that millions of people have read this sensational lie: N. N. Yakovlev's book *The CIA Against the USSR* (200,000 copies) and Yakovlev's articles in the magazines *Smena* (1,170,000 circulation) and *Chelovek i Zakon* (8,700,000 circulation). The appearance of Yakovlev's articles coincided with publication in the newspaper *Izvestia* of a letter signed by Academicians A. A. Dorodnitsyn, A. M. Prokhorov, G. K. Skryabin, and A. N. Tikhonov which deliberately and outrageously misrepresented my views on nuclear war, peace and disarmament. In violation of common sense, my wife was saddled with that burden as well. It has been used to incite popular hatred and denunciation. Thousands of letters, passersby on the street, passengers sharing her compartment on the train savagely accuse my wife of being a Zionist, an agitator, a traitor to the motherland, a murderer.

Elena was subjected to all this shortly after suffering a

heart attack on April 25. The infarct was extensive and severe. Later attacks damaged more heart tissue. My wife's condition is still not stabilized and remains life-threatening. Her most recent attack, a severe one, occurred in October.

We attempted during May and June to secure our joint admission to the hospital of the USSR Academy of Sciences. That would have alleviated at least some of the fears which I have mentioned. Our effort failed, even though a commission of physicians visited me in Gorky and confirmed that my health problems require my hospitalization. My wife has been, in fact, left without medical care. Policemen are stationed at the door of our Moscow apartment just as in Gorky. Doctors hesitate to visit her, fearing the consequences. The telephone in our Moscow apartment was disconnected in 1980, and the nearby coin telephone was disconnected right after Elena's heart attack. This is certainly no sheer coincidence. In case of a sudden attack, she cannot even call an ambulance.

I fear—and I believe the fear is justified—that if Elena were to be hospitalized, some means may be found to bring about her death. The risk would be greater if she were alone, but it would not be completely eliminated by my presence. (The danger, of course, is there at home as well.) Even if I am exaggerating the danger, the public harassment and constant KGB interference preclude any possibility for serious medical treatment. When my wife was a patient in the Moscow Eye Hospital in 1974, she was advised in confidence to sign herself out immediately for the sake of her life and health. The situation has grown many times worse since then! Now the only acceptable solution is for my wife to go abroad. That is the only way to save her. Elena applied for an exit visa in September 1982 when an eye operation became an urgent necessity. Elena's eyes still require treatment. But since her infarct, treatment for her heart disease has taken priority and cannot be postponed. Her application has not been answered despite the regulations in force. I sent a letter on November 10 to the Soviet Head of State Yuri Andropov requesting permission for my wife's trip.

I appeal to my colleagues abroad and in the USSR, to public figures and government officials in all countries, to our friends everywhere. Save my wife Elena Bonner!

Translated by Khronika Press.

ANDREI SAKHAROV'S APPEAL ON BEGINNING HIS HUNGER STRIKE

The following appeal was written by Andrei Sakharov in January 1984. It was released by Efrem Yankelevich on May 8 after he received word that Andrei Sakharov had begun a hunger strike on May 2.

To All My Friends in the World

I appeal to my scientific colleagues, to public personalities and to statesmen, to all who have ever spoken out in my defense or who are willing to speak now, at this tragic moment in our lives.

I am beginning a hunger strike with the demand that my wife, Elena Bonner, must be allowed to travel abroad to get medical treatment and, to see her mother, children, and grandchildren.

On April 25 of last year, she suffered a severe myocardial infarct. She has not recovered from that heart attack, and, in some respects, her condition has become worse and threatens her life. During this entire period she has been denied any real medical care. Under present conditions, with an all-out slander campaign organized against her and with constant KGB interference, my wife cannot receive effective treatment in the USSR. More than that, it might be extremely dangerous. I note, in particular, that official propaganda has saddled my wife with responsibility for my public statements, has proclaimed her an imperialist and Zionist agent, and has spread everywhere monstrous slander about her.

The only possible solution now is for my wife, Elena Bonner, to go abroad.

In September 1982 Elena Bonner applied for a visa. On November 10, 1983, I wrote a letter to the head of the Soviet State, Yuri Andropov. We have received no response.

In 1981 we were forced to go on a hunger strike in order to obtain permission for our daughter-in-law to leave the USSR to join her husband. World public opinion was of enormous help in resolving that tragic problem.

Now, once again, I see no alternative to a hunger strike. My wife's health prevents her from taking part in the hunger strike which I am starting. My hunger strike will be indefinite—I will end it only when my wife is allowed abroad. Her death will be mine as well. Once again, as I did two years ago, I ask for your help. Save us!

CHRONICLE OF DISAPPEARANCE

THE LAST TIME AN ACTUAL EYEWITNESS REPORT of the Sakharovs was received in the West was on May 6, 1984. Since that time, no one has actually reported having seen Andrei Sakharov and Elena Bonner.

Set forth on these pages is a chronological account of the disappearance of the Sakharovs, from the time Dr. Sakharov began his hunger strike to secure medical treatment for his wife, until editing for this journal:

• May 2, 1984—Andrei Sakharov begins hunger strike. Mrs. Sakharov does not arrive in Moscow by train from Gorky, as expected.

• May 4, 1984—TASS* reports that "timely measures" prevented a "ploy" by U.S. diplomats to give Mrs. Sakharov political asylum.

• May 6, 1984—Irina Kristi, a family friend, sees the Sakharovs at their apartment, and learns that Mrs. Sakharov has been charged with defaming the Soviet state and is restricted to Gorky.

• May 8, 1984—The information released by Irina Kristi appears in the Western press. Mrs. Kristi

---

*A U.S.S.R. press agency.

is placed under house arrest for releasing the information to the press.

• May 21, 1984—Conflicting reports on the whereabouts of the Sakharovs are received by French Communist Party leader George Marchais and the First Secretary of the French Socialist Party, Lionel Jospin. Both men received information from Soviet sources.

Soviet government paper *Izvestia* carries a report saying Sakharov is not on a hunger strike.

• May 30, 1984—A friend of the Sakharovs' from Moscow finds their Gorky apartment dark and apparently empty.

A TASS statement provides vague assurances that the Sakharovs are alive and well, but provides no information on their actual whereabouts.

• June 3, 1984—The *London Sunday Times* says sources in Moscow have reported that *Sakharov died May 31* in a Gorky hospital.

• June 4, 1984—TASS reports the Sakharovs' good health and safety, denying responsibility for their whereabouts. *"We are not going to take under protection Sakharov and Bonner,"* the TASS statement said.

• June 6, 1984—USSR Mission to the UN states the Sakharovs are alive and well in Gorky.

At a Moscow press conference, Soviet Academy of Sciences Vice-president Ovchinnikov declares that Sakharov is in Gorky.

- June 20, 1984—German newspaper carries separate photographs of the Sakharovs reported to have been taken within a week of publication. Source of photographs is Viktor Louis, a Soviet journalist linked to the KGB.

  In desperation, the Sakharov stepchildren offer a $10,000 reward *"to the first person who supplies us with information leading to direct contact between us and Dr. and Mrs. Sakharov."*

- June 21, 1984—Soviet spokesman Leonid Zamyatin declares that Sakharov is "alive and well and eating normally," but in spite of these assurances, when visiting French President Mitterrand raises the issue at a state dinner at the Kremlin, he receives no information on the Sakharovs.

- June 26, 1984—A telegram dated June 22, allegedly from Bonner and Sakharov in Gorky, arrives in Newton, Massachusetts, stating: "Don't worry. We are alive and healthy."

- June 30, 1984—Letter from Soviet dissident to friend in West Germany reports Elena Bonner is in her Gorky apartment, and is allowed to leave only in the company of two guards.

- July 9, 1984—Soviet spokesman Zagladin says Sakharov is well and writing a scientific article which will soon be published.

- July 10, 1984—Unidentified source reports that Sakharov is being treated by Dr. Vladimir Rozhnov, a Soviet *psychiatrist* who flies from Moscow to Gorky every other day.

• July 11, 1984—Psychiatric source in Moscow confirms reports about Rozhnov, and states Sakharov is being treated with mind-altering drugs and/or hypnosis to induce him to sign a document recanting his human rights activities.

• July 26, 1984—Exiled Soviet author Lev Kopelev, during interview in Stuttgart, says reliable Moscow sources stated that Sakharov occupies a special room in the Semashko Hospital in Gorky, to which the hospital staff has no access. Kopelev confirms that Sakharov may well be hypnotized and force-fed, in view of twice-weekly visits by Rozhnov, chief of psychotherapy in a well-known Moscow Institute, and a specialist since 1955 in hypnosis and psychopharmacology. Kopelov states that Elena Bonner is not allowed to visit her husband, and that her whereabouts are unknown.

• August 6, 1984—A report of contact made by an acquaintance with Mrs. Sakharov in Gorky was received by a friend of Sakharov in Moscow. It was reported that Sakharov had ended his hunger strike and was being held in the hospital.

• August 7, 1984—Sakharov friend questions that report, citing two letters from Mrs. Sakharov stating that she has not seen her husband since May 7th and is unaware of his condition.

• August 17, 1984—Radio Moscow states that Andrei Sakharov is alive, well, living in Gorky, and receiving not only medical care, but his full pension as well.

- August 22, 1984—Soviet authorities release film showing Sakharov eating in a hospital in Gorky, reading a July 16 issue of *Newsweek* magazine, and depicting Mrs. Bonner separately in Gorky.

- August 23, 1984—Western world views Soviet video film of Sakharov on ABC Network News program.

- August 24, 1984—Reagan Administration reacts to tapes, saying they are aimed at turning attention away from report that Mrs. Bonner has been sent into internal exile for "slandering the Soviet State." State Department spokesman Alan Romberg said the U.S. would continue to insist that independent observers visit the couple, and that the tapes *"prove nothing about the Sakharovs' present condition."*

   Tatiana Yankelevich said that while the narration in the film claims friends are allowed to visit her mother, a woman shown visiting Mrs. Bonner is actually Moscow defense lawyer Yelena Reznikova. *"This shows that either my mother has already been tried or is awaiting trial,"* Bonner's daughter said.

- August 25, 1984—The West German newspaper *Bild* reports that Elena Bonner has been sentenced to five years of internal exile, and quotes an unidentified government official in Moscow as saying Mrs. Sakharov *"was and is in Gorky."* Elena Bonner was apparently arrested on her way to seek asylum in the U.S. Embassy in Moscow, and was tried and sentenced for breaking Article 190-1 of the Soviet Penal Code that forbids "slander of the Soviet state and social system."

• September 11, 1984—Soviet journalist Viktor Louis told West Germany's *Bild* newspaper that Sakharov rejoined his wife in their Gorky apartment, that "considering the circumstances, he is well" and "he has resumed his private life."

• September 13, 1984—The L.A. *Times* reported that Soviet officials published a new article by Sakharov in the August 28th edition of the *Soviet Journal of Experimental and Theoretical Physics*. Western world views this as an attempt to convince the world Sakharov is well and at work, inasmuch as the article was submitted for publication March 14, and there is no official confirmation that Sakharov submitted another article on the same topic in August. Soviet sources who are friends of the Sakharovs reportedly confirmed that Bonner has been tried and sentenced to five years of internal exile—the first such information from Moscow sources with close ties to the Sakharovs since reports in August that Bonner had been sentenced.

• September–October, 1984—Postcards signed by Elena Bonner begin to arrive at the Sakharovs' friends in Moscow and relatives in the United States. The postcards shed no light on the events of spring–summer 1984. Postcards imply that the Sakharovs are reunited in their Gorky apartment around September 7 and are both confined to the city limits.

• November 1984—Photograph of the Sakharovs, made on September 11, and mailed by Elena Bonner, is received by her children in the United States.

Colleagues of Dr. Sakharov from the Lebedev Institute of the Soviet Academy of Sciences are reportedly allowed to visit Sakharov.

• December 15, 1984—Pictures of the Sakharovs are released by the Soviet authorities, again through the German newspaper *Bild*. These pictures, shot by a hidden camera, apparently in the middle of October, show the Sakharovs in a park and at the entrance to a movie theatre.

The release of the pictures coincides with the arrival of Mr. Michael Gorbachev, a ranking member of the Politburo, in Lon-

don, the beginning of his well-pub-
licized visit to England.

"Chronicle of Disappearance" was compiled by the International
League for Human Rights.

WHERE ARE THE SAKHAROVS?

Khronika Press

FROM A VARIETY OF SOURCES, A SOMEWHAT BETter if still tentative reconstruction of what has happened to the Sakharovs over the past eight months is now possible.

Elena Bonner was prevented on May 2, 1984, from leaving Gorky for a scheduled visit to Moscow. Dr. Sakharov began a hunger strike on that day to protest the authorities' action and to secure a response to Mrs. Sakharov's application to go abroad for medical treatment. Her application had been pending for eighteen months, and the Sakharovs had exhausted all possible avenues of help, including personal appeals to Andropov, to Chernenko, and to the USSR Academy of Sciences.

Dr. Sakharov was removed from from the Gorky apartment by the authorities sometime in May. While it is difficult to confirm details, it seems likely that he was hospitalized in Gorky's Semashko Hospital where he was artificially fed through a nasal tube which caused painful blistering. Drugs were administered while he was in the hospital, but their nature and purpose are unknown. Evidently, Dr. Sakharov discontinued his hunger strike after he came to the conclusion that its continuation could serve no useful purpose. He began to take food voluntarily sometime in late June or July. In September, he asked to return to his apartment. When permission was refused, he either threatened to resume or actually resumed his hunger strike, and on September 7 he was allowed to return to the Gorky apartment where he was reunited with Mrs. Sakharov. He was in poor physical and psychological condition, withdrawn and depressed. He began to emerge from this depression and return to his scientific work in October. At Dr. Sakharov's invitation, two or three scientists from the USSR Academy of Sciences visited him in mid-November to discuss his scientific work. At the present time Dr. Sakharov is probably in reasonable physical and mental condition, considering his recent ordeal and chronic medical problems.

On May 2, Mrs. Sakharov was detained in Gorky on her way to Moscow and informed that she was under investigation on charges of slandering the Soviet system (Article 190-1 of the RSFSR Criminal Code).

After May 2, Mrs. Sakharov was kept in Gorky under strict surveillance. In August, she was tried in Gorky and sentenced to five years internal exile. (Her lawyer was the Moscow attorney Reznikova. The charges against her included her alleged activity as a member of the Moscow Helsinki Watch Group.) Since September, Mrs. Sakharov has been permitted to send postcards to her family abroad and friends in Moscow and also receive mail from them, but her correspondence is apparently censored. In November, Mrs. Sakharov's sentence of five years internal exile was confirmed by an appeal proceeding in Gorky. Evidently, Gorky has been designated as her place of exile. She continues to be troubled by serious heart and eye disease.

LETTERS BETWEEN ZBIGNIEW BUJAK AND VLADIMIR BUKOVSKY

SOVIET AND POLISH DISSIDENTS HAVE A STRONG admiration and respect for one another, not only because they know they are fighting for a common cause, but because they know that the fates of the Polish and Soviet peoples are inseparably linked. Poland will be free only if Soviet society undergoes certain changes away from totalitarian dictatorship to at least a limited type of democracy. At the same time, the Poles are providing the Russians a historical example of how to achieve this difficult but noble goal. Andrei Sakharov, Vladimir Bukovsky, Alexander Ginsburg and other Soviet dissidents often speak in support of Solidarity, and, at the same time, Solidarity leaders do not forget about their persecuted Russian friends.

Letter from Zbigniew Bujak, leader of the clandestine Solidarity in Poland, to Vladimir Bukovsky.

Courtesy of Resistance International

Warsaw, May 1984

My dear Vladimir,

I just read your book *And the Wind Stirs Again*. It is a prodigious book. I rejoice at the thought of being able to

293

bring it out in Poland. I would like to see you and have a conversation with you, and not only about politics. In you I found a human being who is Russian and European at the same time and your biography shows many analogies and resemblances to mine. There is one exception, however: I have not yet been in prison.

However, if one day I am locked up, the memory of the heroic combat which you have conducted "over there" will be of considerable comfort and support to me.

Often I ask myself if bolshevism is a direct descendent of the czarist autocratic traditions or if it was spontaneously generated, due to transplanting in Russia of Western European utopias, which Russian society was not able to withstand.

Your book makes it possible to go beyond the cliché which was stuck in the minds of many Poles, a cliché which says that the Russians are men with a slave mentality and, for them, bolshevism is only a natural continuity of their history.

Today, this opinion is changing. More and more, it is becoming clear that bolshevism could not be consolidated in Russia except through an interminable terror with millions of victims. The triumph of bolshevism has exacted the destruction of the whole social fabric of Russia. Your book elicits enthusiasm, because it shows that, in spite of a monstrous toll, there are still men who are ready to fight for the truth. By that, you help us to understand the Russians, whose views are close to our own, and whose combat is an integral part of our combat.

A few years back, I read Vaclav Havel's essay entitled "The Strength of the Weak." For me it was the revelation. It helped me to find my path, had an influence on my conception of things, and braced me in my activity. Reading your book has shown me that all that I have done and continue to do is only a continuance of what you have already done. Testimony like yours and Havel's makes it possible to understand the importance of the impression made by the "Message to the Peoples of Eastern Europe" and the "Declaration on the Question of National Minorities," adopted by the 1st Congress of the Delegates of Solidarity from all of Poland. This being the case, we have demonstrated that moral values must always be placed above everyday political calculations. Our activity is only meaningful if it aims to help man, wherever he is, in the defense of his legitimate rights.

At the moment when I am writing these lines, the combat for the liberty of Andrei Sakharov and Elena Bonner, his wife, is joined, and I fear that their lives will be the stakes of this combat.

Andrei Sakharov may be killed, because there are so many people who need him, and because he is an example to so many, including my friends and myself. Our wish is that he will recover his liberty.

It is with this thought that I finish my letter.

I send you my best wishes for success and I hope to meet you in better days.

With all my esteem,
Zbigniew Bujak

Answer from Vladimir Bukovsky to Zbigniew Bujak

Courtesy of Resistance International

August 14, 1984

Dear Zbigniew,

Thank you for letting me know that my book has come out in Poland. Right now, more than ever before, I feel like a member of the Polish Resistance and I am proud of it.

I felt a somewhat similar sentiment a few years ago when I learned that someone with the same name as myself (and, perhaps, a distant relative) had voted in the Polish Diet against the state of siege. Because, in fact, we are all somewhat in the same family, if only by the similarity of our destinies, of our characters. Independent of our nationality and our age, we are all born in Budapest, went to school in Prague, reached adulthood in the Soviet concentration camps, and maturity in the Gdansk shipyards. Our experience is uninterrupted and the process in which we participate is irreversible, as the process of development of a common organization is irreversible.

It is difficult to judge the degree to which our Muscovite experience can be of practical use to you. Naturally, it is always important to know that there is a living being in the cell next to your own, but your problems, right now, are much broader and more varied than those which we had to solve earlier. In today's communist world, Poland is the only country where Resistance is really general among a whole people, and it is rather up to us now to place ourselves in your school.

In fact, all that we have succeeded in doing in a quarter century of desperate efforts is to show that, under Soviet conditions, it is possible to win morally, and still remain a human being. Above all, naturally, what is involved is a victory over one's self because, I am deeply convinced, we always have the liberty of choice, even in prison, and no one can find a justification if he does not wish to use this liberty of choice. But is not that the beginning of everything?

Nevertheless, it is a shame that the sudden awareness by a man of such a simple fact is usually considered as a proof of heroism and not as the normal reaction. Perhaps it is because of this that our successes continue always to be so modest?

And I think that this is also the reason why the prejudices and stereotypes of which you speak are so strong. Because they also are nothing more than a self-justification.

Well, each of us knows perfectly, in the depths of his soul, that communism is, above all, a self-occupation, and cannot exist without our complicity even if it is only a formal complicity.

In this regard, the Russians are neither better nor worse than the others. We were the just the first to be struck, and,

I think, the first to receive the hardest blow of which few people at the time could predict the consequences. Our fathers did not yet have under their eyes the examples of Kolyma and Cambodia. It took dozens of years of terror, tens of millions of individuals swallowed up by the Gulag, before we, their children, understood that great crimes begin with little compromises.

Now that I have lived in various countries in the free world, I have noticed that there is no lack of fuzzy thinkers there, that there are louses everywhere, and that every man has in himself a slave part and a master part, more slave than master generally. Only we, in the East, have already understood and have already learned many things, while in the West, they have not yet been able to do so. We are already on the road to recovery, while the free world is perhaps still slated to be subjected to this twentieth-century plague (please God that it be a minor infection). And if, for example, it is pardonable for the French communists to reassure themselves with the aid of their prejudices, while seriously believing that their French communism will be better than the examples in Poland, Cambodia, Cuba, Russia, or China (since the French are certainly more cultivated than we others, we Czechs, Vietnamese, Ethiopians, or Nicaraguans), for us, it is not at all the same.

Moreover, we will not be able to move forward until we are freed from these prejudices. I am sure that it is only by becoming aware that our combat is a shared combat that we can free ourselves definitively. It is only when we are fully aware of this invisible front which extends from the Polish shipyards to the Afghan mountains, from the Angolan and Nicaraguan jungles to the Ethiopian desert, from the streets and squares of the occidental capitals to the camps of the Urals and to the Cuban prisons, it is only then that our victories will transcend moral victories.

This is why I consider that the "Message to the Peoples of Eastern Europe" and the "Declaration on the Question of National Minorities," adopted by the Congress of Solidarity from all of Poland, are genuinely historic documents, which testify to the great political maturity of the Polish Resistance. It is not by chance that it is these very documents which have elicited the worst fears from the Soviet ogres, because they are quite aware of the weakest link in their chain of power.

For this same reason, a year and a half ago, we founded Resistance International, in which 26 resistance movements of various communist countries work together right now, with success. Our tasks are very complex and our objectives seem beyond reach. But more than once, we have seen that it is only by breaking through the border of the impossible that results can be attained.

Today, while more and more distressful news comes to us from Moscow, at the moment when we are beginning to think that, apart from Sakharov, nobody remains there, and while he himself is threatened with death, I often think of Adam Michnik, our mutual friend. One day in Paris, shortly before entering Poland, he asked me, in all good faith: "Tell me frankly, just between us, are there many dissidents in the Soviet Union?"

"Well, let us say that there are enough there," I answered him in a evasive way.

"In Poland, there are very few, almost none," Adam told me sadly. And, after a silence, he added: "Everybody there is so conformist."

That happened at the end of 1977, just three years before the appearance of Solidarity and its millions of members.

This is why I think that the "better days" which you mentioned will come well before we might think possible today. And then, in a free Poland, we will finally talk, you and I, and not only about politics. Furthermore, this letter is not completely devoted to it either.

I wish you and your friends new successes in each year of the anniversary of Solidarity.

With all my esteem,
Vladimir Bukovsky

LETTER FROM THE LEADERS OF SOLIDARITY TO KONTINENT

TO: The editors of *Kontinent*

FOR: Elena Bonner and Andrei Sakharov

Dear and respected friends:

It is with the greatest concern and hope that we have long followed your struggle, and we now await any news of your situation with bated breath.

Your struggle, waged in circumstances incomparably harsher than those in Poland, serves as yet one more inspiring example for many of us and thrusts upon us a great responsibility.

We are aware of the common ideals and goals which unite us. It is precisely this unity of purpose which, despite the difficult and complex relationship between our two peoples, gives us faith that the time is approaching when that which unites us will win out over that which divides us.

Please consider our activities in Poland an expression of solidarity with you. We think of you and remember you; we are with you in all our thoughts.

With the greatest respect and admiration and the greatest concern for your plight,

The Executive Committee of Solidarity for the Mazovsze Region:

Konard Belinski
Zbigniew Bujak
Zbigniew Janas
Viktor Kulerski

SOLIDARITY WITH ANDREI SAKHAROV

by Jacek Kuron

IT IS NOT EASY FOR US POLES TO LOVE THE Russians. It is no accident that we look to the battles for independence of the late eighteenth, nineteenth, and early twentieth centuries. These were battles not only against tsarism but against Russians as well. It was the Russians who held Poland enslaved.

My grandfather, a militant in the Polish Socialist Party during the 1905 revolution, would sing a little ditty that went: "Once the Russkies have got ya, you're shipped to Kamchatka." The Bolsheviks include that revolution as one of their high holy days. And while indeed that revolution had spread to nearly all corners of Tsarist Russia, it was just another in a series of spurts toward Polish independence. As early as 1920, my father, then only a fifteen-year-old boy, had volunteered for combat. At that time the Bolsheviks, so it was said, were headed for Warsaw.

Then came September 17, 1939: I saw Russian-speaking soldiers marching Polish prisoners of war down the streets of Lvov. We received cards from my mother's brother in a POW camp for Polish officers in Kozelsk. All of the Kozelsk POWs were brutally slaughtered by the NKVD in Katyn. Today each year several thousand candles are lit in the military cemetery at the site of the symbolic grave of the victims of Katyn, a bare unmarked strip of grass.

It is not easy for us Poles to love the Russians, although

301

soldiers in Soviet uniforms can be seen openly only in the cities and towns in the northwestern part of the country. But they are a permanent part of the Polish national consciousness. Not for a second can we forget what happened in Berlin in 1953, in Budapest in 1956, in Czechoslovakia in 1968. During its forty-year enslavement by totalitarian dictatorship the Polish nation has demonstrated undeniably its thirst for freedom and its yearning for democracy and independence. This is not the first time the Poles have shown themselves worthy of freedom and able to fight for it. If this struggle has been marked by defeats, it is not because the totalitarian dictatorship is supported by the people but rather by the armed forces of the USSR. We are therefore forced to refrain ourselves, to exercise self-control, and to compromise. I believe that this kind of restraint and compromise, which we force upon ourselves out of a feeling of helplessness, is the source of particularly strong psychological crises, which give rise to feelings of aggression and hatred.

It is not easy for us Poles to love the Russians. And yet we must. It is imperative we not give in to the temptation to hate. I am referring here to our duty to love, although I realize that feelings cannot be made to order. Where then are we to find those who could love the Russians? During the first days of the 1830 Decembrist uprising a huge requiem mass was held in Kapucinow Cathedral for the Decembrists who had been executed. The common people of Warsaw paid homage to those Russians who had given their lives for "our freedom and yours." So revolutionary Warsaw perceived the Decembrists' sacrifice.

Our plight was the plight of the Russians, and any struggle waged by one enslaved people was a struggle waged in common. Behind us is a large chunk of shared history. We also share the experience of Siberia, resting place for the ashes of our fathers and their fathers. An awareness of this unity of fates has always been particularly strong in the

Polish national consciousness. Today it appears to be stronger and more widespread than ever before.

The "Message to the Workers of Eastern Europe" issued by the Solidarity congress was politically not the wisest possible step. At any rate, that was my opinion at the time. Even more curious is the fact that later many of the delegates themselves reached the same conclusion. How is it then that such a document was adopted? I witnessed the process, and I understand why. It was an outpouring of the heart. The delegates listened to the proposal and jumped to their feet. There was an ovation, but no discussion followed. These were the real representatives of the entire Polish work force, and they were in fact expressing the will of their constituents. Among others the message was addressed to the Russian worker.

There can be no doubt that the Russian people have suffered more than anyone else from Soviet totalitarianism. Poles, however, became aware of that fact only after they heard the voices of Russians opposing that totalitarianism. Perhaps only those noble people, alone and persecuted, succeeded in restoring to the Poles a love for the Russian people: Russian voices of truth about September 17, 1939, Russian voices of truth about Katyn, Russian voices of truth defending Polish political prisoners. And yet, Poland was far from their first and only concern. I believe it is enough to have discovered that there are people in the USSR who have not yet been defeated. They have become role models for us, a source of hope and courage. In the early seventies my friends and I applauded the Russians. We envied them with their samizdat and their *Chronicle of Human Events,* their Committees for the Defense of Human Rights. It was this feeling of admiration and envy which gave birth to many of our beginnings.

Of those noble, lonely, and persecuted few who restored our love for the Russians, Sakharov occupies a place of distinction. I need not say this to those people fighting for

Russian democracy. They know best of all. In Poland this struggle for democracy is symbolized by two people: Sakharov and Solzhenitsyn. For this they represent the Russian people as a whole. And if in our hearts and consciences we are to weigh all the hate and resentment on the one hand against our empathy for the plight of a people as symbolized by those two names, our empathy would win.

I want to express my deep feeling of solidarity with Andrei Sakharov, not because Sakharov's point of view in the debate following Solzhenitsyn's "Letter to the Soviet Leaders" is closer to mine, and not because we, the members of the Committee for Public Self-Defense (KOR), have worked together with Sakharov both in our writing as well as in person by way of Zbigniew Romaszewski's visit. Rather I would like to express my solidarity—our solidarity—with Sakharov because his life depends entirely on the solidarity of world public opinion. He is old, alone, and sick, and yet he represents a very real danger to the rulers of the Soviet Union. If they fear anything at all, it is free speech. And as long as the voices of people of good will around the world ring out strong, they will never physically destroy him. I stress that we are defending Sakharov from physical harm. Morally he has already won.

ANDREI SAKHAROV AND THE RUSSIAN INTELLIGENTSIA

.

by Valery Chalidze

© *Courtesy of Alfred A. Knopf, Inc.*

WE MUST LOOK TO THE EARLY NINETEENTH century in order to understand the origins of the Russian intelligentsia. Until then, culture in Russia was closely associated with the court and depended on the patronage of the crown. During the reign of Alexander I—perhaps as a by-product of his unrealized liberal tendencies—some creative talents abandoned the court and, while not yet forming a separate social caste, gathered in intellectual circles which were independent of the state power, and even inclined to oppose it.

The rupture was not abrupt. The poet Alexander Pushkin, known for his love for liberty and for his independence, recognized before his death that the alienation of educated society from authority and from the official state hierarchy was strange and unnatural. Pushkin was partly ready for a reconciliation with the Emperor. But the divorce of culture from the Russian state proceeded, although not everyone recognized the process while it was occurring.

Why have I begun with such ancient history? Because we cannot understand Sakharov's role in Russia today unless we know the epic of the intelligentsia. Sakharov is a heroic figure, and admired everywhere for his appeals on behalf of human rights and fundamental freedoms. But he is also a tragic actor in the drama of Russian history and of the Russian intelligentsia.

Who is guilty in the conflict between state and intelligentsia in Russia? Both parties, I believe. The authorities because they want to subordinate culture to their own purposes and turn the intelligentsia into propagandists for imperial greatness. The intelligentsia because in warring against the state for two centuries, they turned their backs on normal politics and have played an exclusively negative role, first as critics of the prevailing order and then as destroyers of that order. The Russian intelligentsia constitute a unique social group. I have not discovered any Western counterpart. Intellectuals do exist in the West, and they may oppose the government, but they do not form a separate, coherent caste.

The intelligentsia fostered the fall of the Russian Empire, but after the Revolution, the intelligentsia remained in opposition and the new regime made war upon the social group which had created it. The very nature and beliefs of the intelligentsia seem to require opposition to the government in power. We have learned much about the bloody persecutions of the intelligentsia during the Soviet era, but we know too that its traditions survived and continue to enrich world culture. But the tragedy for the Russian nation is that the intelligentsia have excluded themselves from practical politics. The intelligentsia as a matter of principle refuse to participate in the decision-making process of the state. Moreover, the intelligentsia scorn the common man's striving for a career and success. I remember my own friends in Russia—they thought the word *career* somehow disgusting. Their ideal is a selfless dedication to culture, to the ideals of art and science with almost no regard for recognition by society.

From one perspective, Sakharov's way of thinking, his

ethical principles, even his opinions, are typical of the Russian intelligentsia. On the other hand, he not only served in official posts; he rose high in the state hierarchy and did much to make strong the existing regime. It is well known that Sakharov made notable contributions to the military applications of thermonuclear reactions. For many years he occupied a leading post in the military-industrial complex, and he received the highest state awards for his accomplishments. Similar cases were known earlier. Intellectuals had served successfully in official posts, but as a rule they were then no longer considered intelligentsia in the Russian sense.

But Sakharov never stopped being an *intelligent*. His faculty for independent thought about society as well as about science never atrophied, although social criticism is a taboo subject for private Soviet citizens. Sakharov made no effort to camouflage his opinions. After working inside the establishment for many years, in 1968 he published his outspoken views on the course of Soviet society and on the dangers threatening the world. His essay "Progress, Coexistence, and Intellectual Freedom" was a sincere attempt to initiate a dialogue to which the regime could well have responded. His act was, however, too unexpected, and the state hierarchy expelled Sakharov. The regime once more displayed the symmetry of its relations with the intelligentsia. The intelligentsia totally reject the regime, and the regime replies in kind. Of course, the symmetry is not complete, because the authorities send the intellectuals to prison and exile.

Sakharov's public activity has turned him into a symbol of liberty, of opposition to tyranny. He had said many wise and good things. But I believe that he will be remembered in future history books as one of those rare intellectuals who dared to break down the wall between power and culture, disregarding the moral taboos of his social group and the lack of understanding of the authorities.

Earlier attempts to build bridges between state and society

foundered because they were out of phase. Alexander II introduced important reforms which should have been welcomed by the intelligentsia, but they disdained gradual progress. In the second half of the nineteenth century, they began sharpening the ax which cut off many heads of the intelligentsia after 1917.

History is ironic. The intelligentsia might have gone to meet Alexander II's reforms or Nicholas II's creation of a parliament. But the moments were lost and instead the current dissident movement had to begin by seeking a dialogue with Mr. Brezhnev. By then the authorities were deaf and blind. They rejected the intelligentsia's attempt, and so the country remains *at war with itself*.

Forecasts are risky, but I believe it possible and desirable that in the future the situation in Russia will lead the regime to undertake cooperation with the intelligentsia without insisting that they abandon their principles or tell lies. And perhaps circumstances will change sufficiently so that in Russia as in other civilized countries the intelligentsia will no longer consider participation in the political process shameful and will be willing to assist in the government of their country. This may sound utopian, but Sakharov's example shows that it is possible. He worked within the government establishment and still remained an honest man and a member of the Russian intelligentsia.

Sakharov's tragedy is not his interrupted career, not the lack of success of many of his human rights initiatives, not even his current exile in Gorky. His tragedy lies in his attempt to overcome the two-hundred-year antagonism between the intelligentsia representing the culture of society, and the authorities representing the power of society.

No single cause can explain the tragic course of Russian history for the last two centuries, but the hostility, the lack of mutual understanding, between the state and the intelligentsia was surely a significant factor. Elimination of this conflict is absolutely necessary for Russia's health in the future. The ice must be broken by brave individuals. Sa-kharov was the first and most prominent man of our age who—while holding important state posts—remained a member of the intelligentsia and openly expressed his be-liefs.

HUMAN RIGHTS AND FOREIGN POLICY

by Max M. Kampelman*

IN THE SPRING OF LAST YEAR, WHILE PHYSI-
cally still able to function, Soviet leader Yuri Andropov, in
addressing his Communist Party cadres, urged them to remember that there was a vital battle under way "for the
hearts and minds of billions of people on this planet." We,
too, must never forget that reality. It is also a part of that
reality that the Soviet Union is today the major threat to
our security and values—an aggresive society seeking, with
its massive military and police power, to expand its influence; and a repressive society determined to defend its totalitarian power, whatever the human cost.

It is not useful to deny this reality. The task is, rather,
how constructively to face it. I suspect that we and our
friends who value freedom will pay a heavy price and suffer
great anguish as we come to grips with this hard fact and
seek to do so constructively. The integrity and strength of
our society and of our people will undergo perhaps the most
serious challenge of our history as we learn how to live with

---

*Max Kampelman made this speech on October 1, 1984, to
the National Committee on American Foreign Policy in honor of
Ambassador Jeane Kirkpatrick.

311

Soviet military power, meet it, challenge it, and simultaneously strive to maintain the peace with liberty that we seek.

The object of diplomacy in a democratic society is to preserve peace at the same time as it protects and pursues vital national values and interests. This is the supreme challenge to statesmanship. In our nuclear age, the significance of these words is overwhelming.

History has demonstrated that diplomacy can fail and frequently has failed. The price of that failure in the past has too often been a loss of human life, the destruction of property, and the erosion of human values. But that price, tragic as it was, did not include the direct threat to our civilization, and perhaps to our planet, costs that could well be exacted for the failures of diplomacy today and tomorrow. And yet today, diplomacy is weaker in the resources that it can command to meet its awesome responsibilities. It is undermined by skepticism on the part of the body politic; and, more importantly, by the threat of internal divisiveness as partisanship and its temptations lead to excesses in language and in policy conceptions.

We still look upon ourselves as a young and developing nation, even though we are now one of the oldest stable systems in the world. We did not seek the role of world leadership, and our people today still tend to shy away from it. At the end of the Second World War, our relative geographic isolation, our democracy, our bountiful natural resources, and our productive people made us strong. We were somewhat like a young giant among nations, and being a giant is not easy. It is not easy living with a giant, and our friends are aware of that. It is hard to find shoes to fit if you are a giant; and the bed is always too short. Being strong, the giant can afford to be gentle, but he is also, at times, awkward. His good intentions are not always so interpreted by others.

We make mistakes because we are unaccustomed to and hesitant about the responsibilities of leadership. As a result, our behavior is at times one of fits and starts that frequently bedevil our foreign policy and confuse both friend and foe.

We look upon ourselves as a nation committed to the values of liberty. Some of our more sophisticated friends, modern-day Metternichs, see this linkage of values with world *realpolitik* as a form of naïveté. But liberty to us is not an abstract value. We also know it is not abstract to those unable to enjoy it. These values, in fact, distinguish us from the totalitarians and authoritarians of the world.

But let us explore for a moment whether our "Rights of Man" values, which we look upon as a source of our strength, may not complicate our pursuit of peace and international stability. What are the implications of injecting morality considerations into American foreign policy? Is there not a tension created when we engage in moral condemnation of totalitarian societies and then undertake to negotiate toward understanding with those we condemn?

The charge has been heard that raising human rights issues is a form of "confrontation" which runs contrary to the spirit necessary for serious negotiation. I respectfully suggest that negotiation without confrontation, where the objective facts require blunt talk, is not a serious negotiation at all. It is a charade. A purpose of negotiation is obviously to reach agreement. Where difficult issues are involved, however, that agreement may not be possible in the short run. The negotiating process must, therefore, be used to illuminate the differences, lessen the ambiguity, and, in time, possibly lead to later agreement. Absent this clarity, there is no reason for the other side to take seriously the depth of our concerns.

The alternative, furthermore, is silence. But can we be silent when silence, in effect, becomes acquiescence and even complicity? And if silence is morally unacceptable, is verbal condemnation adequate when we know it is likely to be ineffective? Is "action" by us then called for? If so, what kind? Do we have the moral right to encourage people who live under repressive regimes to seek to change their conditions? Is it possible we have the moral duty to help them change their conditions when they ask for help? Is intervention ever called for? If so, what kind? Or does this depend on whether the intervention will work and at what cost?

I am aware of the assertion that the best way to help those who are victims of authoritarian or totalitarian regimes is to set a fine example. I suspect this avoids the issue. The example we set, no matter how noble, will do little to alleviate the condition of those victimized by repression. We should also understand that even setting an example can produce international tension. The good example set by West Germany only led to a wall of concrete and fire around Communist Germany. The existence of a good example is, in effect, a threat in the eyes of those who control repressive regimes. That threat, in turn, produces fears and frequently leads to increased repression and more police and armed force. The example set by free societies may well be perceived by totalitarian leaders as subversive of their authority.

The peoples of the Soviet Union, who comprise hundreds of different nationalities, share the same values of human dignity that we proclaim. They are as dedicated to the elimination of war as any other peoples. They have no wish to be isolated from their neighbors and from the forward movement of civilization. But this creates an insecurity on the part of their authorities, who then go to great lengths to restrain, punish, fence in their citizens.

There is a related set of questions. Are we consistent with our values if we have and support allies who do not share them? Our founding fathers accepted an alliance with a France governed by a tyrannical monarch, at the same time as we forcefully expressed our detestation of absolute monarchies. During World War II we entered into an alliance with Stalin, whom history will record as perhaps the most brutal human butcher of the twentieth century, certainly a close competitor with Hitler for that title.

Must we be consistent? Some would have us seek to

improve our relations with Castro's Cuba, increase our trade with totalitarian Soviet Union, and also apply sanctions against racist South Africa.

I raise these questions not to undermine the legitimacy of injecting morality into our foreign policy. Morality must be a major component of our foreign policy. It may well be an indispensable ingredient for the domestic consensus that is required if any foreign policy in a democracy is to be effective. But strategic self-interest must also be a major consideration of an effective and desirable foreign policy.

Thus, the dilemma and the opportunity. There are some who may respond to the danger to us represented by Soviet military power and theology by ignoring or minimizing its existence. That would be fatal for us. There are others who are so overwhelmed by the difficulties as to place all their trust in military power and its use alone. That view carries with it the seeds of tragedy as well.

We dare not and cannot blow the Soviet Union away. We cannot wish it away. It is here and it is militarily powerful. We share the same globe. We must try to find a means under which we can live together in dignity.

The Soviet Union is not likely soon to undergo what Jonathan Edwards called "a great awakening," or see a blinding light on the road to Damascus. Yet, the imperatives for survival in the nuclear age require us to persist—through the deterrence that comes from credible military strength, through critical dialogue, through negotiation—to persist in the search for understanding, agreement, peace.

We hope the time will soon come when Soviet authorities comprehend that repressive societies in our day cannot achieve inner stability or security. We hope they will come to feel the need to show the rest of us that the cruelty is not an indispensable part of their system and is, indeed, thoroughly counterproductive to their interests. Just as the Leninist aim of achieving world communism through violence is an anachronism in this nuclear age, so must it be understood by an evolving Soviet leadership that in the long run it cannot survive without humanizing its controls. Included in our message must also be the understanding that new opportunities exist for cooperation with us on all levels if Moscow will live up to its international responsibilities so clearly delineated in the Charter of the United Nations, the Helsinki Final Act, and in the Madrid Concluding Document, all of whose words they accepted.

We hope, but if we are to be prudent, we cannot trust. We must negotiate; and negotiating means more than talking. It means listening as well. We must also be politically, economically, socially, and militarily strong. The Soviet Union respects military power. Its incentive for negotiating an agreement is greater when the positions taken by its negotiating adversary have the added dignity of being supported by military strength.

But we must understand that diplomacy in a democracy requires public support, particularly where the use of force is an option. We are entering a period in which this public support may well be the ultimate determinant in whether we are able to achieve the peace with dignity that we seek. No democracy can achieve the broad domestic consensus required for its foreign policy to proceed unless that policy is grounded in moral principles as well as vital national interests. That is certainly true of ours.

The problems that divide us are real, serious, and numerous. We trust our negotiating efforts will produce results. By the nature of things, however, we must appreciate that even with agreement we will still be nearer to the beginning than to the end of our pursuit of peace. We need patience.

Patience is indispensable. We must be prepared to remain in any negotiation with the Soviets for one day longer than they. We must be bona fide negotiators in good faith; anything less is transparent and damaging to our political interest. We must always be reasonable and also appear to be reasonable in what we seek. We should appreciate that superpower status does not always bring with it superwisdom.

But we must be clear, unambiguous, consistent. It is more important to be direct and candid and even sharply critical when called for. It is risky to soften or minimize our real concerns so as not to offend or inject a discordant note.

Soviet leadership, attempting to obscure the depth of their own responsibility for destroying the "détente" we all hoped to achieve, loudly calls on us for deeds rather than words. It is essential, if we are ever to achieve understanding, that we remind them that it is Soviet deeds that undermine stability in the world: 120,000 Soviet invading troops in Afghanistan brutalizing an innocent people; Soviet use of psychiatric hospitals as a form of political punishment; Soviet-sponsored anti-Semitism; Soviet persecution of Evangelical Christians, Baptists, Seventh-Day Adventists, Pentecostals, Catholics; Soviet refusal to permit the reunification of families by cruelly restricting emigration; Soviet harassment of Andrei Sakharov and Elena Bonner; Soviet violations of agreements against the use of chemical and biological weapons.

"Yes," our government must constantly assert as we negotiate, "it is deeds rather than words that count with us." The deeds to which we object are deeds in violation of international agreements and agreed-upon rules for civilized international behavior.

It is time for our genius as a people to rise to the challenge. We can find a revitalized American consensus in support of our values and our national security. We must lift ourselves above the polarity and divisiveness that too frequently become a characteristic of partisan politics. The primary task of leadership today is to rebuild the vital American political center which James Madison argued for in *The Federalist Papers* and which has kept us united in the face of our adversaries.

As we do so, guided by the values that unite us as a government and as a people, we will have the added strength that comes from the respect, admiration, and affection of the peoples of the world. That strength is there ready to be expressed and warmly channeled in our direction. It remains for us to provide the leadership.

The "correlation of forces" has moved against the Soviet Union. The credibility of its system as a viable alternative has collapsed for sensible people. The gas has largely escaped from its ideological balloon. The future lies with freedom. There can be no lasting stability in societies that would deny liberty. Only freedom can release the constructive energies of men and women to work toward reaching new heights. A human being has the capacity to aspire, to achieve, to dream, and to do. He cannot be permanently prevented from stretching his muscles to exercise his human right to attain ambitions for himself and his children and thereby fulfill his evolutionary destiny. That is our strength. Human rights is our strength.

REMARKS FROM CLOSE FRIENDS

NOT LONG BEFORE MY DEPARTURE FROM RUSSIA, a remark appeared in an American newspaper, or maybe a journal, to the effect that Sakharov, after all, is only a general without an army. An American correspondent in Moscow asked me what I thought about it. Is it true? Of course not, I said—but not because Sakharov has an army, but because he is not a general. Outstanding public figures who leave their imprint on history may be divided into two categories: leaders and saints. The leaders show other people what they can (although they, maybe, should not) do. Thus they are followed by masses. The saints show others what they should (although they, maybe, cannot) do. Thus, they are followed, if at all, by a handful of dissidents.

Sakharov is from the category of saints. I had the privilege of closely knowing Andrei Dmitrievich. His is a personality which makes everyone better who comes in touch with him. His human kindness, his noncompromising, absolute honesty has been a shining beacon for all of us. When you speak with Sakharov you keep wondering at his amazing simplicity, his absolute artlessness. To understand Sakharov, it is essential to remember that he is a scientist, a scientist to the marrow of his bones. He started his life as a scientist *par excellence;* Sakharov the public figure is the result of the evolution of Sakharov the scientist. Essentially, he took the high standards and values of science, first of all that of truth, and applied them to problems of social life and politics. It was not easy, and it required tremendous courage. The crowd of his former colleagues betrayed and ostracized him.

I remember an episode. It was in September 1973, soon after the infamous letter of forty academicians condemning Sakharov. I was sitting with the Sakharovs—in their kitchen, as usual—and discussing the letter. The Sakharovs had just returned from a Black Sea resort, and Lucia (Elena) told me about a funny occurrence which took place a couple of days before they left. They were taking sun at the beach, when a short man ran up to Andrei Dmitrievich, showed him how glad he was to meet him, shook his hand, and several times repeated how fortunate it is that such a person is among them. "Who was that?" asked Lucia when the short man departed. Andrei Dmitrievich answered that it was an academician so-and-so. Three days later, when the letter of forty was published, that academician was among the signers.

Lucia, who is generally emotional, spoke with contempt and indignation, which were cetainly well justified. I looked at Andrei Dmitrievich: what is his reaction? It was very typical for him. Sakharov was half-smiling and pensive. He showed no contempt. He was not indignant about the episode. He was *thinking* about it.

Though Sakharov's name is universally known, the full impact of his personality on the developments on the world's scene is still to be appreciated in the future. We know from history that when new civilizations emerge, it is the saints and prophets who come first; leaders come later. Humanity is in desperate need of a new and more sound basis for the goals and values of the new global civilization that is now in the throes of birth. I see Andrei Sakharov as a prophet of this coming civilization. He demonstrates that the heights of moral strength, courage, and self-sacrifice are not necessarily based on any of the traditional religions which now separate the human race. Nor do they require a belief in the supernatural or in life after death. They may take root in the sober and critical but compassionate human thinking so characteristic of Andrei Dmitrievich.

VALENTIN TURCHIN

I do not know anyone else with the same look in his eyes. I met him at a time when he was just beginning to lose all his privileges. He chose this cross to bear knowing full well what lay ahead. First he turned back into an average person who would have to wait in line to buy potatoes ... like me. We shared a dacha. Now his situation is far worse than average. And all of these sufferings are for us. That is why I believe we now are all responsible for his survival.

MSTISLAV ROSTROPOVICH

THE AUTHORS

Edward D. Lozansky. Graduated from the Moscow Institute of Atomic Energy in 1969. Emigrated to the United States in 1976. Currently Professor of Mathematics and Physics at Long Island University in New York and the Executive Director of the Andrei Sakharov Institute in Washington, D.C. Editor of the English Edition of *Kontinent*. Lives in Washington.

Natalya Gorbanevskaya. Russian poet, activist of the human rights movement in the USSR. Spent several years in prison and mental institutions for participation in the famous Red Square protest demonstration against Soviet invasion of Czechoslovakia. Deputy Editor of *Kontinent*. Lives in Paris.

Vladimir Maximov. Russian writier. Author of many novels translated into several European languages. He was expelled from the Writer's Union in 1972 and allowed to emigrate in 1974. Maximov is the founder, publisher, and editor-in-chief of *Kontinent* which is published in Paris.

Eduard Kunetsov. Russian writer and journalist. One of the leading Soviet dissidents. In 1970 was sentenced to death for the attempt to hijack the plane with Jewish Refuseniks from Leningrad to Stockholm. The sentence was later commuted to fifteen years in jail. In 1979 was exchanged for two Soviet spies. Currently works as the News Director for Radio Liberty in Munich.

Lawrence Elliott. American writer of eight books, the latest a biography of Fiorello La Guardia. He is a roving editor for *Reader's Digest*. Lives in Luxembourg.

Kevin Klose. Harvard graduate. Moscow bureau chief for the *Washington Post* from 1977 to 1981. He is coauthor of several books. Now lives in Chicago, where he is Midwest and Canada bureau chief for the *Washington Post*.

Edward Teller. Born in Budapest, Hungary. Graduated from the University of Leipzig. Emigrated to the United States in 1935. In 1942 joined the Manhattan Project. Widely known as a "father of the H-Bomb." Currently a Senior Research Fellow at Hoover Institution, Stanford University, and a consultant at the Lawrence Livermore National Laboratory.

Natalya Gesse. Russian children's writer, close friend of the Sakharovs, emigrated to the United States in 1984. Lives in Detroit.

Vladimir Voynovich. Russian writer. Author of many books translated into several European languages. His more popular book in English is *The Life and Extraordinary Adventures of Private Ivan Chonkin*. In 1974 he was expelled from the Soviet Writers Union. In 1980 he was deprived of his Soviet citizenship and allowed to emigrate. Lives in Munich.

Vassily Aksyonov. Russian writer. Graduated from Leningrad Medical Institute in 1956. Author of many novels. Editor of *Metropol*, the literary almanac of uncensored Soviet writings. In 1980 was forced to emigrate and immediately thereafter was stripped of his Soviet citizenship. His latest book in English, *The Burn*, was published by Random House. Lives in Washington.

Robert Kaiser. Graduated from Yale and London School of Economics. From 1971 to 1974 served as a Moscow bureau chief for the *Washington Post*. Now the associate editor of the *Washington Post*.

Valentin Turchin. Physicist and one of the closest associates of Sakharov. Former Chairman of the Moscow section of Amnesty International. Professor of Computer Science at Queens College, New York.

Jacek Kuron. One of the founders of the Polish Committee for Self Defense and one of the leaders of the banned trade union Solidarity.

Zbigniew Bujak. Leader of the clandestine Solidarity.

Vladimir Bukovsky. Author, scientist, one of the most prominent Russian dissidents. Spent eleven years in Soviet Gulag. In 1976 was exchanged for General Secretary of the Chilean Communist Party Louis Corvallan. Founder and President of the Paris-based organization Resistance International. Currently working on his Ph.D. in brain psychology at Stanford University.

Valery Chalidze. Physicist and human rights activist who helped Sakharov to found the Moscow Human Rights Committee. Publisher of the *Chronicle of Human Rights* in the USSR. Lives in Vermont.

Max M. Kampelman. Prominent American lawyer. Served as ambassador and head of the U.S. delegation to the Madrid Conference on Security and Cooperation in Europe. Now heads the American delegation to the disarmament talks with the Soviet Union.

Dr. Sidney D. Drell. Physicist and close personal friend of the Sakharovs. He is Deputy Director of the Stanford Linear Accelerator Center, a long time adviser to the U.S. government on national security and arms control issues, and a member of the National Academy of Science.

DATE DUE